"This profound, delightful, and thought-provoking exploration of life's values and goals, challenges and trade-offs, and dilemmas and contretemps is likely to become required reading not only at business schools but for professionals generally."

DAN ROSE,

CHAIRMAN, ROSE ASSOCIATES

"McCoy's forte for business managers should not be underestimated. He has done the deals and climbed to the very top of the corporate mountain. Voices such as his, especially ones that have done considerable soul searching over the years into the deeper aspects of business ethics, are rare."

THOMAS M. DONALDSON,

MARK O. WINKELMAN PROFESSOR,

THE WHARTON SCHOOL

"In masterful style, *Living Into Leadership* offers an antidote to the dominant greed-sickness in business culture. McCoy uses a real voice of experience to explore an extensive and authentic range of ethical settings and dilemmas."

LAURA L. NASH,

MANAGING PARTNER, PIPER COVE ASSET MANAGEMENT, LLC;

FORMER PRESIDENT, SOCIETY FOR BUSINESS ETHICS

"McCoy draws on his personal experience as well as the work of a range of intellectual giants—from Dante and the Rule of Saint Benedict to Immanuel Kant, Peter Drucker, and Lynn Sharpe Paine—to offer a compelling answer to the fundamental ethical question 'How shall we live?'"

OLIVER WILLIAMS,

DIRECTOR, CENTER FOR ETHICS & RELIGIOUS VALUES

IN BUSINESS, UNIVERSITY OF NOTRE DAME

"In a world that has seen corporate abuse from the top, insider trading, and a breakdown in moral and ethical leadership at many levels of government, now is the time for a book that concerns itself with ethics, morality, and the law. Buzz McCoy covers all aspects of ethics, told through his personal experiences as an undergraduate student at Stanford, serving in the army during the Korean War, studying at Harvard Business School, leading a successful career at Morgan Stanley, and, more recently, teaching and lecturing. *Living Into Leadership* demonstrates that ethics is something deeper than complying with the law. We need the law in order to keep us honest and provide a level playing field, but true ethics involves some sort of compassion. Ethics is not what we *have to* do, but rather what we *can* do."

A. EUGENE KOHN,
CHAIRMAN, KOHN PEDERSEN FOX ASSOCIATES

LIVING INTO LEADERSHIP

A JOURNEY IN ETHICS

Bowen H. "Buzz" McCoy

Published in association with the Center for Social Innovation,
Stanford Graduate School of Business

STANFORD BUSINESS BOOKS
An Imprint of Stanford University Press
Stanford, California
2007

Stanford University Press
Stanford, California

Excerpt from "Little Gidding" in *Four Quartets* copyright 1942 by T. S. Eliot and renewed 1970 by Esmé Valerie Eliot, reprinted by permission of Harcourt, Inc.

Excerpt from "The Dry Salvages" in *Four Quartets* copyright 1941 by T. S. Eliot and renewed 1969 by Esmé Valerie Eliot, reprinted by permission of Harcourt, Inc.

"The Parable of the Sadhu" was originally published in *Harvard Business Review,* September–October 1983. Copyright ©1983 by the Harvard Business School Publishing Corporation; all rights reserved.

Excerpt from *Good Work: When Excellence and Ethics Meet* copyright 2001 by Howard Gardner, Mihaly Csikszentmihalyi, and William Damon; reprinted by permission.

Printed in the United States of America on acid-free, archival-quality paper

Library of Congress Cataloging-in-Publication Data

McCoy, Bowen H.

Living into leadership : a journey in ethics / Bowen H. "Buzz" McCoy.
p. cm.
Includes bibliographical references and index.
ISBN-13: 978-0-8047-5576-4 (cloth : alk. paper)
ISBN-10: 0-8047-5576-0 (cloth : alk. paper)
1. Business ethics. I. Title.

HF5387.M345 2007
174'.4--dc22

2006031229

Designed by Bruce Lundquist
Typeset at Stanford University Press in 9.75/15 Sabon

Special discounts for bulk quantities of Stanford Business Books are available to corporations, professional associations, and other organizations. For details and discount information, contact the special sales department of Stanford University Press. Tel: (650) 736-1783, Fax: (650) 736-1784

To Barbara—my muse, my Beatrice, my love

Contents

Changing World, Changing Ethics?

THE TIME OF MY GENERATION has been termed the "age of conformity." Certainly from today's perspective, my business school class would appear to be amazingly homogeneous; yet there were vast differences in outlook and experience lying just below the surface. But some of my differences were wildly apparent. For one thing, I was coming from California. For another, I had just completed thirteen months of serving in the Army in Korea. My scant civilian wardrobe, which consisted of wide lapels, padded shoulders, and less than subdued shades, was sure to set me apart, especially given that the 1950s "gray flannel suit" conformity was still dominant—and the group norm was for us to wear business suits to class. But as it turned out, a large proportion of us had just returned from military service, and that experience had been a great leveler. In addition, Harvard seemed to delight in throwing in a few "wild cards," including those who were admitted without a college degree, based on their life experience. All of us were expected to learn from one another, and learn we did.

We have been open to the vast changes that have occurred in the past fifty years. Some of my peers pushed hard to get women and minorities into business. These activities require sustained effort over many years, and the culture at many firms remains resistant to such changes to this day. Yet in a smaller, globalized world, openness to diversity has become a required norm. In a sense, the uniformity of background and shared experiences of the 1950s and 1960s made it easier to teach or to lead. These days when I teach ethics in graduate business schools, I have some fun with the students by comparing them with my classmates of forty-five years ago at Harvard. I set this up to demonstrate the wide swings in societal behavior that are tolerated from time to time. I exaggerate the differences, describing my class as all male, mostly Anglo-American, wearing gray flannel business suits (even to class), and smoking cigarettes. I then describe their typical class. Often at least a third of it is women; in some cases, more than half.

Students are a range of ages and nationalities, including native Chinese, Korean, Indian, Kenyan, Nigerian, Mexican, Brazilian, Argentine, Polish, and Russian, to name a few.

Most of my current students, casually dressed in t-shirts, baseball caps, cutoff jeans, and tennis shoes, cannot imagine coming to class in suits—never mind wearing fedoras en route. Many arrive drinking Starbucks coffee or eating noodles. Even with the wild cards, my class would have been surprised to see a forty-two-year-old black mother of two coming back for her M.B.A.; my present students would be horrified at how overwhelmingly white and male my Harvard class was.

The deep diversity of current classrooms provides opportunities for learning about differences and styles. It becomes impossible to stereotype one another and to have the "correct" prototype of a USC or Harvard M.B.A. student. Issues are no longer clear-cut. Beyond that, today students' experiences are much more broad. For example, few of my compatriots at Harvard had ever been encouraged to bribe someone. These days, every ethics class I teach contains seasoned students from India, China, or southeast Asia for whom the experience is common. They understand that if they do not participate in local bribery, they will lose their jobs or worse. Simplistic answers are no longer satisfactory. The diversity of the classroom forces us to deal with the depth and reality of the issues.

As the chapters throughout the book explore, I believe that ethics is contextual and is derived from the faith and value system of a particular culture. Thus what is deemed appropriate in a Judeo-Christian ethical culture may or may not be appropriate in a Muslim, Buddhist, Confucian, or animistic culture. With less common ground, perhaps business ethics in a global environment requires more explicit guidelines. There is a need to better understand the value systems of our counter parties when we are dealing globally.

Even my own classmates, operating in what appeared to be a simpler world, have had to deal with dramatic changes, unpredictable events, and unforeseen contingencies. Indeed, the essence of what Harvard attempted to teach us was how to make decisions under conditions of uncertainty, when all that needs to be known cannot be known. To live contingently and successfully one must develop a moral compass. We are beginning to understand that it is not a Harvard or a Stanford M.B.A. that is of critical importance. What is important is to develop over time a sense of integrity. The great business leaders of the future must have abiding integrity if they are to be counted on to make the correct moral decisions even when the way is not clear.

OVERVIEW

The book that follows is organized in three parts. Part One covers how we develop a sense of our integrity, focusing in Chapter One on such issues as developing the habits necessary to discover our personal ethics and dealing with autonomy versus group values. Chapter Two deals with developing an intentional plan for our lives, built around core values. Chapter Three discusses sustaining an ethical self in a changing contextual environment. The precepts are grounded in the reality of my personal experiences, especially during my earlier years at Morgan Stanley.

Part Two is concerned with putting ethics into action. It begins with a rather exotic tale, "The Parable of the Sadhu," that describes an ethical situation I encountered at 18,000 feet in the Himalayas while on an extended six-month sabbatical from Morgan Stanley. Chapter Four is involved with leading while holding onto core values, Chapter Five with living your ethics through a balanced life, and Chapter Six with living your values in the workplace. Examples are drawn from my growing experience as a business unit leader at Morgan Stanley.

Part Three describes ethical trade-offs in the real world. Chapter Seven deals with ethics in the face of resistance; Chapter Eight with ethics in business practice at a more senior level, and Chapter Nine with ethical behavior in the face of changing societal values. Once again real-life situations illustrate the text and are drawn from senior leadership decisions at Morgan Stanley as well as my experiences teaching values-based leadership at graduate schools of business.

Without being presumptuous, I might flatter by imitation my hero, Dante. One can read this book in the manner Dante wrote to a friend describing how he would like his *Divine Comedy* to be read. Initially, one may read for the *surface story* of my twenty-seven-year career at Morgan Stanley, following my successes and pitfalls and hearing stories such as the sale of the Irvine Ranch or the restructuring of J. I. Case. One can also follow the paths of some of my other heroes, such as Trammell Crow, Harry Cunningham, John Gardner, Bill Hewlett, or Charlie Shaw. In an *allegorical sense*, the book takes the motif of life as a journey. As Cervantes demonstrated in his immortal allegory, *Don Quixote*, it is about the road, not the inn. On the normative, or *moral level*, one can follow the struggles of Morgan Stanley attempting to survive in a deregulated environment: pushing the envelope, doing things it had never done before, and attempting to change its culture without violating its values. Finally, there is the *deep level of religious and spiritual growth and formation*, of attempting to live out one's deepest values in the workplace, which becomes the source of one's courage and steadfastness when all else seems to fail.

Above all, in a time of well-publicized scandals and moral failures, this book is intended to tell the story of one person who is not a well-known business icon but who has found in a business career an immensely satisfying way to build life-long relationships and to participate, not always with elegance, in a worklife filled with adventure, humor, personal growth, and the opportunity to test and live out one's deepest personal values.

Finally, although this book is complete, the journey is not over, either for me or for you, the reader. We are always growing and becoming and dealing in new contexts. A specific gripe of mine about "business ethics" is the complaint that graduate students are too old to learn ethics—that their values have been embedded long ago. That has not been my experience. What a shame to think we know all there is to know at age twenty-five, or forty-five, or seventy. Life is a continually unfolding journey. There is always the potential for new relationships, new ideas, new adventures, and new failures. The drama of the journey is discovering where we stop wandering and take our stand. I thank the reader for being willing to share a small part of my journey, and I wish you continuing *bon chance* on yours.

A WORD ON THE TITLE

Leadership is not a genetic gift or a family legacy; we have sympathetically observed some failures of those assumptions. It is not a warranty with a degree from an excellent graduate business school, though the rigor of that experience can provide valuable returns. Becoming a leader is an intentional process of growth that must be lived out experientially. One must have the will to say "yes" and even "no" to an unending series of tests, large and small, each demanding that we take one more step toward a definition of who we are. We must be ready to define our values, our character, and our leadership style. For durable, strong leaders, the process will not end. It will become a way of life, not only in business, but within our families, our various communities, and the world.

So if you are contemplating a career in business, or if you are already in a position of business responsibility, I trust that what follows will give you confidence as you begin, grow, and live into leadership.

Acknowledgments

MUCH OF THIS BOOK concerns events and stories that took place at Morgan Stanley and elsewhere twenty-five to forty years ago. Although I still feel I have my wits about me, I have no doubt that some of my former associates will see these past events from a perspective different from mine. I ask their indulgence and forgiveness for any of my sins of omission or commission. I also would like to thank all those who worked with me, especially in building the Morgan Stanley real estate platform, over those years. We can be very proud of what we accomplished, and of how we treated one another while doing it. It was a rare privilege to be associated with so many women and men of such intelligence, high energy, and integrity.

I have tried assiduously to acknowledge sources, attribute credit, and quote accurately throughout this book, but it is possible that some attributions may have been overlooked. In such cases, it was certainly not my intention.

I especially wish to acknowledge the powerful role played by Morgan Stanley's leader during much of the period discussed, Robert H. B. Baldwin. He had what Peter Drucker describes as "a passion for the enterprise." I doubt we would have made it without him. He is a man of great character and integrity, as well as personal intensity. He gave us the chance, and he showed us the way.

The two great heroes in my early life were my father and my grandfather. My grandfather, with an eighth-grade education, enlisted in the Spanish American War, served in the Philippines, served with General Pershing on the Mexican Border, and saw heavy combat in World War I, including at Belleau Woods and Chateau Thierry. He retired a brigadier general.

My father served the American Red Cross for forty-five years. In World War II he was in charge of U.S. Red Cross aid to England and France in 1940–41. He took a train of Jewish refugees out of France into Spain and ended up directing aid to England during the Blitz. He then served for

General Mark Clark in Italy, where he was present at the Battle of Casino. Finally he directed all Red Cross aid in the South Pacific, serving on Admiral Nimitz's staff. In that capacity he landed on Iwo Jima the first day, with the fifth wave of Marines, just to see what was happening in the field.

Heroes take us only so far. Also of great importance to me are those who helped form my faith. My mother heads this list. Her sense of fairness and truth, and her deep sense of spirituality, have remained with me throughout my life. My father-in-law in my first marriage, Henry B. Arthur, deceased professor emeritus at Harvard Business School, showed me that one could be a successful businessperson while retaining a strong faith commitment and an abiding interest in ethics. His daughter, Janice Arthur McCoy Miller, shared thirty-one years of life with me and endured my constant struggles and questions with grace.

My minister in Connecticut, George Pera, introduced me to Dietrich Bonhoeffer, the German theologian, who the reader will see is another of my heroes. This led to a friendship with Paul Lehman, a theologian who was a close personal friend of Bonhoeffer's. Paul led me to Charles McCoy (no relation), another theologian, who became a close friend and joined me on a Bonhoeffer pilgrimage in Germany.

The Reverend Charles Shields was my pastor in California for fifteen years before his untimely death. We shared so many things together: visiting monasteries, traveling to the Holy Land, praying, laughing, running, hiking, drinking. He showed me more of Jesus Christ than any other man in my life. My closest spiritual advisor at present is Fr. Luke Dysinger, a Benedictine monk and much more. We have taught together in his monastery, St. Andrew's Abbey, for several years, and he is an anchor in my life.

Harvard Business School has had an important impact on my life. Among those faculty who supported and sustained my interest in ethics are Steve Fuller, John Matthews, my classmate Tom Piper, and Lynn Paine, whose tenacity and intelligence in expanding the role of ethics in the curriculum have made her another of my heroes. I also wish to acknowledge the role of my friend Michael Josephson, who did much to teach me how to teach ethics.

There have been so many who have shared life with me and formed the stories in this book and helped me attain whatever level of wisdom and balance I have achieved. My running buddy and neighbor, Jim Fixx, who talked as much as he ran. My six-hundred-mile Himalayan trekking partner, Stephen Richardson, with whom I shared a true lifetime adventure. My jazz buddy and pianist extraordinaire, Shelly Berg, who expanded the horizons of a hobby beyond measure.

Finally, there are patient editors to thank. First is Lisa Collins, who did such a superb job on "The Parable of the Sadhu." It is a miracle to me that it has lasted so long in the business ethics canon, and the miracle is in large part Lisa's. In the case of this book, two early editors, Linda Seger and Judith Searle, took the beast emerging from my stream of consciousness and brought discipline and control to it. Then there is Jan Hunter, who took what was essentially a memoir and made a book out of it. Thanks also to Terry Pierce for putting us together, a great gift. Finally, I wish to thank Geoffrey Burn, Alan Harvey, and the staff of Stanford University Press for seeing the potential of this book and enthusiastically endorsing it while making it better.

Over the six years I have been working on this book, several individuals have encouraged me to keep on going, even when it appeared impossible. These include, among others, David Brady, Tom Donaldson, Mary Fleischmann, Kirk Hanson, Michael Keller, and Laura Nash. Others who have supported and encouraged my efforts in business ethics over the years include David Gergen, Peter Gomes, Maryanne Jennings, Larry King, and Fr. Ollie Williams.

Then there is my conscience and editor superior, my wife, Barbara, to whom this book is dedicated.

LIVING INTO LEADERSHIP

PART ONE

Setting Your Compass

MY LIFE JOURNEY TO DATE has, in many ways, been a search for values and vision. How do we gain values and a personal vision? Obviously at our parents' knees, but also in the myriad of experiences and personalities we encounter throughout life. We can be intentional about what we read, who our friends are, and what our spiritual practices are in an attempt to refine our values, but cannot discount the existential happenstance of life as having an equal impact. Life is an adventurous pilgrimage during which we are formed and re-formed. Some values and behavioral patterns are picked up and then discarded as they become inappropriate to contextual twists and turns. Others are sustained throughout, and they determine what we are willing to lose for. They trump the intermediate goals of the pilgrimage.

Business and economics education in general is oriented toward winning—maximizing profits, optimizing outcomes, and prevailing over competition. The emphasis on outcomes rather than values tends to create an impression on students (and teachers) that issues of ethics, spirituality, or religion are inappropriate in a business situation. The only way out of the miasma of corporate scandal is to elevate ethics as a rational input in a business discussion. To do this we must reorient our thinking to focus also on what values are so important to us, either individually or corporately, that we are willing to suboptimize the results and lose for. It becomes another short-term versus long-term trade-off. How much are we willing to lose in the short term in order to preserve our values and our corporate culture?

An ethically sensitive person does not live in isolation. Indeed the essence of ethics is to take oneself out of self-absorption and into community with others. In my own case mentors and deep friendships were indispensable in sustaining me through the vicissitudes, triumphs, and failures encountered in military service, graduate school, an almost thirty-year career as an investment banker, a rather large nuclear family, and recent years of semiretirement. As we progress on our journey we become part of multiple communities. We have social friends, sports friends, play friends, and work friends; spiritual friends, intellectual friends, love relationships, and family. The truly deep relationships occur when the connections are on multiple levels. We can be said to have integrity when we are perceived as the same person by all of our constituencies, including those at work.

CHOOSING AN ESTABLISHED ETHICAL FRAMEWORK
VERSUS ESTABLISHING YOUR OWN

On my own journey I have traveled from being a student of leadership to being a leader to being a teacher of values-based leadership. Each group to which we attach ourselves, including society in general, has an embedded sense of values that form its ethical underpinnings. A successful leader attempts to align the values of the enterprise with those of the individuals who form it, striving to facilitate a sense of deep meaning and commitment in their work. A precondition is a heightened degree of sensitivity on the part of the leader to the values of society, the enterprise, and the individuals who constitute it. Also required is a willingness to tinker with the business plan, if necessary, as well as a sense of trust in gaining support for changing individual values, if necessary, to align the individual to the enterprise.

There are several basic types of ethical frameworks. While most of us tend to default to a particular model, we also shift our behavior patterns contextually. In discussing ethics it can be very useful up front to have a basic understanding of the predominant models as a means of assessing, or even predicting, behavior in a given situation.

A problem in discussing ethics is that most of us are not trained in it, nor are many of us exposed to deep ethical discussions on a regular basis. Few of us are accustomed to exposing our individual ethics before a group. And in today's norm of cultural relativism—"I'm OK, You're OK"—we are reluctant to publicly criticize the value systems of others. If we can't discuss ethics on a personal level, how are we to learn to discuss it at the organizational and business levels? In a graduate business school, learning is compartmentalized into marketing, production, control, finance, human behavior, and more. Ethics reaches into all these areas—or should—but full discussion is hindered by the fact that students do not start with a common language for ethics. In the following text, I will attempt to frame a definitional language by discussing types of ethics. The types described are by no means inclusive; I provide them as a way to gain a primitive hold on a possible common language.

Normative Ethics

In simple terms, normative ethics is that behavior to which society at large conforms over time. Normative ethics may be codified as the law, but it embraces large areas of behavior not codified by the law. It encompasses our behavior in groups (do not yell "Fire!" in a crowded theater), expressions of our sexuality, our dress, and other conventions. Cultural relativism is a current norm, as is situational ethics. There are those who would say that today's norm is that there are no rules, no easily identifiable broad set of values to which we can all agree. It is easy to go along with the norm, but the norm can fall into pluralistic ignorance or lead to the incremental gradualism of bad practice. Years ago, the Kitty Genovese case in Queens, New York, shocked the public. People were horrified to learn that a young person's cries for help had been ignored by over thirty listeners, each of whom thought (or hoped) that someone else would handle the situation. Today, when drive-by shootings occur in full sight, are we surprised that none of the witnesses come forward to describe the vehicle, the driver, or the weapon?

Economists have utilized terms such as the "tragedy of the commons" or the "fallacy of composition" to describe the behavior of those who do not believe that their actions, even in the aggregate, can make a difference. Thus we continue to litter national parks and local squares, fail to vote, dodge jury duty, avoid taking a stand, put off writing that letter to the editor, lulling ourselves into thinking we do not count when, in the aggregate, we all do.

A very important aspect of normative ethics is that it changes over time as people's attitudes change. Observers such as historian and social critic Arthur Schlesinger Jr. have described long wave rhythms of societal norms swinging back and forth between conservatism and liberality. This applies to a wide variety of societal issues including how we dress, express our sexuality, or deal with minorities; our expectations of government; and a host of other issues. Thus if we base our behavior purely on societal norms, we must be prepared to have the rug pulled out from beneath us. Somewhat arcane but valid illustrations would include price fixing, antitrust behavior, insider trading, executive compensation, document-shredding policies, or the nonpayment of social security taxes for part-time domestic employees. If we base our future behavior solely on current norms, we might find ourselves considered criminals twenty years hence.

Kantian Ethics

Named after the famous nineteenth-century moral philosopher, Kantian ethics has come to mean rigid ethical rules or duties. Attributed to Immanuel Kant is the categorical imperative—which is to say, there are certain things we simply must do to maintain our basic humanity. As much as certain elements of our normative society are crying out for at least some rules to live by, others would say that Kant's approach is too rigid and duty bound for contemporary society.

I tell a story to my students to illustrate an apocryphal extension of Kantian ethics. I have the students imagine themselves in Amsterdam during World War II. There is a knock on the door. They answer and find Anne Frank standing there. Without hesitation, they hide her in the attic to save her from the Gestapo. Later, when the Gestapo knocks on the door and inquires as to Anne's whereabouts, they must tell them she is hiding in the attic. According to Kant, there is never a good excuse for a lie.

When the group quiets down, I tell them they are each Kantians. Naturally, they object. As living practitioners of normative ethics, they could never be so rigid. Yet we are all Kantians. The trouble is, we are each Kantian about different things: each of us has certain things we could never cause ourselves to do, for in doing them we would lose our personal sense of our humanity. Yet for each of us the limits are somewhat different. This is what makes governance so difficult for any type of social structure, and this is why, in an age of cultural relativism, we often come together at the lowest common denominator or at the worst bad practice.

Utilitarian Ethics

Stemming from Jeremy Bentham and John Stuart Mill, utilitarianism (the greatest good for the greatest number) is a powerful shaper of our normative ethics, particularly in the business world. Utilitarian ethics drives government policymaking, economic input-output modeling, and cost-benefit analyses, and basically determines how our world works.

As but one example, health care policies are based on utilitarian ethics. Health care managers are constrained economically from paying $500 for a unit of blood when it is commonly available at $200 a unit. In theory, for example, the odds of contaminated blood may be 1:100,000 at $200 a unit, and, if we perform more costly testing, 1:1,000,000 at $500 a unit. We as a society do not think that is a good cost-benefit ratio. Health care costs are out of control. But if our loved one is infected through contaminated blood, we will sue the hospital for millions of dollars for not using the more expensive blood, assuming it is available.

We can calculate the value of a human life and enter the sum into our input-output models to determine how many kidney dialysis machines we can afford as a percentage of our gross national product. Statistical analysts can calculate your future earning power. They can also calculate how much you should be willing to pay to save your own life. A result is that people's lives are calculated to be worth more in wealthy countries than in poorer countries.

The Economist, for example, reported that in 1993, a human life was calculated to be worth $2.6 million in America and $20,000 in Portugal.[1] Robert McNamara ran the Vietnam War on an acceptable kill ratio of 20:1. They killed 56,000 of ours, and we killed over a million of theirs.[2] The First Gulf War was a prized case of a successful kill ratio (unless, of course, someone you loved was killed).[3]

Utilitarian ethics, focusing on consequences, are pervasive in our society. The majority wins. The only real losers are the minority.

Social Justice Ethics

Social justice ethics is an antidote to the excesses of majority rules utilitarianism. It gives rights to those who otherwise lose out to the mainstream of society by coalescing their power behind a single issue. Most would agree today that the Civil Rights Movement was a constructive use of such power. The social safety net, or the negative income tax, is another good example of social justice. Even a conservative like Richard Nixon, working with Daniel Moynihan, felt it was good politics to care for the poor. Critics of social justice politics point to unresolved issues such as abortion rights or gun control, which tend to defy closure, and they brand the process as "single-issue politics," or the "tyranny of the minority."

Religious Ethics

Moral philosophy and theology play a major role even in normative ethics. Will Durant writes in *The Story of Civilization*, "Conduct deprived of its religious supports deteriorates into epicurean chaos; and life itself, shorn of consoling faith, becomes a burden alike to conscious poverty and to weary wealth."[4]

The issue for society is, Which religion do we choose? Even in countries such as Nepal that have an announced state religion, religious diversity is present. We are taught to embrace diversity, yet nothing has divided mankind more throughout history than religious differences. In the United States, where religion is pervasive in our normative culture, we continue to attempt to preserve the notion of the secular state. Indeed, we are a country founded on the idea of religious freedom, with separation of church and state key to the founders, yet maintaining that separation is a never-ending process.

In his book *The Culture of Disbelief*, Stephen L. Carter writes of the ubiquity of religious language in our public debates as a form of trivialization of religion, as our politicians repeat largely meaningless religious incantations.[5]

Like insider trading, faith is a state of mind. How do you know if a person is truly faithful or merely bringing in pseudo-religious language as a means of gaining support? People who use faith as a means to an end are subjecting themselves to a higher standard of scrutiny in all of their daily actions and must be prepared to live with the consequences. Trust is not freely given, and it is easily taken away.

Just as a politician needs to seriously consider whether he or she has a truly felt religious ethic shared with the populace, so should any leader be sensitive to the deeper values and beliefs of those to whom his or her leadership is entrusted.

Communitarian Ethics

A more secular and perhaps less controversial approach to moral theology, but based purely on the social sciences, is communitarianism. Most recently espoused by Amitai Etzioni in his book *The Moral Dimension* and reported by *Time* magazine, communitarianism relies on (1) the individual, (2) society, and (3) transcendental values.[6] Transcendental values can be any of the world's religions or even a deeply rooted humanism.

Religious Ethic: In Search of the Transcendent

The great Protestant theologian Paul Tillich discussed evil in terms of isolation, loneliness, and alienation. We must be in harmony with ourselves, our communities, and our God. Tillich summarized all of Christian (as well as Jewish and Islamic) theology in the One Great Commandment and its corollary: "Love the Lord your God with all your heart, all your mind, all your strength and all your spirit; and love your neighbor as yourself." If we unpack this timeless command, it sounds quite Greek: be in harmony with yourself, your neighbors, and some great transcendent spirit that draws you out of yourself and that we choose to term "God." Its chief purpose appears to be to take us out of ego-centeredness and into relationship with all the others, including the divine Other, which Tillich termed "ultimate reality." Tillich would say that is all we need to know. Indeed, virtually all religions attempt to draw us out of ourselves while remaining in harmony with ourselves. This theology is validated by the great depth psychologists such as Freud and Jung.

It is interesting that a deeply committed Christian such as Paul Tillich would describe ethical challenges in almost the same language as a highly secular individual such as Carl Jung. In *My Search for Absolutes*, Paul Tillich wrote, "no moral code can spare us from a decision and thus save us from moral risk. . . . Moral commandments are the wisdom of the past as it has been embodied in laws and traditions, and anyone who does not follow them risks tragedy. . . . Moral decisions involve moral risk. Even though a decision may be wrong and bring suffering, the creative element in every serious choice can give the courage to decide. . . . The mixture of the absolute and the relative in moral decisions is what constitutes their danger and their greatness. It gives dignity and tragedy to man, creative joy and pain of failure. Therefore he should not try to escape into a willfulness without norms or into a security without freedom."[7]

Likewise in his autobiography, *Memories, Dreams, Reflections*, Carl Jung wrote of the existential anxiety of moral decision making, saying "we must have the freedom in some circumstances to avoid the known moral good and do what is considered [that is, "normative"] to be evil, if our ethical decision so requires. . . . As a rule, however, the individual is so unconscious that he altogether fails to see his own potentialities for decision. Instead he is consistently looking around for external rules and regulations which can guide him in his perplexity."[8]

In *The Leader of the Future*, Peter Drucker writes of the need for leaders to believe in themselves, love people, and have a passion for the enterprise.[9] Such a philosophy appears aligned with both the communitarian movement and the great Biblical commandment. Drucker went on to state that such leaders experience a clarity of personal values and the emotional strength to manage anxiety and change. One source of such emotional maturity and strength can be the deep faith, peaceful orientation, and detached sense of self that some gain from their religious practices and beliefs.

The universality of all great world religions and their integrity with personal values can be found in their common approach to The Golden Rule, the simple statement of "Do unto others as you would have them do unto you."[10]

> Christian: And as ye would that men should do to you, do ye also to them likewise (Luke 7:31).
>
> Jewish: Do not do to others what you would not want them to do to you (Shabbat 31a).
>
> Islam: None of you is a believer as long as he does not wish his brother what he wishes himself (Forty Hadith of an-Nawawi, 13).
>
> Hindu: One should not behave towards others in a way which is unpleasant for oneself: that is the essence of morality (Mahabharata XIII 114, 8).

Buddhist: A state which is not pleasant or enjoyable for me will also not be so for him; and how can I impose on another a state which is not pleasant or enjoyable for me? (Samyutta Nikaya V, 353.35–342.2).

Confucian: What you yourself do not want, do not do to another person (Sayings 15.23).

Aristotle: We should behave to others as we wish others to behave to us.

Thus, despite great cultural differences, virtually all organized societies have evolved over time the fundamental notion that one must be in community with others and sacrifice one's own ego for the good of the whole. All organized religions also contain elements of spiritual discipline and contemplative practices, in which practitioners attempt to be in harmony with their inner selves and develop a fundamental set of values and beliefs that guide their daily lives. In my teaching of spiritual literature, I have been impressed with the thoughts of both Dante and Kierkegaard in this regard.

When Dante was in exile from Florence, he wrote a letter to one of his protectors, Can Grande from Verona, in which he provided guidance for reading *The Divine Comedy*. Dante said his great poem was polysemous and should be read on four levels at the same time. He described the four levels as follows:

The surface level: Where we each spend most of our time, dealing with the superficialities with which we must all cope in our daily lives and being socialized.

The allegorical level: The level where we determine meanings of life from our heroes and the stories they tell.

The moral level: This is the level which Dante associates with custom, society, and the law. It is that behavior which society as a whole is willing to condone from time to time. It sets limits defined by those living around us.

The deep level of ethics, spirituality, and religion: This is the level from which we draw our deepest meanings of life. This is where we define what we are willing to lose for. It is where we derive our personal voice. This is the level of the transcendent, or what many call God.

I find Dante's formula useful as a metaphor for life. We live on all four levels simultaneously. Most of us spend the bulk of our time in the surface level and the least amount of time in the deep level. Each of us has our personal mythology of heroes and stories that move us. We are deeply attuned to culture and society and what is expected of us. While we have no wish to break the law, there is something deeper that drives our being.

Those with the ability and the support to decompartmentalize their lives and bring the fourth level into all that they do, including their work, can be said to lead fully integrated lives. Others are, as Carl Jung might put it, "unconscious" of the deep level, and they glide along on the surface of things.

Most of us move in and out of the different levels. Organized religion can help us get to the deep level, as can spirituality. Art, music, nature, and transcendent beauty of all sorts can take us to these depths. Few of us, unless we are contemplative monks, spend much time in the deep level. But we can spend more time there intentionally, and the time we spend there defines who we are.

Søren Kierkegaard, the nineteenth-century Christian existentialist, paralleled Dante in his thinking, although he had but three levels: the aesthetic, the ethical, and the religious. His aesthete skims over the surface of the world, becoming culturally adept at enjoying art, wine, food, sexuality, music, and nature but missing the deep richness of life with others. One attains the ethical life by beginning to cease living purely for oneself and stepping up to the responsibilities of career and family. The religious level is attained for Kierkegaard when one develops a spiritual nature and comes to live in the presence of God, achieving maturity. This level, with deep knowledge of the transcendent, is what Dante strives for in his great poem. Rather than being pulled by societal whims, one is rooted in the wisdom of the ages.

The greater the extent to which friendships and relationships are based on a commonality coming from the respective deep levels, the greater sense of support and well-being an individual is likely to have. It is too easy for a kind of hopeless cynicism to emerge and create self-oriented worlds for each of us. Such attitudes narrow the field of choices, as we are always suspecting that others will let us down. A business leader who resonates with the deep foundational values of the enterprise and those working within it is far more likely to break down these walls of cynicism and provide inspired possibilities. The deep sense of the other that comes out of all deep religious convictions helps to take us out of pride and greed. We can become whole, complete, and more relaxed when we discover that we can live out our foundational beliefs.

THIS BRIEF REVIEW of a few ethical systems can, at best, only begin to elevate awareness of different ethical systems and provide a bit of clarity to our thinking. But it is helpful to begin developing a language of ethics if we are ever to reason together. It is also a useful practice to consider which ethics are behind decisions, discussions, and debates. Listen to political candidates debate each other, for example, and you may observe that they unintentionally are constantly shifting their viewpoint from that of utilitarian to Kantian to religious incantation, and so forth. Having a frame of reference for ethics may make such debates more meaningful, and it may also add clarity to events in our daily workplace. We each develop our own ethical code, which often contains elements of all the systems just described. We form our ethical model through those we choose as our heroes, those we respect and deem to lead successful lives, as well as through the actual experiences of our lives, especially those that involve stress and even failure. If we do not intentionally choose models, both personal and intellectual, for our behavior, our journey will continually be subjected to the winds and tides of the moment. When the good people are unwilling to speak out and be counted, the bad people drive the day. Groups of individuals, organizations, and even society itself can be defined by their ethical code and how they live it out.

CHAPTER I

Establishing a Personal Ethic

THERE IS A PARADOXICAL CONNECTION between solitude and togetherness. Dietrich Bonhoeffer, the great German theologian and World War II resistance leader, wrote elegantly about this tension. We need to be "alone together," he said, recognizing our conflicting needs for both and for cultivating each aspect of our lives.

Bonhoeffer ended up with more time alone than he had bargained for. A son of an aristocratic Berlin family, he studied theology at the University of Tubingen and Berlin University and became a Lutheran priest. He traveled twice to the United States, studying at Union Theological Seminary at Columbia University in New York. The eminent social philosopher and theologian Reinhold Niebuhr arranged for Bonhoeffer to sit out World War II in the United States. Yet Bonhoeffer returned to Germany in 1939, writing to Niebuhr, "I will have no right to participate in the reconstruction of Christian life in Germany after the war if I do not share the trials of this time with my people."[1]

Bonhoeffer became a leader in the small portion of the German Lutheran church that went underground and resisted Hitler's regime. The last years of his life were filled with living out the tension between obeying the requirements of his faith and plotting tyrannicide and lying to the Gestapo under torture to protect his friends and relatives. He was imprisoned for eighteen months, initially by the army authorities in Berlin and later by the Gestapo. Hitler held Bonhoeffer a responsible party in the July 20, 1944, attempt on his life. Bonhoeffer was sent to Buchenwald concentration camp and ultimately to Flossenburg, where he was hanged at age thirty-nine on direct orders from Hitler—just three weeks before Patton's army of liberation arrived at the camp.

Bonhoeffer's collected writings portray the brilliance of a young theologian whose potential was never achieved. Indeed, his contemporaries who survived the war in Germany, Great Britain, the United States, and elsewhere felt that he would have become a powerful voice in the post–World War II ecumenical church movement. His thoughts concerning the character of postwar religion are only partly formed in his books *Ethics* and *Letters and Papers from Prison*. Because of their incompleteness, his thoughts have been used by others to support a wide range of theological positions, ranging from support for the contemplative life in the midst of secular community to support for liberating, antiestablishment movements throughout the world.

The drama and poignancy of his life, together with the unfinished nature of his intellectual work, have created widespread and enduring interest in his life and writings. I was one of those drawn to him.

ESTABLISHING A PERSONAL ETHIC

As a young investment banker, I was strongly interested in Bonhoeffer's writings. Here was an active, highly privileged man of the world who brought his faith into everything he did and attempted to use that faith to make a difference in a world that he considered corrupt. Over the past twenty-five years, I have read everything I can find by him or about him, toured all the places in Germany where he lived and worked, met with some of his close associates, and helped fund a project to translate his complete writings into English. I have found Bonhoeffer very useful in my life. He served as a model for me in how he brought his contemplative and theological concepts into the sometimes frightening, hard-edged reality of the secular world of Nazi Germany. Through him I discovered the potential for living an integrated religious life and still being an authentic investment banker.

Bonhoeffer's writings helped me to recognize the conflicting needs for solitude and community within myself and to act out of those tensions. As my responsibilities grew within Morgan Stanley I found myself more and more in conflict with the various internal assignments given me by the firm, the demands and needs of my clients, and the priorities which I had previously set for myself. Well before the dawn of e-mail and cell phones, I found too much of my time being dictated by telephone messages and my in-box. The barrage of daily data became increasingly irrelevant without a deeper sense of purpose. I felt the need for time for contemplation, for reading books rather than memos, for broadening beyond the everydayness.

Bonhoeffer's words spoke to me. As he wrote in his most popular work, *Life Together*, "One who wants fellowship without solitude plunges into the void of words and feelings, and one who seeks solitude without fellowship perishes in the abyss of vanity, self-infatuation and despair. Let him who cannot be alone beware of community. Let him who is not in community beware of being alone. . . . One does not exist without the other. Right speech comes out of silence, and right silence comes out of speech."[2] Bonhoeffer helped me to set my moral compass. He had to make decisions far more difficult than any I ever encountered, and he did so with courage and a deep faith commitment. He made religion seem relevant to me. It no longer was important that I had difficulty with some of the assumptions of my Christian faith, issues I had puzzled over. What mattered was that I could use his image in my mind's eye to validate my own spiritual and religious feelings in the midst of the highly secular world in which I was living. Bonhoeffer was a real man, with a sense of humor and a love of wine, tobacco, women, gospel music, travel, hiking, reading, and more. He had learned to deal with wealth. He had at least two love interests. He lived an active, engaged life. And yet he brought his religion in a meaningful way into the very crisis of his life. He was an intellectual theologian, a pastor, and a spiritual contemplative, spending time in monasteries in England and Germany and replicating monastic life in his underground seminary.

How does one operate with a strong sense of mission, purpose, and autonomy while at the same time developing the skills required to lead teams and establish deep trust relationships? We need time alone to think, gain perspective, and figure out what we stand for. Ironically, Bonhoeffer honed this experience during his eighteen months in prison. We also need time together to build and sustain relationships. Bonhoeffer was close in age to his illegal seminarians. They engaged in sports together, and he introduced them to American jazz music. Being successful in business demands an extroverted nature: the ability to engage others, to be convincing, to make the sale, to prevail. Being successful as a leader also demands an introspective nature: the ability to determine one's basic values, where to take a stand, what one is willing to lose for. For me, Bonhoeffer modeled all these traits, leading me eventually to teach in my church, serve in residence in a seminary, and become a lay member of a Benedictine monastery, all while running a successful business unit at Morgan Stanley. Bonhoeffer showed me that I could intentionally try to live a rich spiritual life and still be an authentic business person.

SETTING FORTH ON A PILGRIMAGE

We all need touchstones in order to remain centered on the true reality of life. We cannot find our way alone. While on our life journey, we each need an *internal compass* as a way to deal with tension and change both in business and in our lives. There are, of course, many opportunities to get knocked off course. A correct moral compass enables us over time to instinctively see the ethical issues in each situation and complete our journey safely. The compass can—and indeed should—be developed from all sides of our lives. No course in ethics can fill in all the spots. Upbringing, education, and even casual activities all factor in, if one is alert to the possibilities. Even the decidedly nonbusiness writings of Charles Williams, who was a close friend of C. S. Lewis and T. S. Eliot, have lessons for us all. In his seven novels, which some people refer to as "theological thrillers," he depicts the significance of small, unimportant daily acts leading either to grace and redemption or into a pattern of evil behavior. The choices are there every day. It is far too easy for us to lose our ethical sensitivity and walk right through them. We also need to achieve a balance and not become the "house nag." When and where we take our stand defines who we are, both to ourselves and to those around us.

As Bonhoeffer has so aptly described, we must learn to live in tension with ourselves and with our various communities. To be successful at investment banking, for example, it helps to be a "type A" personality, dedicated to persuading others, prevailing and getting things done. Such persons have a strong sense of the self, especially in the moment. Yet to be truly successful, they also must develop a deep sense of the needs and desires of others. This comes from participating in community and listening to others. They must develop a deeper sense of the self beyond the current moment. This comes from self-reflection and time alone, whether in nature, humanism, or spirituality, developing those values that trump expediency and determine who we want to be.

At an early stage in my career at Morgan Stanley, I was working on the financing of a new aluminum company in Australia. During the course of the assignment, the company went public. It was then the custom in Australia to award "founders shares" of common stock at an extremely low price to friends of the company just prior to the public offering. Shares were given to several individuals in the United States, including three individuals at Morgan Stanley—two partners and me, a junior associate. The dollar amount allocated to me by the Australians was fairly small, but so was my salary. I knew that my relatively miniscule junior associate salary and bonus was calibrated by the partners with great precision, and any subtle distinctions in the amounts of compensation within my group were meant to convey significant messages. It made me uncomfortable to be receiving something that was not offered to my peers.

I did not yet own a television set or a car, and those "founders shares" sure looked good, but I knew I had to divulge my windfall to one of the senior partners. I hoped this might be an ambiguous issue that could go my way. I really wanted the shares, but my own moral compass was pointing me toward full disclosure and transparency. In making this decision, which was primarily intuitive, I had to begin to develop a sense not only of who I was but of what the norms and values of the firm were as well, and of how I could be true to my own values while still meshing with those of the group. Another issue was that what might have been legal under then existing Australian securities laws might not have been legal if the issuer had been under the jurisdiction of the Securities and Exchange Commission. At this early stage in my career, I did not have the judgment to discern between possibly conflicting global rules. How could I sustain my own values and still fit in as a constructive part of the group?

Part of the reconciliation was in how I framed the issue. I did not state that there was anything wrong. I knew I needed some help. I went to a senior partner whom I trusted and asked him for an interpretation of the issue, stating that, on the margin, it made me uncomfortable. A precondition for a successful interpretation of the rules is that trust relationship, which is invaluable. Later, as a leader at Morgan Stanley, I tried to emulate the behavior of the senior partner to whom I had turned for advice in this instance. I was very uncomfortable receiving the shares "under the table," and I knew that full disclosure would only cause resentment and ill will among my peers. In a way it was trading short-term gains for long-run relationships. The situation was ambiguous; there was no one right answer, other than the one that I could live with.

I felt I had to divulge my windfall in a way that would not cause the shares to be taken away from the partners I was working with. I outlined my dilemma to the senior partner, stating that I did not wish to receive additional compensation to which I was not entitled, nor did I wish to interfere in any way with the other individuals involved. The senior partners reallocated my shares to the two partners, nothing was said, and there was no change in my year-end bonus. The senior partner in whom I confided became a good friend and, ultimately, a CEO of Morgan Stanley.

Not everyone would have made the same decision that I did. There was nothing wrong in receiving founders shares by the norms of that day. I had a taste of what was to come, and I felt I had done the right thing. It was fair to give the additional shares to the two partners who had worked on the deal. It might also have been fair to put the shares in a firm investment account for the benefit of all the partners, but I was not then knowledgeable about such practices. My autonomous values caused me to have the ethical sensitivity to feel uncomfortable about the offer of the shares. I was still discovering the values of the Morgan Stanley culture and the ways in which its values were harmonious with mine.

Ethical sensitivity is a state of mind and needs to be developed. Because someone who raises ethical issues in every circumstance and every day quickly becomes a genuine pain in the neck and unemployable, the true art of ethical sensitivity is knowing where and when to make a stand. Taking a stand can require a great deal of courage; you have to be sure of what you're willing to lose for. We each need a group of peers, in the workplace and elsewhere, with whom we can discuss the everyday issues without putting ourselves in jeopardy. As we work out our values, we will be tested and retested; each test is an opportunity to learn. Great leaders are tested time and again, and they learn from their failures. They have been through the crucible.

An underlying core ethic is what differentiates a profession from a job. A true professional is someone who can be trusted by others to provide unbiased and objective advice that is generally acknowledged as fair. Such individuals are not viewed as being out for themselves, but rather as willing to sacrifice some degree of current success for the long-term betterment of the enterprise. They have a sense of purpose and mission beyond themselves. The force of their perceived integrity draws others to them. Professional firms are regarded in the same way. Such trust and reputation, once accorded to an individual or to a firm, becomes binary: we do not trust a person or a firm 45 percent of the time; we either honor them with our trust or we do not. This explains the irony that when "good people" stumble, they seem to fall farther than individuals with lesser reputations.

FINDING THE DRIVERS

Having a strong sense of personal values is not always enough. If the personal values are not supported and lived out by the organizations in which one participates, the result can be great frustration, isolation, and bitterness. Not long ago I attended a lecture on the leadership style of John Wooden, the great UCLA basketball coach. The speaker boasted that Wooden could be effective running any large business concern. I spoke up and objected. Wooden's deep values of work, self-discipline, and even prayer could be effective only in an organization that honored such values. I stated that, for example, l did not believe Coach Wooden would have been a very effective leader within the culture that existed at Enron.

If we think of life as a pilgrimage, we discover we need the support of those taking the journey with us, for companionship, even safety, but we also need the time alone to develop and refine our core values. I am reminded of a humorous tale told by a Benedictine monk of "hermits having conventions." At a particular hermitage, hermits lived alone in huts during the week and got together on Saturday evenings for dinner, when they raised a hubbub of conversation concerning their experiences and the best practices of hermit-hood. Thus we need to be together to be alone; and we need to be alone to be together.

A key task of a business leader is to get inside the ethical culture of the organization. Individuals will be far more productive if they can align their personal values with those of the enterprise. The most difficult challenge for a leader is to change that culture if appropriate, especially when the values are deeply entrenched. Once an individual has found personal congruence within an organization, a significant change in the culture, even if it is for the better, can be viewed as a betrayal of trust. Neither of these highly sensitive and paramount tasks is possible if the leader does not have a sense of purpose and mission for the business or personally beyond making money or getting promoted. Without having a core ethic in place, a leader cannot successfully create a valid ethic for the business and the employees who make the business work.

It thus becomes important for a business leader to be sensitive to the needs and values of the employees. A Drucker Foundation book, *Leading Beyond the Walls*, concludes that getting rich is not a deep enough motivation to sustain most employees throughout a demanding career. The book reports that the principal factors involved in creating a culture that breeds trust, inducing individuals to stay in a firm, include (1) maintaining integrity, (2) openly communicating a vision and values, (3) showing respect as equal partners, (4) focusing on shared goals, not personal agendas, (5) doing the right thing regardless of personal risk, (6) listening with an open mind, (7) demonstrating caring compassion, and (8) maintaining confidences.[3] As employees we need to feel that we and our work product are important. We need affirmation at work. We need to be trusted. If we are to go the extra mile, we need to know we will be treated fairly and supported if we make a mistake. Managers and leaders must become sensitive to the needs of employees for empowerment, trust, and integrity. The reminders are everywhere; one need only be alert to them.

In a recent speech, Radha R. Basu, CEO of SupportSoft.com, a Silicon Valley software developer, recounted lessons she'd learned while observing her Sherpa support team during her two treks to the Everest Base Camp in Nepal. She found these lessons helpful in her business. Basa recounted, "The lessons you acquire while trekking include resilience, endurance and teamwork. Working with Sherpas and seeing their selfless teamwork was an inspiration. Their fulfillment comes from being part of a team, not being the one who reaches the summit. You are only a success because of your team. You just happen to be the point that's visible. The people who do the 'small' things are as important as those who do the big things."[4] Acknowledging that lesson and then keeping it alive in a business environment is the challenge before many leaders.

Ian Mitroff, Distinguished Professor of Business Policy at the Marshall School of Business at the University of Southern California, describes the top five items that give meaning and purpose to employees at work as (1) having interesting work to perform, (2) realizing one's full potential as a person, (3) being associated with a good organization, (4) being associated with an ethical organization, and (5) making money.[5] These human needs overlap. Individuals truly want to make their work their vocation, their outlet for expressing their individuality, creativity, and moral sensitivity. Rather than operate in a command-and-control environment, they want to be able to define their own limits and be trusted. If given the freedom to cocreate their work, they will be more productive than otherwise. They don't want to "put their game face on at the office." They want to be able to be the same person whether at work, at home, at play, or at their place of worship.

Much as it can be a powerful short-term and intermediate-term driver, financial wealth ranks below the top motivational drives in the studies we have cited. As a long-term business school recruiter, I looked for fire in the belly: focused energy, the drive to succeed. I was careful to watch for how people defined that characteristic, though. It cannot be defined solely by financial remuneration; instead, it must be linked to a strong sense of personal integrity.

In my own case, financial rewards were more important as a measure of my relative success within the firm than for their own sake. Certainly I enjoyed the prospect of a new car, a nice home, and travels—but I also have always loved the simplicity and stripped-down nature of the backpacker's life. I don't want my journey cluttered up with too many things. Yet as a result of the boom market for financial services since financial deregulation in 1975 and Morgan Stanley's highly successful public offering of its equity in 1986, those of us who struggled in the early 1960s and stuck it out became wealthy beyond our wildest imagination. I was enabled to retire at age fifty-three and pursue a whole new portfolio of activities, much as I had outlined in an early written personal life plan. A couple of partners retired in their mid-forties and went to divinity school. Others stayed on, further enhancing their personal wealth, even though they are now past their mid-sixties. Everyone has a number at which they feel financially secure, and the range of numbers—even among successful investment bankers—is broad indeed.

For some who stayed on, their work had become a vocation, and they thrived in the role of senior counselor and trusted friend to clients and younger associates. Many grew into the creative uses of wealth, living outside themselves, serving the needs of others. Wealth can create disposable time, and one becomes challenged to use that time in ways meaningful to others.

There are dangers in making financial rewards the chief driver. As firms like Morgan Stanley became larger and more specialized, it was increasingly difficult to gain whole-task involvement. When wealth becomes the overriding goal, it becomes easier to be disappointed, and burnout seems to occur much earlier. We require something deeper to sustain us, an underlying ethic that will support us through our lives, through our careers, and over time.

ETHICS AND INCLUSION: STAKEHOLDERS AND THE PUBLIC TRUST

Great leaders will have the sensitivity to recognize ethical issues and the self-confidence and courage to raise up such issues as a part of their customary business decision model. They will create an atmosphere that supports questioning "the plan" from an ethical perspective. Individuals will raise issues and speak up only if they feel they are working in a trust environment. How does a leader create this trust? Through demonstrated fairness, promise keeping, genuine interest in others, and a consistent record of small acts that build up a pattern of integrity. Individuals must be convinced that it is okay to bring their personal ethics into the workplace. The more open the discussion and the more thoroughly the analysis considers the broad range of possibly affected parties, the better chance there is of coming up with the right solution. As we increase our influence on the direction of the enterprise, our sensitivity to the needs of the stakeholders is at a premium. The more inclusively and creatively we can define the web of affected parties, the better chance we have of making a tough decision correctly. Conversely, the more narrowly we define our constituency, the greater our chance for error. If the affected party is always a universe of one—*me*: my wealth, my status, my power—the answers will invariably become less ethical over time.

Over time leaders develop an intuitive sense of what is right and what is wrong, a deeper level of ethical awareness and sensitivity, and the courage to act on hunches, knowing that on occasion those hunches will prove incorrect. One gains this ethical courage through practice and experience. Group norms need to support ethical inquiry, foster discussion of ethical issues, and tolerate occasional misjudgments. One litmus test for the ethics of a situation is to define as broadly and creatively as possible the list of affected parties, or stakeholders, to a business decision or practice. Are customers regarded as individuals to be served or as individuals to be outsmarted? A leader who has the ability to listen and align the enterprise with the values of the employees, customers, and society as a whole will have an empowered enterprise.

Johnson & Johnson

A strong case in point is Johnson & Johnson. That firm has done a better job than most in making its values explicit to all employees through the Johnson & Johnson "Credo." All employees are expected to read, discuss, and sign on to the Credo as they enter the company's workforce. Thus there can be little ambiguity in what the firm stands for (so long as the firm lives out the Credo).

In both 1982 and 1986, through no fault of the firm, certain lots of its Tylenol product were tampered with and poisoned, resulting in the deaths of a small number of consumers and a nationwide scare. One hundred million people had taken Tylenol the year prior to the initial problem. The product was withdrawn from the market, repackaged, and successfully reintroduced to consumers. The overall cost of the reaction to the poisoning was calculated as high as $500 million. Tylenol represented about $100 million a year in profit to the company. From the very beginning and during the some twenty-five hundred calls from reporters that came in the early weeks, the company was completely open and candid with the press. All available information was given to the press so that the public could be informed and protected. The company took immediate steps to protect its customers, withdrawing the product from the market without losing the public's trust and reintroducing it to become once again the most popular over-the-counter pain remedy.

A major factor in this success story was the character of the CEO, James Burke, and his deep concern for core values. When he first became CEO he challenged what was known as the Johnson & Johnson Credo. He stated that if the Credo, which was by then thirty years old, was not still meaningful to managers, it would be better to "tear it off the wall" than to have it stand for nothing. Thus he was striving for alignment between personal values and corporate values. The result was a series of meetings culminating in a rewording and reaffirmation of the Credo. The Credo was then promulgated to all employees. In brief, the current Credo, now over fifty years old, states, "We believe our first responsibility is to the doctors, nurses and patients, to mothers and fathers and all others who use our products and services. . . . We are responsible to our employees. . . . We are responsible to the communities in which we live and work and to the world community as well. . . . Our final responsibility is to our stockholders."[6] The Credo is notable in that it encompasses a broad range of stakeholders and in that it puts the shareholder (making money) in last place.

The Tylenol crisis was the real Credo challenge. As James Burke said in a classroom visit to the Harvard Business School, "I do know that running through my mind throughout . . . was how the hell after we'd had everybody in the world challenge the system, buy into it, and say, 'Yes, we believe in it,' could we sit in our offices and say, 'Well, in this case we're just not going to do it.' So we locked ourselves in. . . ."[7]

Johnson & Johnson's success with the public was due to a number of factors. The facts were on its side: the company had not been negligent and there was nothing to cover up. Second, the company reacted very quickly to the problem. It did not engage in "analysis paralysis." Instead, there was quick consensus to do the right thing. The company entered into a partnership with the media. The third factor was the reputation for trust the firm had established prior to the tampering. The fourth factor in saving the brand was James Burke himself. He took responsibility for the firm, all its employees, and the lives of a number of consumers. He took full command. It was a situation for which probably no one inside or outside the company was prepared. Finally, the firm had the financial resources to get through the crisis.

Burke put forth three principles that he felt underlay successful management at Johnson & Johnson:

Decentralization: "You must give people freedom to do what they are capable of and stay out of their way. . . ."

The Credo: "Without a moral center that you can recognize and understand, I am absolutely convinced you can swim in chaos."

Time horizon: "The company really has to want to manage for the long term."

Of the Credo, Burke stated, "If you really read the Credo, it doesn't say anything very profound except in its simplicity. It just says that everybody is responsible to all those that are dependent upon them."

As Harvard Business School expresses in a teaching note to the case, "The real power of this material is that students should be brought to understand that hard choices lay ahead. But these choices are just that—choices. Students are not in the grip of an evil system that compels them to sacrifice their finer instincts and impulses in order to put bread on the family's table. To the contrary. They can—if they have a sense of themselves and force themselves to challenge their own views of right and wrong—be true to their better selves and make a perfectly good living as well."[8]

Enron

In direct contrast to Johnson & Johnson is Enron. Some of the Enron issues involved highly technical infractions of securities regulations, a slippery area since the rules and regulations have not been written definitively to cover all the technicalities of hedging and the use of derivatives. However, the main issue at Enron, as it was with the insider trading scandals, does not lie in technical aspects of laws and regulations; one can live within them and still commit fraud. Like insider trading, fraud is a state of mind, and a state of mind is beyond the scope of the legal system. As Dante and others have written, fraud has the face of an honest man.

The bad practices at Enron did not emerge all at once but developed incrementally. Beyond the unconscionable sums some Enron executives were paid in relation to their contributions to society, the great crime at Enron is the breaking of the public trust. This has, in turn, raised issues of public trust with respect to public accounting firms, law firms, management consulting firms, boards of directors, financial reporting, business leadership, and the stock market itself. Because in this age of globalization of money and capital markets the U.S. capital markets are looked on throughout the world as the model to be emulated, Enron thus broke trust with institutions throughout the world.

The leaders at Enron appeared to encourage a reckless, no-holds-barred trading culture in many ways, not the least of which was encouraging the establishment of a fake trading floor, staffed with clerical and support help, to defraud visiting financial analysts and bond-rating agencies. One senses from reports that the leaders at Enron winked at excesses and viewed the law not as a constraint but as something to be gotten around. Theirs is a classic example of the fact that without ethical leadership, bad practices can drive out good ones.

We can only speculate how different the outcome might have been with a different ethical base. It takes people of exceptionally strong ethical discernment, courage, and character to blow the whistle when, at least superficially, everything appears to be going well. What was needed was leadership with a moral compass, leadership that would set limits and establish controls. At its highest level, the role of leadership is to establish a transcendent goal for the enterprise that rises above annual bonuses and momentary success. A true leader has a deep sense of purpose, calm, and even detachment during a crisis; the trust that has been built up sustains employees during a time of high anxiety and stress. In contrast, the atmosphere at Enron seemed to have been one of chaos and confusion, leading to shredding; bailouts; last-minute bonuses; and hasty, false reassurances that all was well. Enron lacked both a Credo and a James Burke.

By any measure, the fallout on shareholders and many employees at Enron was not fair: they suffered both financial loss and loss of reputation due to events and deceits beyond their control. But the idea of fairness is not always so clear.

FAIRNESS AS CONTEXTUAL

At Morgan Stanley I was often involved in determining "fairness" and learned early in my career that fairness is contextual. A major lesson in this regard came during my first big real estate assignment on taking over leadership of the real estate finance unit. It involved the sale of the Irvine Ranch. We were retained by the James Irvine Foundation (the "Foundation"), which owned 54 percent of the common stock of the James Irvine

Company. The Company, in turn, owned the Irvine Ranch, which comprised about one-fifth, or ninety-three thousand acres, of Orange County, south of Los Angeles. The Foundation carried its 54 percent ownership of the James Irvine Company on its books for the total value of one dollar. Our assignment at Morgan Stanley was to value the asset for purposes of complying with the Internal Revenue Service and paying the newly required excise tax. The Tax Reform Act of 1969 contained several provisions aimed at charitable foundations requiring them to update valuations of their assets to current market values, pay an excise tax on the revised value of the assets, and diversify their investments, among other matters.

Our five-person assignment team spent months valuing the Irvine Ranch, touring the property, visiting with senior management, and examining their business plan. We determined that all land of greater than thirty-degree slope was not developable. We made assumptions as to annual absorption rates for single-family homes, apartments, retail shops, industrial parks, and office buildings. We figured that it would take thirty years to develop the entire ranch. We had to come up with the correct interest rate with which to discount future years' cash flows into present-value dollars.

At Morgan Stanley we were aware that our mission from the Foundation was to come up with a value we could support in court—and that would be in the lower end of a valuation range, since it was to be used as the basis for excise tax payments by the Foundation. We were not bound to come up with the highest number a buyer might possibly pay in an auction process, for example. For some, there is only one fair value, no matter the purpose of the valuation. The problem, as demonstrated by the process we went through internally, is that individuals can come up with widely varying notions of what that "perfect" value may be. Our analysis comprised hundreds, if not thousands, of judgments as to the timing of development, rental rates, expenses, and other factors. We also had to consider the possible impact of zoning disputes. The City of Irvine was then attempting to slow or stop further growth. In addition, the Sierra Club and other environmentalists were already intervening to stop the James Irvine Company's five-year plan, which called for the commencement of resort and hotel development along three-and-a-half miles of the Pacific coast by the end of the decade.[9] Aside from these unknowns, we understood that assets can have more value for certain owners depending upon their financial capacity, the blend with assets already owned, and their particular ideas of how to develop the asset.

In framing our valuation, we had three lengthy meetings of all the partners of Morgan Stanley. The end product, in which we placed a value of less than $200 million for 100 percent of the property, was a consensus view of all the senior partners in the firm. We ignored the extremes of opinion on both the high and the low ends. Although in today's market this number seems bargain basement, almost twenty-five years ago we felt we had come up with a fair and appropriate valuation and one that would serve our client well in terms of IRS requirements and taxes due.

Several months after we delivered our valuation, an opinion letter, and backup materials to the Foundation trustees in San Francisco, a couple of the trustees called me. They were quite excited, and they were speaking rapidly, but as I understood it, they had used our IRS valuation materials as a "selling document" and offered the Foundation's shares to CNA, Gulf Oil, and Mobil Oil. Mobil Oil had come back with an offer of $200 million for all of the shares of the James Irvine Company, including the 46 percent of the shares held by individuals and not by the Foundation, and the trustees required a Morgan Stanley written opinion that the transaction was fair in order to validate their deal.

I was concerned. The trustees had misused our document. They had approached the market on a very limited basis, among their close friends, without adequately covering the market. They had used a document written for the IRS that attempted to support a value at the low end of a fairness range rather than a document that promoted the sales features of the property and could be used to solicit higher offers.

The obvious query back was, What is a fair price? That we would not know until the property was fully exposed to the market and we obtained, through a well-orchestrated auction process, a market-clearing price. The current price might or might not be fair; it probably was not. The process was clearly flawed and would not, under normal circumstances, produce the highest price.

Thus I was learning that both rational business decisions and fairness are contextual. It is not always easy to discover the truth, even through concerted efforts. If we were to value an asset for the purpose of paying a tax based on the valuation, we would correctly come up with a much different value than the price that might be paid for the asset in an orchestrated auction with ample time for discovery. In the case of Irvine, we needed time and a process that would find the one buyer in the world for whom the ranch provided the greatest value. Following a prolonged court process and a nine-month auction period in which we made 113 offerings of the property throughout the world, we sold the property for $336 million to an investment group that included Henry Ford, shopping center developer Al Taubman, and local Orange County developer Donald Bren.

Donald Bren subsequently bought out his partners. His long-term outlook, deep knowledge of local Orange County markets, and concerned stewardship of the land made him the best buyer for acknowledging the long-term value of the property. The court process brought together the IRS, the State of California (having purview over California foundations), and Joan Irvine Smith, a minority owner of the Irvine Ranch, who was seeking a court adjudication of the fairness of the transaction. The judicial process along with the orchestrated auction effectively cleared the market and validated the final price. There was no issue raised as to our previous IRS valuation, as it had occurred seven years earlier and without the market process.

We were operating in a fishbowl. Every single event in the long-orchestrated auction, which took many months, was reported on the front pages of the financial press. I appeared for several days as a witness in the court case, and I was constantly engaged in the courthouse lobby by individuals claiming to represent Arabian princes and the like who would pay much higher prices for the property. Each of these dubious leads had to be checked out so we could prove their veracity and convince the judge of our serious intent to get the highest price.

The Irvine Ranch sale raised numerous issues. The drawn-out court process took almost three years, which meant I had to make a sustained commitment of resources to the deal without receiving any current income. The IRS valuation had to be reasonable so as to avoid sustained further litigation or payment of fines by my client. (Our client actually expressed the view that our valuation number was high.) Once the trustees of the Foundation had unilaterally put the property on the market, we had an obligation to ensure that the price received was not only fair but the best price obtainable at that time. In fact, the James Irvine Foundation has, since the sale, become a very important benefactor to charitable institutions throughout California. As a lover of the land and the California coastline myself, I always faced the issue of how much weight to attach to a responsible land developer as against someone who would skim the cream and engage in poor land use. In many ways, through the use of the land and the ongoing charitable work of our client, the stakeholders to the transaction included all the citizens of California.

During the Irvine transaction we were continually determining fairness (in an ever-changing world), while attempting to make sure that what we were doing fit with our personal ethic.

WE CONTINUALLY ARE CHALLENGED to test our own values against those of the groups in which we become involved. At times we may be involved in unhealthy groups or relationships, and we are challenged to terminate our involvement with them, or at least to minimize their influence. At times we may be called on to help change the value system, or to go against the prevailing set of values. Such matters require courage and a willingness to take personal risk. There are times when we may assert our personal autonomy and turn out to be wrong ourselves. Thus a strong sense of who we are is necessary, not only in taking a personal stand but also in surviving the times when we turn out to be in error ourselves. Sustaining nurturing values, through literature, relationships, nature, music, art, and even religion and spirituality, is an important issue on our lifelong journey.

CHAPTER 2

Living with Intention

AS YOU ENTER into any community, whether it's a new business environment, a new business unit, or simply a new group of people, you are entering a new culture. If it's a strong culture, its members will attempt through a variety of methods to "socialize" you into buying into the customs, rules, and mores of that culture. This can be a positive development so long as there is goal congruency, since such socialization makes you a more effective player within that culture. To establish the prerequisite correspondence of goals, you must first know yourself.

In his book *Leading Out Loud*, Terry Pearce reports the answering machine greeting of a friend, Gary Fiedel, as follows: "Hi, this is Gary, and this is not an answering machine, it is a questioning machine! The two questions are, 'Who are you?' and 'What do you want?' . . . and if you think those are trivial questions, consider that 95 percent of the population goes through life and never answers either one!"[1] Answering these questions is work for a thoughtful individual. Important as these questions are on a personal level, they become even more critical for one who is or hopes to become a leader, for leaders must know the answers to these questions to be able to pass their own inspiration on to others.

It is difficult to become intentional about all the various experiences we will have in life, but striving toward that can certainly be a goal. These efforts and our reactions to the unexpected crises help to define who we are. Out of these experiences we can begin to shape patterns in our consciousness about who we are and who we hope to be.

DEMONSTRATING CHOICES

In the 1950s ROTC was active on campuses throughout the country, and upon graduation I was commissioned as a second lieutenant in the United States Army. A six-month active duty program together with an obligation to serve an additional seven-and-a-half years in the reserves had just been promulgated, but I opted for two years of active duty. I knew I wanted to go to graduate school, and I also felt I needed a break from academia. As a volunteer, I looked forward to military service. My father, two of my uncles, and my grandfather had all served in military-related activities.

My eyesight precluded combat specialties, so I applied for military intelligence and ended up attending the Army intelligence school in Baltimore for seven months. On completion of that course, I volunteered for thirteen months of duty in Korea. At that point, I had never traveled outside the United States, and Asia—and in particular Asian religions—had an appeal to me. Even within the rigidity of the military system, I was able to control my experience to a degree, in that I chose a two-year commitment and I chose Korea. Feeling I had a role in where I went empowered me to seek to learn as much from the experience as possible.

I was stationed on the demilitarized zone in support of the South Korean Army, on full combat alert. I was the youngest person in the platoon, which I commanded. The military provided a powerful experience in honing skills in leadership, teaching, teamwork, and adapting to changing circumstances and stressful situations. The opportunity to work in close contact with older men who took their mission seriously was also a maturing experience for me. Upon my completion of the tour, the Army offered me a fully paid scholarship and a salary to attend Harvard Business School if I would extend for six more years. Although I was now independent and had insufficient funds, I opted to try my luck on my own.

TESTING YOURSELF

While in Korea I was accepted at two business schools—Stanford and Harvard. I chose to attend Harvard, since I had already spent four years at Stanford and it seemed the greater challenge. Also, I had retained the memory all those years of a conversation I had with my father when I was in the eighth grade. Presumably suffering from premature angst, I had, out of the blue, asked him: "What shall I do?" He paused for a long moment, and replied, "I don't know what you should do, but all the guys I know who have made it big in this town went to Stanford, then Harvard Business School, and ended up owning a piece of the business they worked for."

This offhand comment may well have been just his way of encouraging me to set my sights high and do well in school. But in the back of my mind that became my plan. At each critical juncture a door was opened, and I went to Stanford, then Harvard Business School, and then landed a job at Morgan Stanley. In reality, I played out variations on a theme. I did not know what an investment bank was until I arrived at Harvard. In the early days, I was a fish out of water in the heady atmosphere of a small Wall Street partnership. I required a great deal of socialization. I was fortunate in that there were those at Morgan Stanley who were patient with me as I found my way. So, in time, I did end up owning a piece of the business I worked for.

As I look back on the process of selecting a career and a firm within that career, I realize how fortunate I was that, at the time, my personal vision for a business career encompassed a vision of a good firm that I picked up in my reading and incorporated into my journal. That vision was of a learning organization where I could grow and meet my potential; a successful organization where I could free myself from financial anxieties; a trust organization where I could form deep personal relationships with individuals for whom I had respect and affection; a well-run organization with articulated and agreed-upon rules and sanctions that were administered fairly; and an organization with a vision of serving others to which I could become committed. I was fortunate that, during the time I was there, Morgan Stanley met those criteria.

I was also fortunate to live in a society that honors merit and hard work. The institutions we have nurtured and sustained in the United States provide unparalleled opportunity for individuals. In my case it was the United States Army, Stanford and Harvard universities, and even Morgan Stanley. Although I initially was intimidated by that firm's reputation and atmosphere of money and privilege, I came to realize that many of the senior partners had come from middle-class backgrounds similar to mine. My contemporaries and I were given a wonderfully generous opportunity to learn and grow and participate in the success of that firm.

In contrast, in many countries throughout the world, there are no institutions on which individuals may base their education and livelihood and trust they will be treated fairly and in proportion to their value, whatever their background. As a result people in these areas must rely on family relationships and connections and "payback" of various forms. What we might call "crony capitalism" may be the only rational response in such an environment. We in the United States are empowered to determine what we do. It matters little who our parents are or where we are from. We tend to lose sight of how fortunate we are, transforming the great opportunities we have into entitlements.

Who are you? What do you want? One way to establish what you stand for is to test your attitudes toward such things as wealth, time, fame, and power. These are concepts one must become comfortable with in a successful business career. How do we test such attitudes? One way to begin a testing process is to formally write out a personal business plan that addresses these issues. Such a self-imposed discipline can help us think through the issues and become more purposeful in living them out. It has been said that a vision without a plan is a hallucination.

A PERSONAL BUSINESS PLAN

I wrote a personal business plan in my second year at Harvard Business School, when my business policy professor, Steve Fuller, had each of us write a plan for our lives. He suggested we have a strategy for the next three to five years, in which we focused on continued learning; an intermediate-term strategy over, say, eight to ten years, in which we made substantive career decisions; and a long-term strategy for our lives, in which he urged us to come to terms with the benefits of leading a balanced life. He wanted us to think through how we viewed such matters as marriage, family, wealth, "success," philanthropy, community, health, hobbies, reading, music, or adventures and their relative importance for us.

I was surprised and pleased to have a prestigious second-year professor emphasize the importance of such activities. This process of thinking through a plan for my life was a watershed event for me, so much so that I have held on to the plan itself through forty-five years of moves around the country. Mine was not a rigid plan, but the process of thinking it through and writing it down expanded my concept of what my life as a professional businessperson might become. As a result I gave myself permission to pursue activities meaningful to me outside of work, at every stage of my life. At that time, I had formed strong interests in hiking and mountaineering and jazz music, and I was an inveterate reader. Although I was reared in a lower-middle-class family and surroundings, my parents had steeped me in the practice of philanthropy. I began to gain a different perspective on the value of time, especially discretionary time, and the responsible use of time. Among other things, I was able to sustain a career as well as fulfill a boyhood dream by organizing treks into the Himalayas. In my early forties I was brave (or reckless) enough to insist on a six-month sabbatical from Morgan Stanley so I could indulge myself in a six-hundred-mile Himalayan trek. While on the journey I had an experience with a Hindu holy man that has continued to shape and direct my teaching of business ethics, an experience I wrote about in my *Harvard Business Review* article, "The Parable of the Sadhu."

Having a life plan also provided a firm yet flexible foundation as my interests broadened into new areas while I grew older, areas that include ethics, theology, and spirituality. Giving myself the freedom to use time in these ways undoubtedly sustained my interest in a business career over the long term and provided me with a sense of detachment and independent thinking that proved invaluable in a complex professional life.

I came into this second-year course at Harvard Business School having just spent the summer working on Wall Street, and it looked as though I was going to receive several offers to join investment banks in New York City. The placement officer at Harvard Business School had listed the qualifications for such positions as "blood, money, and brains." I knew my blood was O positive and that I had successfully completed the Harvard program, but I was flat broke and in debt. My parents were social workers and had never owned a common stock. My background was far from the norm in my class, in which it seemed everyone was the son of someone important, or at least knew someone important. Beyond that, it seemed that everyone else had gone to a proper Eastern prep school followed by Harvard, Yale, or Princeton. In those days Stanford was regarded as a regional university and lacked its current standing. San Francisco was considered a charming place to be from, but Southern California was out of the question. Regional differences were greater than at present, perhaps in part due to the absence of commercial jet aviation. All told, I had serious doubts that I would fit into the rarified atmosphere of a small private New York banking house.

Accordingly I wrote in my personal business plan that I would work as hard as I could in New York City for a minimum of two years and learn as much as possible. If my credentials were deemed suitable, I would be prepared to stay much longer. If not, I would return home to Southern California with some excellent training under my belt.

My desire was to become a successful New York investment banker, if the culture would support me, retire fairly early (money being a secondary objective for me), and devote the remainder of my active life to teaching and philanthropy. In fact, I was a general partner or managing director of Morgan Stanley for twenty years, I retired at age fifty-three, and I have spent the years since teaching, writing, traveling, and engaging in senior business counseling and philanthropy. And yet, the choice of Morgan Stanley was not an obvious one for me. While some of my fellow employees had attended Groton and Harvard and had known since young adulthood that Morgan Stanley was the place to be, I had no notion even of what investment banking was until my first year at Harvard. I soon learned that access to Morgan Stanley came through relationships or from going through the Harvard interview process, Harvard being the only graduate school where the firm interviewed at that time. Investment banking had suffered from the relative inactivity of the Great Depression and World War II, and the firms were all private, small, and undercapitalized. The boom in investment banking and consulting was to come later. In some ways the options for employment coming out of business school were more limited than at present. This was true not only of investment banking and consulting but also in the not-for-profit field, for example.

It is good to have a plan. It is also good to be in the right place at the right time. By the time Morgan Stanley began its immense growth in headcount, capital, and business opportunities, I had mastered a profession and become an owner. Over time and in order to support the expanded opportunities for growth, Morgan Stanley became far less insular and opened employment to large numbers of women and men from diverse backgrounds. You could say it came my way.

As my career developed, I was fortunate to have spent quality time, prior to committing to a full-time occupation, contemplating my reaction to such things as wealth, the use of time, fame, and power. As my journey progressed I continually took time out to retest these reactions in light of my experiences. If we do not formulate and retest our own values, we are left in a situation in which the organizations and individuals with whom we relate will define them for us. Once again, it is extremely useful in formulating such values to have a couple of deep trust relationships with people with whom to discuss your conclusions. Absent such mentors and trust relationships, one might consider keeping a private journal reflecting personal values and ethical issues to ensure that you are dealing with these deeper issues in a timely and disciplined manner.

What Is Wealth, for You?

Attitudes toward financial wealth are deeply personal and complex. For me, when I started out, the idea of wealth was just that: an idea, not an experience. My family had never enjoyed wealth. We lived in a small one-bathroom house in central Los Angeles. The concept of living on capital was totally foreign to me. It probably helped me that, in the early 1960s, when I entered investment banking, it was a relatively low-paying profession. Although we heard tales of J. P. Morgan partners in the 1920s making a million dollars a year, such income levels appeared a fantasy to us, probably a once-in-a century happening that was unlikely to be repeated. As a result of the Great Depression and World War II, investment banking had become far less lucrative. The firms had not grown much. Morgan Stanley had only 140 employees in total. In going to work for Morgan Stanley, I went to participate in what was generally deemed the best training in finance one could possibly receive. I figured that if I continued to sop up as much learning as possible, it would one day serve me well and the financial rewards would be enough to sustain a good life for my family and me. Financial security for one's family is obviously very important. Wealth for pure wealth's sake, or keeping score, or having more toys was, for me, a less important objective.

Wealth remains a great driver, especially in production- or sales-oriented cultures. It is very satisfying to own a great home, drive a hot car, and travel to Tuscany. The issue becomes whether continually accumulating wealth can, of itself, prove to be a valid long-term goal, especially if it means sacrificing self-esteem and empowerment both on and off the job. The bottom line becomes, How do I like to spend my time? If it is playing with kids, reading a novel, and going for a hike, your answer is going to be different from one who finds satisfaction in amassing net worth and participating in power lunches.

How Valuable Is Time?

There is never enough time for a person who leads an intentional, proactive life. We are always dealing with trade-offs. As I became a business unit leader, I realized that the bureaucracy would allow me to "coast" for a while on the credibility I had achieved within the firm. If I were fully responsive to all the demands on my time, dealt with the entire content of my in-box, answered each and every telephone call, and attended all the internal meetings that were expected of me, I would be viewed as a good corporate citizen—and my unit would accomplish nothing of lasting significance.

I soon learned that to actually run my business, I had to be in tension with the rest of Morgan Stanley and not do all the things they expected of me. The same was true if I hoped to attain any balance in my life concerning work, family, intellectual pursuits, physical well-being, and philanthropy. Thus I came to view my time as a precious asset to be rationed among competing demands.

A seasoned leader must become comfortable with these tensions, even to the point of walking away from matters for which there simply is no time. A successful leader learns, through trial and error, when it is safe to do this. A truly mature leader learns the significance of taking time off to gain refreshment and a new perspective.

This attitude toward time is important in the early years as well, but it must be dealt with discreetly. The risks are greater, especially before one has established credibility. There are times when one must conform to the demands of the situation, including "all nighters," weekends, and intense workweeks. One must be willing to pitch in and support the project team. At the same time, I always took my full allotted vacation each year, spent time with my family, attended church on a regular basis, and engaged in at least a limited amount of philanthropy, all the way through. One must be able to sustain a personal life in order to avoid early burnout.

Do You Have a Taste for Fame?

Andy Warhol stated, "In the future everyone will be famous for fifteen minutes."[2] This is obviously elitist, since most of us are never famous at all, yet the concept of fame itself holds allure for many; others want no part of it. Whether that fame is desired or not, a successful businessperson does create a reputation and sometimes even a following. Being profiled in *Business Week*, *Fortune*, the *Wall Street Journal*, or *Barrons* for your business accomplishments can be a heady experience. And it is the fortunate person who, after such an experience, is brought rapidly back to earth by a boss, a colleague, or a spouse.

Some business organizations tolerate and perhaps intentionally cultivate a star system. The problem is that there are never more than a few "stars," and creating such a system diminishes the value of the many other fully capable professionals in the organization. The "stars" can become fast-burning candles that self-extinguish or leave for more glamorous, profitable positions. The stars' commitment is to the self and not to the strength and well-being of the organization. In contrast, when everyone is in tune and the goals are shared, the entire organization can benefit. I think of Chanticleer, a small group of twelve choral singers, standing together on the huge, otherwise empty stage of Walt Disney Concert Hall. Individually, each is a star, but they sublimate their "star" power to attain the combined power of the group in harmony. At Morgan Stanley we were trained to subordinate our own egos to the banner of the firm so as to make the franchise more valuable. Because this was a private partnership, these benefits accrued to all the partners. And when I became a leader of a small business unit, it became abundantly clear to me that the more I spread around the credit and empowered others, the more we could accomplish together.

That is not to say our egos were always under control. One common pitfall in working on Wall Street is to believe that you have accomplished something important when the markets go up. It would be tempting, for instance, and seem easy to claim credit for a major stock offering that you spearheaded, but one is never acting alone. There are always many professionals in the firm involved in a large transaction and a major commitment of capital to finance the risk, as well as several hundred underwriters representing literally thousands of brokers throughout the world. How could any single person claim credit for all of that? One has to guard against a desire for fame to be sure credit is duly divided.

Some individuals take great satisfaction from being singled out for fame. Others are satisfied to be productive members of a winning team. There can be huge enjoyment from participating in a string quartet or choral group, or a championship sports team, when you know the others will do their bit and not let you down. Lifelong deep relationships from such a team can prove more durable than the fifteen minutes of fame.

We always need to listen to that small voice within us and to the wise counsel of trusted friends and associates. Be oriented to something outside of yourself. Had he been attuned to them, what voices might have signaled to Ken Lay, CEO of Enron, that he was pushing too far?

Power is addictive. Like all addictive experiences, it is hard to relinquish. It must be a powerful experience to have your own private jet aircraft and the names of scores of powerful chief executive officers at your fingertips. Unless one is very fortunate, however, the price is a narrowing of one's interests and depth of experience. For some of us the cost required to attain power is too great. It is not important enough to sacrifice the joy of a Himalayan view, a rhapsodic concert, or the love of a child.

BALANCING CAREER DECISIONS
AND FINDING YOUR PATH

At some point in a career it is important to define the degree to which you will surrender your other interests and discretionary time in a trade-off for wealth and power. I worked on charities, took a lengthy and unprecedented sabbatical, walked in the woods. To some, I seemed a bit eccentric; it's true I did not completely fit in. But the decisions I made were intentional and did not happen by accident. I firmly believe that it is a good idea to place limits on what you will trade off.

Just as we were instructed to do in that personal business plan, it's important to organize our life goals into layers of short-term, intermediate-term, and long-term objectives. Such prioritization is exemplified by the triage approach of medical care on a battlefield or after a natural disaster. In such a situation one is taught to segregate the injured into three categories: those who will benefit most from immediate care, those who will benefit from care but can wait a while without serious consequences, and those for whom care is likely to be futile. In the case of a personal business plan we can think of activities that must be performed in the short term to get through the day and meet deadlines, those that must be accomplished but have more relaxed due dates, and those that can be put off. If we try to accomplish everything at once, we will overload and accomplish nothing. If we do not have a tickler file for the long-term things, they will never get done. Planning is a matter of focus and prioritization, and the wisdom that not everything is going to get done. What we choose not to do can be as important as what we accomplish. We need to adopt different attitudes toward today's "to do" list and our lifetime preoccupations and be sure that we give attention appropriately.

An important aspect of goal setting is leading a balanced life. It's necessary to have flextime, down time, and restorative time. Taking the time to explore the deeper nature of life provides us with the ethical muscle to make tough calls when they arise. We also need to take time to develop relationships of deep trust with others. We will need that trust when we ask for help or make the mistakes everyone eventually makes.

I began to learn the uses of time during the period I was stationed in Korea. We all knew we were going home in thirteen months, and that was the overwhelming time issue. We settled into the daily boredom of routinized garrison duty only to be reminded each evening, as we left our weapons cocked and our combat boots half-laced, that we were hair-trigger hostages to the Cold War. We could not live for thirteen months on the edge of anxiety, yet we had to bring some of the tension and immediacy of our mission into our daily exercises. We also had to create lives for ourselves out of meaningful relationships, responsibility, and even having fun.

When I first arrived at Morgan Stanley I knew that the socialization process would be difficult for me—and that my time there would be a powerful educational experience, whatever the outcome. As mentioned earlier, I privately committed myself to sticking it out at Morgan Stanley for two years. I had made a major decision not to go back home to Southern California, and I felt that two years would be a powerful learning experience no matter the outcome. It would also provide a time for building relationships. At the end of two years, I would make a conscious decision: "go" or "no go." I would not burden my daily life with that decision.

At the end of two years I decided to stay for three more years, under the same formula. The learning curve was still very high, and the work was becoming enjoyable. I was being given increasing responsibility and traveling to places such as Paris and Australia. At the end of five years I saw a fighting chance to make partner, and at the end of eight years, at age thirty-two, I did. For me, the self-discipline of imposing staged, intermediate-term goals removed the strain of the decision from my day-to-day activities. Without that goal, each small setback or discouragement might have assumed more importance. Even giving such a decision an arbitrary due date makes it easier and less stressful to stick with and complete in comparison with a completely unknown or unpredictable time frame.

Studies have indicated that indeterminate time periods cause a higher level of anxiety than predictable time frames. In their book *The Leadership Challenge*, Kouzes and Posner relate a study of groups of soldiers performing long marches. Different groups are given wildly different information regarding how long the march is to be and how far they have progressed. Invariably the best performers were those who knew exactly how far they had to go and where they were during the march. Those who performed worst were the soldiers who received no information about the goal (total distance) or the distance that they had already traveled (feedback).[3]

Similar principles can apply to discrete tasks or, especially, to prison sentences. On a different scale, not forcing myself to make the "cosmic" decision every day freed me up to focus my energy on completing the task at hand. Many of the more important transactions I was involved in were complex and took a year to complete, several took three years, and the Irvine Ranch sale occupied me for seven years. In such circumstances, it's important to maintain a focus on longer-term goals and be comfortable with less-than-instant gratification.

When I took over the real estate unit, I wrote down on a pad of yellow paper all the things I saw there that seemed wrong to me. The unit had no organized customer files, no records of past years' bonus payments, no business school recruiting, no pension plan, no annual budgeting or planning— the list seemed endless. I soon realized that I couldn't get it all done at once. I had to choose short-term, intermediate-term, and long-term goals.

I kept that pad of paper for the thirteen years I ran the business unit.

Each year I prioritized the list and added to it. I needed to make certain we achieved closure on some matters each year. The key to success was choosing wisely the tasks I would insist on completing each year.

Just as a business plan must be aligned with the goals of a company, we must make sure our career direction fits our overall goals for life. Becoming a general partner of Morgan Stanley was, for me, a valid intermediate-term goal, but it would not have been a valid long-term goal. For me it was a means to an end. I have seen too many cases in which individuals sacrificed their personal lives for several years to earn that one promotion only to discard it a few years later on discovering no deeper meaning in their work beyond the title. We need to have a plan for life with sustaining and self-reinforcing activities built around it. We can always "get our loving at home," but those whose work goals are congruent with their life goals can attain an ease of accomplishment that can make the journey easier.

CHAPTER 3

Sustaining Influences

WHAT WILL SUSTAIN US over a lifetime of attempting to make the tough choices and do the right thing? Can we count on our set of core values—our internal compasses—to sustain us on the journey? What else should be in the mix? How and when do we adjust our values to assimilate our ongoing life experience as well as the changing norms of the society and organizations in which we live? Do we let the changing relative norms of society determine our own values? When and how do we take a stand if we disagree with the values that surround us?

Our core values are formed at an early stage. How do we make them explicit and viable in our day-to-day behavior? How do we proactively sustain them, renew them, adapt them to changing circumstances and personal growth? What impact does our choice of friends and mentors have on our personal values? Where do we find the courage to take time away from the demands of a career and listen to the voices of our family as well as our own inner voices?

Our priorities shift as we mature. We may become less accomplishment-oriented and more deeply philosophical, or even spiritual. Where do we find the support and affirmation to make such changes in our worldview? Can we grow and change inside the community and career relationships we have developed or do we need to find new relationships that sustain us as we reach out for balance and depth in our lives?

HONORING YOUR BELIEF SYSTEM

For me, as for most of us, family is the obvious early influence on the belief system that controls the compass and is a significant part of the foundation. It was not by chance that I was part of the Junior Red Cross program. My parents had met while working for the American Red Cross on the 1933 Long Beach–Compton earthquake in Los Angeles. They spent a total of ninety-five years between them working professionally and volunteering in the service of the Red Cross to aid others in need. My parents and almost all of their friends were active in helping others. They were not antibusiness, but they did not know very much about the business world. Nevertheless, when he assumed the responsibility of running the Red Cross in Los Angeles, my father depended upon the community business leaders to support his organization's activities. In the years following World War II, the Los Angeles Red Cross had the strongest volunteer board in town, filled with CEOs of all the leading businesses. As a result of these associations, my father was offered the position of vice president of one of the leading banks. He turned it down in part because he deeply loved his work with the Red Cross; his job was his calling. In an interesting way, growing up in the Red Cross organization in Southern California exposed me to the common experiences of earthquake, fire, and flood. I thus learned early about the contingent nature of life. Much as I am a great believer in planning, I learned that unforeseen events require one to adapt quickly to a changed environment. Our journey does not always take a straight course. This ability to improvise is also a quality of a good leader.

My maternal grandfather had also turned down opportunities to enter the business world, including running the New York Port Authority, in order to continue to serve his country. He saw extensive combat in World War I and ended up as a brigadier general. I saw my father and my grandfather as examples of what could be accomplished through will, energy, and personal vision. The fact that they both strongly believed they obtained deeper satisfaction in aligning their professional life in service to others than they might have in business was not lost on me.

I also saw that my parents' religious convictions helped sustain them, both personally and professionally. My father was raised a Quaker, and he used Quaker precepts in building teams and avoiding confrontation when possible. Perhaps as a result, his coworkers and employees had tremendous loyalty to him. My mother, raised a Congregationalist, changed her religious allegiance over time, becoming a Presbyterian and then, on my father's death, a Catholic convert. I shared part of that journey with her, staying a Presbyterian and, in more recent years, becoming an oblate in a Benedictine monastery. From my mother I received a deep sense of right and wrong and fairness. I also shared with her a sense of the more mystical aspects of religion, which appeared to be totally alien to my father.

At a certain point, peers begin shaping one's values. In my experience, values among my young male friends had an almost Spartan nature. We were expected to be loyal, truthful, strong, courageous—and to keep our emotional life out of sight. Through athletics, socializing, storytelling, and other, more risky activities, we were affirmed as young males. Our role models tended to be warlike, with physical prowess. In the military we became focused on duty and the mission. The "softer," more lasting virtues were acquired later. Further on in life, we find mentors who help show us the way into more substantive trust relationships. The deeper sense of institutional trust takes time to develop. And today, at least in some institutions, it may never occur. This cannot be laid solely on the institutions. Many of the young people I teach in the M.B.A. classes tend to have greater loyalty to their peers and friends than to the organizations that employ them.

Trust takes time to establish, and is derived from protracted, consistent behavior that one comes to depend on. The current reduction of trust in institutions derives in part from downsizing as well as the tendency of professionals to job hop. Instincts of self-preservation reinforce personal autonomy and a reluctance to turn one's fate over to an organization. I also question the effectiveness of "fungible" corporate leadership that can come into an organization and effectively take over without building sustaining relationships.

Starting in my early days in the real estate unit at Morgan Stanley, I was fortunate to have Trammell Crow, the renowned Dallas real estate developer, as a client-teacher. We were in continual relationship, whether there was a pending assignment on the table or not. He would help me secure business from others, and I did the same for him. Ours was not an exclusive arrangement—each of our firms was too large and powerful for that—but it became a relationship of considerable depth, based on trust.

Over those years, Morgan Stanley performed over a billion dollars' worth of financial transactions for Trammell, and he and I traveled together several times for pleasure to Nepal, China, the Caribbean, and elsewhere. On our Himalayan trek in Nepal, we walked for hours together, discussing everything from our personal spirituality and family to wide-ranging and sometimes intimate business issues affecting our respective firms. I learned that Trammell's parents had wanted him to become a preacher, and although he had deep spiritual feelings, Trammell did not see himself as religious. He was, however, as enthralled as I with the Buddhist culture, and he would sit at length in contemplation in the various temples we visited.

I had felt that one's business and spiritual natures had to be compartmentalized. I had my church friends and my business friends. Trammell trusted me to the point of sharing his deep feelings with me, and he empowered me to do the same. Like Bonhoeffer, he taught me there need be no separation between the secular and the sacred. I grew as a person because of our friendship. Trammell asked my advice on the sharing of his wealth. He was concerned about the balance between caring for his family and his philanthropic interests. What is a fair proportion to leave to a family? How much is too much? What criteria might one use to differentiate among family members? Does one favor the eldest, the neediest, or the most talented? Should everyone receive the same share? Although we could find no one correct answer, we concluded that equality, while simple, does not necessarily equate to fairness. In my experience, such discussions with clients are rare, and they create a strong relationship that can survive the rocky times that always come along. In addition, such deep trust and understanding make a business career more meaningful and sustainable.

Trammell was brilliant at empowering others—clients, employees, tenants, lenders, or investors—to do things they had never done before or had any intention of doing. Trammell reinforced for me the positive roles of personality, focus, intensity—and love.

He loved to tell a story about himself in which a student at Harvard Business School asked him the secret to success: What is the most important quality that a business leader can have? As Trammell related in a video, "I knew what to say but I was timid to say it, until finally, after a pause of a few seconds, I said, 'Well, I'm going to say it and the answer is *love.*' The most important factor in the success in business is love. Love your partners, love your customers, love each other."[1] As Robert Sobel explained in *Trammell Crow, Master Builder,* "Crow firmly believes that if you truly have love for people you will be more successful with them. If you love what you are doing, you will be successful at your job. If you love yourself, you will be a better person."[2]

Trammell did not exhibit love at every moment; like most of us, he could get angry, mean, and even downright ornery when things did not go his way. But he did always exhibit a passion for the enterprise.

The man brought richness into my life. I learned many things from him, including the power of a long-term relationship, the power of a leader who has a genuine passion for his people and his work, and the value and import of developing and empowering younger people. Long before I began to consider retirement, I wrote in my trekking journal something Trammell once said to me: "When a person turns over the reins, it's good if he has enough spirit to take on a lesser job and still glory in it."

About the time Trammell and I trekked in Nepal together, I began my interest in Dietrich Bonhoeffer, and started reading his books. I also visited my first Benedictine monastery in an attempt to find again that spiritual place Trammell and I had enjoyed in the Buddhist monasteries in the Himalayas. And I spent three months as executive in residence at the Pacific School of Religion. I was ready for a period of both intellectual and spiritual growth, and I proactively went after it. Time spent with this good friend and the spirituality I had experienced in the Himalayas had a profound impact on my life.

DEVELOPING COMMUNITY:
SOUNDING BOARDS, SUPPORT, AND SUSTENANCE

Even with a strong and well-anchored belief system, we need community, on many levels. Having at least a handful of fundamental trust relationships is key at any stage of life. When we face stressful decisions, we are less likely to be in error if we share our decision making with at least a few "partners" whom we can count on to follow ethical principles.

In the longer run, it is important to develop activities that can sustain us throughout our career stages and afterward. It is useful to engage in activities—whether music, writing, philanthropy, athletics, or others—that help us connect with people of different backgrounds and interests than those we know at work. Thornton Wilder, in his novel *Theophilus North*, wrote that to stay attuned to life, "A man should have three masculine friends older than himself, three of about his own age, and three younger. And he should have three older women friends, three of his own age, and three younger."[3] I would add that this quote holds true for both men and women, and that the friends should not be all of the same occupation or interests. Like much of my reading, Wilder's statement validated behavior that was instinctive to me, but that I had not thought through or articulated well myself. Such relationships become signposts on our journey, with the younger reminding us of the past and the older giving us hope for the future.

With whom should one attempt to develop such trust relationships? My own experience is episodic. If you are open to them, they happen—but to become too intentional or manipulative at the beginning can become awkward and self-defeating. Trust relationships seem to develop out of intense, shared experiences. They are more likely to come out of difficult problem solving rather than easy wins. They evolve out of multiple connections: adventures, intellectual discussions, shared spirituality or religion, and a variety of other shared experiences. Note that Wilder suggested that only a limited number of such relationships can be sustained. Otherwise we begin trading off against each other.

Connecting Ages

As an only child, I grew up quite comfortable in the presence of adults; and that ability to relate to people much older than I became a real advantage for me. At Morgan Stanley our clients were often chief executive officers or chief financial officers of major corporations, so that as young associates, we were often dealing with a generation older than ours. When I first arrived in New York City, a group of senior Stanford alumni, including several chief executive officers, reached out to encourage me. In addition to friends in the firm, it seemed that most of my hiking buddies, jogging buddies, church buddies, and Stanford alumni buddies, female and male, were older than I. In later years of recruiting, training, and running the business unit at Morgan Stanley, I was in constant touch with younger people to whom I listened and who continually challenged me on the appropriateness of our actions.

A major function of my job was teaching. Despite their illustrious business school pedigrees, young associates at Morgan Stanley spent much of the early years engaged in on-the-job training. Clients continually had to be briefed on new financing techniques. Good teaching is good salesmanship. In more recent years I have taught several hundred M.B.A. students, and there is always a group who stay in touch and seek my advice on career matters. They also keep me up to date on what is going on in the real estate industry.

I have benefited from a number of deep trust relationships along the lines Wilder discussed. Some have been with young people. Several of these relationships have lasted twenty-five, thirty, and even forty years, and the longevity and consistency of these friendships provide great mutual satisfaction. Of particular satisfaction are the ongoing relationships with most of the folks who worked with me in the real estate unit at Morgan Stanley from 1973 until 1985. Even twenty years later, the bonds and mutual information sharing remain strong.

From Friend to Mentor and Back

Often the line between friendship and mentor is nearly indistinguishable. I've been fortunate to have had very strong mentors when I most needed them.

Early in my career I had a marked need of mentors. Many people were there, both to acclimatize me to the firm and to help me through my gaffs, personal and professional. Soon after I started at Morgan Stanley, I worked on a public offering of convertible preferred stock for Detroit Edison. As a result of the senior partners' ethic that all equity securities must first be offered to existing shareholders, we managed a seventeen-day subscription offering to all current shareholders of common stock. When the subscription offering was completed, we would sell the remaining shares in a public offering. We would estimate the shareholder response throughout the period and sell shares to the public as we went along, to mitigate the risk. As a result, on the last day, the underwriters were always either long or short shares, and an adjustment was made through an offering to either buy or sell on the New York Stock Exchange.

Thus on the last day of the Detroit Edison offering, I made the calculation of how many shares Morgan Stanley had to buy or sell. I had never done this before, and I did it wrong. I had us selling shares when we should have been buying them. But by then I had developed such credibility for accuracy that, even though my calculation was checked, no one caught the bigger error in direction. After we had mounted the operation and published an announcement on the Dow Jones news tape, I realized my error. I told everyone to stop and reverse course. At first they did not believe me, but I finally got it straightened out. This was a public error of the kind Morgan Stanley simply did not make. At the end of the day, I went home, extremely distressed, and warned my wife that I would be fired. I knew that what I had done would make it easy for the partners to eliminate me from the large pool of us coming up for a promotion decision in a few months. But I was not broken. I had an inner calm because there was nothing I could do about it. I had certainly learned my lesson; it was not just the math. I knew I could do the business. I could not change what I had done; there was no reason to torment myself about it. Whatever was going to happen was to be; it was not the end of the world.

The next morning, sure enough, I was summoned to the office of John Young, a founding partner. He shook my hand, gave me a seat—and told me about one of the dumbest things he had ever done. As a senior partner of Morgan Stanley, he received five-year operating projections from the CEO of a New York–based client company, and he was sworn to secrecy on their contents. He went downstairs and took a cab back to our office. When he returned, he realized he had left the confidential document in the cab. In concluding his story, Young told me he knew just how I felt. I thanked him for his kindness and said I would do my level best to keep anything like that from happening again. When I got home that evening, I told my wife what had happened, and that I believed it meant I was going to become a partner.

I was lucky to have a senior partner who took an interest in me and was willing to forgive my mistake. Sadly, several years later a promising young partner was moved into a new area, where soon thereafter a trader report-ing to him sustained a large loss. The young partner had to leave the firm, as there was no senior partner watching out for him.

Why do some of us gain the support of mentors and others do not? There are ephemeral aspects to this. Why does one couple fall in love and another reject one another? There are doubtless many factors, but in a business set-ting, a major input has to be a sense of shared values. It does not work to parrot what you believe to be the values of your boss. You actually have to believe in those values yourself and live them out. One strong element of success involves forming your own core values and working in an enterprise that esteems and acts upon similar values. I was indeed fortunate, as it turned out that my values became aligned with not only my firm but also many of my clients. We need to make conscious choices about those we emulate. We are formed over the years by the experiences and relationships we participate in. We also become an influence on others. Over the long run, through the seemingly trivial daily acts we perform or observe in others, we become the person others see.

Another mentor of mine was John Gardner, founder of Common Cause and, coincidentally, a fellow high school and Stanford graduate, although a generation older. When I first came to New York, John was head of the Carnegie Foundation, and he watched out for me in my early days with Morgan Stanley. John always took a keen interest in younger people, and he thrived as a mentor to them. We kept up our friendship until his death. He maintained a sincere interest in me, sitting in on a couple of my lectures at Stanford Business School and reading and commenting on my ethics articles. Although we had different political outlooks, his grace and wisdom made a deep impression on me, and I listened to what he had to say. Two of his books, *Excellence* and *Self-Renewal*, had a major impact on my life; I have read them each at least three times. John's notion of "repotting" and rechallenging oneself every ten years became a catalyst for both my sabbatical and my early retirement.

You are fortunate if early on you perceive the value of experience and wisdom, seek it actively, and find it. Alec Wilkinson, prize-winning writer and frequent contributor to the *New Yorker*, decided at age twenty-four that he wanted to write. He asked his father for the help of his closest friend, William Maxwell, widely regarded as one of the twentieth century's great American writers and an editor of fiction for forty years at the *New Yorker*. In his recent book, *My Mentor*, Wilkinson describes his twenty-five-year experience with Maxwell.

> He taught me to be a writer, he provided me, when I was young, with a model of masculinity that was sensitive and appealing and courtly and had great dignity and was graceful. (If you wonder what kind of graceful,

I can tell you that John Updike once described Maxwell as a figure resembling Fred Astaire.) . . . The day before Maxwell died I sat on his bed and, holding his hand, said what I had tried to keep in and instead it came out of me all at once: "How will I ever do without you?" Before I could add, "You don't have to answer that," he started to speak. "You won't have to" he said, "because I won't ever leave you."[4]

Indeed, Maxwell's words ring true: Strong mentor relationships remain with us all our lives, transcending distance and time. While this was clearly a case of male-to-male bonding, it is obvious that there is perhaps even a greater need for young women to have role models to help them deal with the large questions, such as about the trade-offs between career and parenthood.

How does one choose a mentor—or become chosen? It seems all relationships are a combination of luck and intentionality. First one must have developed that personal value system to know, in a general sense, whom one is looking for. In the case of my great friendship with Trammell Crow, we first met jogging together on a beach, during which we talked the whole time. We each had a great deal to say to the other, and we sought out opportunities to meet, do business, travel, and continue talking. Neither was embarrassed to expose his feelings, beliefs, or uncertainties. A willingness to share one's values and feelings openly and without pretense is important. One must choose carefully, however, as it is not possible to sustain more than a handful of such relationships.

TIMING AND TIME:
ALLOWING FOR GROWTH AND RENEWAL

Highly energized, successful individuals are not likely to become dormant during their free time. The challenge is often in finding the time and then using it well. If we are not proactive in our use of time, we won't be able to fit everything in; deadlines will slip, relationships will suffer, opportunities will be lost. We will always be operating behind the power curve, and we'll arrive back at work tired or restless, without having been renewed.

But we needn't let time get away. The use of time can be intentional and goal-directed. Working hard at something entirely different from our career responsibilities can be a form of relaxation. It is important to find activities, such as volunteering or philanthropy, that can absorb our energy and interests and that provide satisfaction in the possibility they may leave some lasting positive impact in the world.

Early in my career, a very senior partner advised me to save time in my life for one or two charities and for my family. When I became a business school recruiter for Morgan Stanley, I cautioned potential candidates that if they could not succeed at their work and still take time off for other interests in their lives, they would fail in the long term. They would be competing with individuals who could excel at the work and create flextime for other things. Thus there is a balancing point between diligence and the joy of life. We cannot endure over the long term without both.

We need to allow ourselves the time to freewheel, to be creative, to be in touch with our deepest nature, and to experience the sheer joy of life. We need to spend time with family and friends, including friends at work. Time spent sustaining and renewing relationships outside of ourselves is not wasted. When we have to make the tough calls and test our moral compass, we will need those trusted friends and family to help us sort out our thinking; if we're lucky, they'll rely on us in the same way. Fame and the other trappings of the business world are fleeting. Friendships—solid friendships, nurtured over time—are not. We cannot allow ourselves to become so burdened by the trivia of daily life that we neglect those relationships that can sustain us during the hard times.

Managing Your Time

Time is your greatest asset: therefore, time management is important. If one "works smart" and intentionally, the chance for success is far greater. While these traits might appear self-evident, they are often overlooked, even by sophisticated and intelligent people. One classic course at Harvard Business School, taught by a leading professor, contained a module in which students were taught "how to read a newspaper." Rather than lackadaisically flipping through the pages, we were encouraged to always read with a goal in mind, such as how to turn the day's news into our business advantage.

Harvard Business School also taught us how to focus and prioritize. So much reading was thrown at us, we could not possibly do it all. We had to train ourselves to perform triage on the documents, learning what to skip, what to skim, and what to study. I have always favored the elegance of the 80-20 rule. As I interpret it, one can gain 80 percent of the benefit in 20 percent of the time if one correctly discerns where to expend the effort. Implementation of this rule assumes a keen ability to focus and prioritize and a willingness to risk focusing in the wrong place. With the Internet, Bloomberg screens, Palm Pilots, Blackberries, and the rest of today's technology, the amount of raw data thrown at us has grown exponentially. It is now even more important to be able to draw back from the cacophony and discern longer-term trends, not getting lost in the noise and confusion.

An active person attempting to lead a balanced, multifaceted life will have far more things on his or her "to do" list than can possibly be accomplished. Those who deal most effectively with the burden have developed the knack of selecting which tasks need to be accomplished and which do not. How does one develop this skill? In part through trial and error. It is also important to attempt to live out a vision that transcends the noise and confusion of the present. What a shame it would be to carry the day-to-day burdens of the office along with you on a three-week trek to Nepal! We need to develop the self-confidence and positiveness to know that all will be well when we return. This ties in with the concepts of focus and prioritization outlined earlier. For example, great investors focus on long-run trends before selecting particular investments. An "old-fashioned low-tech" investor such as Warren Buffet is a master at this.

Balancing Time

I have always felt that the principal use of wealth is to "buy" discretionary time. Free time is more valuable to me than money, in large part because it allows for personal growth. Knowing ourselves, we know when we need that time—and we need to listen to our inner voice that tells us. Failure to recognize our need for time can lead eventually to poor performance, burnout, addiction, or even suicide.

So if you recognize the need and find the time, how do you then use this personal time? In many ways we define ourselves by how we use our personal time. At some level, we can often share this precious time—or at least the benefits from it—with the interests of our business enterprise.

I figure I have hiked or trekked some ten thousand miles in the mountains of the world, including a thousand miles in the Himalayas. My restless nature calls me to see what is over the next hill. As a part of my sabbatical from Morgan Stanley, I trekked six hundred miles in the mountains of Nepal. Each day I passed through a couple of mountain villages. Over the eleven weeks of my journey, I became adapted to the rhythms of Himalayan Buddhist life. In many ways, the life of these villagers became my life. Their days were occupied with procuring water and food, and they would walk for hours to bring in a supply of firewood. These people were living as all my ancestors had lived just a few hundred years earlier, or fewer in the case of my Celtic forbears. I saw that we were all truly members of a great community stretching through time and space. I was touched by their strong intragenerational relationships and their joy in sharing the burdens of survival. I was impressed by the outward feelings of unity, wholeness, and harmony in village life, centered always on the small Buddhist temple.

I recall one afternoon when my traveling companion and I were beckoned into a village home to gain shelter from a downpouring of rain. We spent the afternoon sitting around the fire pit, drinking homemade beer and eating popcorn, sharing the warmth with three generations of a family—and the goat—and there was no place I would have rather been. We were made to feel welcome to take the time to refresh ourselves and, for a few hours, become a part of the family. There was no pressure to go anywhere or do anything but enjoy the languorous moments.

It struck me that even an American businessman like me had much in common with these hill people. I spend a major portion of my days sleeping, eating, dressing, and preparing for these activities. I also work eight to twelve hours a day. The difference—and it is huge—is in how much discretionary time we are able to create for ourselves.

An extensive trip in the wilderness, in a different culture, provides us with the time to examine ourselves, make adjustments to our goals and timelines, and better understand our values and priorities. This is what the existentialist philosopher Søren Kierkegaard terms a "rotation," or what T. S. Eliot describes as returning to a time or a place in the past and recognizing it for the first time. It is testing your values through a different prism. The prism need not be a powerful adventure. It may be a vacation, a book, work for a not-for-profit, a spiritual experience, or any type of rotation out of your own everydayness.

When I ask myself why some of my successful contemporaries are still in the struggle long after they could have retired, one possible answer is their need to satisfy a craving for power. They are replaying the same unending series of deals through a different prism—a prism of power rather than of wealth accumulation or a desire to get promoted. Yet power comes at a cost, and it's one I was not willing to pay.

It is always possible that if I had not placed a premium on creating and sustaining a personal life for myself, I might have risen further at Morgan Stanley. I am content that I met my potential in that environment. I ran an important business unit, became a "senior partner," and served on an operating committee that ran the several businesses of the firm. The two individuals from my peer group who ultimately ran Morgan Stanley were, in my mind, better qualified than I for the position.

An epiphany occurred for me a couple of years after I retired from the firm. By then I had picked up a half-dozen consulting assignments; I was serving as chairman of the Red Cross in Los Angeles, along with other philanthropic pursuits; and my teaching load was expanding in good order. I received a telephone call out of the blue from the dean of a respected law school. He was serving as chair of a search committee for a new dean for that university's graduate school of business and advised me I had been recommended to be a business candidate for the position of dean. He wanted me to go "on the short list" for the position.

Had I received the call when I first retired from Morgan Stanley, I would have jumped at the offer. I was still then, in my own mind, building a resume. But now, as laughter bubbled up inside of me, I realized, for the first time, that I did not want to be dean of a graduate school of business or to have any other full-time job. I loved the flexibility, variety, freedom, and creativity of the life I had made. I apologized for my reaction, thanked him profusely, and declined the invitation.

Finding Import, and the Sacred

Truly deep thinkers and creators learn to avoid being controlled by time. Harry Cunningham, the great innovator of K-Mart, had the courage early in his career as CEO to take a year off to study the retailing industry. Great philosophers and theologians have pondered the meaning of time over the eons. Augustine wrote a famous meditation on time in his *Confessions*, which, paraphrased, states that there are not three separate times, past, present, and future. Rather there are (1) a time present of things past, (2) a time present of things present, and (3) a time present of things future. Thus only an infinitesimally small and fleeting moment of the present can be said to actually exist.[5]

T. S. Eliot's famous set of poems, *The Four Quartets*, is itself a meditation on time. In "The Dry Salvages" Eliot writes

> For most of us, there is only the unattended
> Moment, the moment in and out of time,
> The distraction fit, lost in a shaft of sunlight,
> The wild thyme unseen, or the winter lightning
> Or the waterfall, or music heard so deeply
> That it is not heard at all, but you are the music
> While the music lasts.[6]

I do not expect active business people to spend long hours pondering sacred time, but I suspect that the most deeply rooted leaders in any organization do find time for such serious thinking. If they do not, they can become rootless and unable to deal effectively with the institutional anxiety that is inevitable in these agitating times.

To successfully plan for a business, one must escape from everydayness and ordinary time. Retreats and "weekends in the woods" are commonly utilized, yet they often do not serve the desired purpose. To do so, somehow the group must be awakened to the deeper reality of the enterprise and taken out of the everydayness that stifles deep thinking. Sometimes this can be accomplished by a very special speaker or by group activities that are taken seriously. The Outward Bound movement, for example, has been successful in moving small groups out of the ordinary and building teamwork and trust.

At its deepest level, work can be seen as vocation, service, and choice—as creative activity. We become stewards who serve a greater purpose with the human and other assets with which we have been entrusted. We are here to serve others, and in so doing, we serve ourselves. In giving ourselves away, we find ourselves.

In his recent book, *Human Accomplishment*, Charles Murray states, "Human beings have been most magnificently productive and reached their highest cultural peaks in the times and places where humans have thought most deeply about their place in the universe and been most convinced they have one."[7]

Murray goes on to relate that "A story is told about the medieval stone masons who carved the gargoyles that adorn the great Gothic cathedrals. Sometimes their creations were positioned high upon the cathedral, hidden behind cornices or otherwise blocked from view, invisible from any vantage point on the ground. They sculpted these gargoyles as carefully as any of the others, even knowing that once the cathedral was completed and the scaffolding was taken down, their work would remain forever unseen by any human eye. It was said that they carved for the eye of God. That, written in a thousand variations, is the story of human accomplishment."[8]

Nothing defines us more than the actions we perform when under stress. A true ethical dilemma often has no textbook response. We and our organization may be caught up in a situation we have never encountered before. A leader must show courage and calmness, even when he or she does not feel them personally. A decision is called for; it cannot be postponed. Ethical leaders in such a situation can be counted on to act instinctively out of their beliefs. In still other cases an ethical leader is called on to behave ethically under stress over a long, possibly indeterminate, period of time. Such was the case of Admiral James Stockdale, leader of the "Hanoi Hilton" for seven years, and also of Dietrich Bonhoeffer, who in 1939 returned voluntarily to Nazi Germany to participate in the church resistance.

We never know where or when we will be called to draw upon our inner resources. Sometimes it is when we least expect it. We need to know that our intuition has been properly nurtured and will sustain us when we need it.

PART TWO

Preparing for the Ethical Dilemma

FOR MOST OF US and the organizations we belong to, whether in business or in other aspects of our lives, an ethical dilemma can intrude abruptly when we are not expecting it and are not prepared to deal with it. I found myself living an unanticipated ethical dilemma during a long-distance trek in the Himalayas. I was taking time out from the journey of life for an inward, private pilgrimage—a journey within a journey. We were episodically thrown together with three other groups of differing religious and cultural backgrounds and with whom we had no chance to develop a sense of community or shared values, other than to successfully climb up a high mountain pass. The nature of the dilemma was such that our own group lacked adequate resources to gain closure. We needed the support of the others to do what my partner deemed to be "the right thing." That support from the others was not forthcoming, as we had not developed shared values, nor did they have any basis for trusting our views in what became an ambiguous situation. They saw no reason to be flexible in deviating from their goal of climbing the high pass.

THE PARABLE OF THE SADHU

As the first participant in the new six-month sabbatical program that Morgan Stanley had adopted, I spent the first half of the sabbatical in Nepal, walking six hundred miles through two hundred villages in the Himalayas and climbing some 120,000 vertical feet. The Nepal experience was more rugged than I had anticipated and significantly more difficult than the typical commercial trek, which lasts only two or three weeks and covers a quarter of the distance. My sole Western companion, Stephen, was an anthropologist who shed light on the cultural patterns of the villages that we passed through.

We were halfway through the sixty-day Himalayan part of the trip when we reached the high point, an 18,000-foot pass over a crest that we'd have to traverse to reach the village of Muklinath, an ancient holy place for pilgrims. The Himalayas were having their wettest spring in twenty years; hip-deep powder snow and ice had already driven us off one ridge. If we failed to cross the pass, I feared that the last half of our once-in-a lifetime trip would be ruined.

The night before we were to try the pass, we camped in a hut at 14,500 feet. The last village we'd passed through was a sturdy two-day walk below us, and I was tired. Beyond that, I was worried: six years earlier, I had suffered pulmonary edema, an acute form of altitude sickness, at 16,500 feet in the vicinity of Everest Base Camp. What would happen at 18,000 feet? Could I make it? During the late afternoon, two backpackers from New Zealand joined us, and we all spent most of the night awake, anticipating the climb. Below, we could see the fires of two other parties, which turned out to be two Swiss couples and a Japanese hiking club.

To get over the steep part of the climb before the sun melted the steps we would be required to cut in the ice, we departed at 3:30 A.M. The New Zealanders left first, followed by Stephen and myself, our porters and Sherpas, and then the Swiss. The Japanese lingered in their camp. The sky was clear, and we were confident that no spring storm would erupt that day to close the pass.

As we began the day it looked to me as though Stephen was shuffling and staggering a bit, both of which are symptoms of altitude sickness. (The initial stage of altitude sickness brings a headache and nausea. As the condition worsens, a climber may encounter difficulty breathing, disorientation, aphasia, and paralysis.) I felt strong—my adrenaline was flowing—but I was very concerned about Stephen, about all of our party, and about my ultimate ability to get across the pass. A couple of our porters were also suffering from the height, and Pasang, our Sherpa *sirdar* (leader), was worried.

Just after daybreak, while we rested at 15,500 feet, one of the New Zealanders, who had gone ahead, came staggering down toward us with a body slung across his shoulders. He dumped the almost naked, barefoot Indian holy man—a sadhu—at my feet. He had found the pilgrim lying on the ice, shivering and suffering from hypothermia. I cradled the sadhu's head and laid him out on the rocks. The New Zealander was angry. He wanted to get across the pass before the bright sun melted the snow. He said, "Look, I've done what I can. You have porters and Sherpa guides. You care for him. We're going on!" He turned and went back up the mountain to join his friends.

I took a carotid pulse and found that the sadhu was still alive. We figured he had probably visited the holy shrines at Muklinath and was on his way home. It was fruitless to question why he had chosen this desperately high route instead of the safe, heavily traveled caravan route through the Kali Gandaki gorge. Or why he was shoeless and almost naked, or how long he had been lying in the pass. The answers weren't going to solve our problem.

Stephen and the four Swiss began stripping off their outer clothing and opening their packs. The sadhu was soon clothed from head to foot. He was not able to walk, but he was very much alive. I looked down the mountain and spotted the Japanese climbers, marching up with a horse.

Without a great deal of thought, I told Stephen and Pasang that I was concerned about withstanding the heights to come and wanted to get over the pass. I took off after several of our porters who had gone ahead.

On the steep part of the ascent where if the ice steps had given way I would have slid down about 3,000 feet, I felt vertigo. I stopped for a breather, allowing the Swiss to catch up with me. I inquired about the sadhu and Stephen. They said that the sadhu was fine and that Stephen was just behind them. I set off again for the summit.

Stephen arrived at the summit an hour after I did. Still exhilarated by victory, I ran down the slope to congratulate him. He was suffering from altitude sickness—walking fifteen steps, then stopping, walking fifteen steps, then stopping. Pasang accompanied him all the way up. When I reached them, Stephen glared at me and said, "How do you feel about contributing to the death of a fellow man?" I did not completely comprehend what he meant. "Is the sadhu dead?" I inquired. "No," replied Stephen, "but he surely will be!"

After I had gone, followed not long after by the Swiss, Stephen had remained with the sadhu. When the Japanese had arrived, Stephen had asked to use their horse to transport the sadhu down to the hut. They had refused. He had then asked Pasang to have part of our group carry the sadhu. Pasang had resisted the idea, saying that the porters would have to exert all their energy to get themselves over the pass. He believed they could not carry a man down 1,000 feet to the hut, climb the slope again, and get across safely before the snow melted. Pasang had pressed Stephen not to delay any longer.

The Sherpas had carried the sadhu down to a rock in the sun at about 15,000 feet and pointed out the hut another 500 feet below. The Japanese had given him food and drink. When they had last seen him, he was listlessly throwing rocks at the Japanese party's dog, which had frightened him.

We do not know if the sadhu lived or died.

For many of the following days and evenings, Stephen and I discussed and debated our behavior toward the sadhu. Stephen is a committed Quaker with deep moral vision. He said, "I feel that what happened with the sadhu is a good example of the breakdown between the individual ethic and the corporate ethic. No one person was willing to assume ultimate responsibility for the sadhu. Each was willing to do his bit just so long as it was not too inconvenient. When it got to be a bother, everyone just passed the buck to someone else and took off. Jesus was relevant to a more individualistic stage of society, but how do we interpret his teaching today in a world filled with large, impersonal organizations and groups?"

I defended the larger group, saying, "Look, we all cared. We all gave aid and comfort. Everyone did his bit. The New Zealander carried him down below the snow line. I took his pulse and suggested we treat him for hypothermia. You and the Swiss gave him clothing and got him warmed up. The Japanese gave him food and water. The Sherpas carried him down to the sun and pointed out the easy trail toward the hut. He was well enough to throw rocks at a dog. What more could we do?"

"You have just described the typical affluent Westerner's response to a problem. Throwing money—in this case, food and sweaters—at it, but not solving the fundamentals!" Stephen retorted.

"What would satisfy you?" I said. "Here we are, a group of New Zealanders, Swiss, Americans, and Japanese who have never met before and who are at the apex of one of the most powerful experiences of our lives. Some years the pass is so bad no one gets over it. What right does an almost naked pilgrim who chooses the wrong trail have to disrupt our lives? Even the Sherpas had no interest in risking the trip to help him beyond a certain point."

Stephen calmly rebutted, "I wonder what the Sherpas would have done if the sadhu had been a well-dressed Nepali, or what the Japanese would have done if the sadhu had been a well-dressed Asian, or what you would have done, Buzz, if the sadhu had been a well-dressed Western woman?"

"Where, in your opinion" I asked, "is the limit of our responsibility in a situation like this? We had our own well-being to worry about. Our Sherpa guides were unwilling to jeopardize us or the porters for the sadhu. No one else on the mountain was willing to commit himself beyond certain self-imposed limits."

Stephen said, "As individual Christians or people with a Western ethical tradition, we can fulfill our obligations in such a situation only if one, the sadhu dies in our care; two, the sadhu demonstrates to us that he can undertake the two-day walk down to the village; or three, we carry the sadhu for two days down to the village and persuade someone there to care for him."

"Leaving the sadhu in the sun with food and clothing—where he demonstrated hand-eye coordination by throwing a rock at a dog—comes close to fulfilling items one and two," I answered. "And it wouldn't have made sense to take him to the village, where the people appeared to be far less caring than the Sherpas, so the third condition is impractical. Are you really saying that, no matter what the implications, we should have changed our entire plan?"

DEEPER DIMENSIONS OF THE SADHU

Despite my arguments, I felt and continue to feel guilt about the sadhu. I literally had hiked through a classic moral dilemma without fully thinking through the consequences. I've since seen that the parallels and relevance to a life in business are many.

I excused my actions by pointing to a high adrenaline flow, a superordinate goal, and a once-in-a-lifetime opportunity—all common factors in corporate situations, especially stressful ones. Had we mountaineers been free of stress caused by the effort and the high altitude, we might have treated the sadhu differently. Certainly we were stressed, yet isn't stress the real test of personal and corporate values? Just as in many business situations, an immediate response to the crisis was mandatory. Failure to act was a decision in itself. Business is not philosophy; it involves action and implementation—getting things done. The instant decisions that executives make under pressure reveal the most about personal and corporate character. Managers must come up with answers based on what they see and what they allow to influence their decision-making processes. On the mountain, while most of us were concerned about our personal well-being, Stephen instinctively focused on the deeper dimensions of the situation we were facing.

One of our problems was that as a group we had no process for developing a consensus. We had no sense of purpose or plan. The difficulties of dealing with the sadhu were so complex that no one person could handle them. Because the group did not have a set of preconditions that could guide its action to an acceptable resolution, we reacted instinctively as individuals. The cross-cultural nature of the group added a further layer of complexity. We had no leader with whom we could all identify and in whose purpose we believed. Only Stephen was willing to take charge, but he could not gain adequate support from the group to care for the sadhu.

The lessons that might move us forward on our journey are there, and hinge upon the moral dilemma. Real moral dilemmas are ambiguous, and it's all too easy to walk right through them, as I did, unaware that they exist. And so, the questions must be asked:

What are the practical limits of moral imagination and vision?

Is there a collective or institutional ethic that differs from the ethics of the individual?

At what level of effort or commitment can one discharge one's ethical responsibilities?

Not every ethical dilemma has a right solution. Reasonable people often disagree; otherwise there would be no dilemmas. In a business context, however, it is essential that managers agree on a process for dealing with dilemmas.

Some organizations do have values that transcend the personal values of their leaders. Such values, which go beyond profitability, are usually revealed when the organization is under stress. People throughout the organization generally accept its values, which, because they are not presented as a rigid list of commandments, may be somewhat ambiguous. As discussed in the chapters that follow, it is these values that then are called on when split-second decisions are required, when the organization finds itself in new territory that is not clearly marked. These values help people find meaning and purpose and align their individual and corporate values—even in the gray areas.

In contrast, organizations that do not have a heritage of mutually accepted shared values tend to become unhinged during stress, and individuals bail themselves out in any way they can. Can we identify the difference between an impersonal organization, apparently opposed to individual values and needs, and one in which people's values and beliefs are respected and their expressions encouraged? Knowing this, can we then manage more effectively?

People who are in touch with their own core beliefs and the beliefs of others can be more comfortable living on the cutting edge. At times, taking a tough line or a decisive stand in a muddle of ambiguity is the only ethical thing to do. If a manager is indecisive about a problem and spends time trying to figure out the "good" thing to do, the moment—and the enterprise—may be lost.

Effective managers, therefore, are action-oriented people who resolve conflict; are tolerant of ambiguity, stress, and change; and have a strong sense of purpose for themselves and their organizations. That sense of purpose and ultimate goal make all the difference.

When I return to memories of my four trips to Nepal, I realize that my most interesting experience occurred when I lived in a Sherpa home in the Khumbu for five days while recovering from altitude sickness. The high point of Stephen's trip was an invitation to participate in a family funeral ceremony in Manang. Neither experience had to do with climbing the high passes of the Himalayas. Then why were we so reluctant to try the lower path, the ambiguous trail? Perhaps it was because we did not have a leader who could reveal the greater purpose of the trip to us. Without that, without some support system that encompassed our involuntary and episodic community on the mountain, it seemed beyond our individual capacity to do more than we did.

For each of us the sadhu lives. Should we stop what we are doing and comfort him, or should we keep trudging up toward the high pass? Should I pause to help the derelict I pass on the street each night on my way home? Am I his brother? What is the nature of our responsibility if we consider ourselves to be ethical persons? Perhaps it is to change the values of the group so that it can, with all its resources, take the other road.

In Part Two, we will deal with the issue of holding onto core values amidst the daily distractions and changing contexts of organizational life.

CHAPTER 4

Leading in the Gray Areas

A LITERAL SADHU may not often appear in anyone's life, but each of us is faced with daily decisions that have no easy answer, decisions we need to make in split seconds. At the time, there is no way of knowing what the ripple effects may be. Some compromises you might be tempted to make could be detrimental to you personally, to your organization, or to your profession. But they don't announce themselves. They come unexpectedly. How then do you hold to your values, how will you define unethical practices and hold the line against them? What does it take to stand for your values if you're not the one in charge of the organization or the group? Or what does it take if you are?

Fairly early in my position as leader of the real estate unit at Morgan Stanley we were given the responsibility of liquidating a large real estate portfolio for a Baltimore-based publicly owned insurance company. The Internal Revenue Service had approved a tax-free reorganization of the business into two separate entities—an insurance company (Monumental Life) and a real estate company (Monumental Properties Trust)—with the proviso that all the real estate assets were to be sold within one year. If we missed the timetable, the shareholders would be forced to pay a double tax. We spent the first third of the year performing detailed analysis of the assets and the middle third in a marketing effort; the final third was set aside for closing the transaction. The prospective transaction was widely reported in the financial press, and interest was high.

We attempted to impose a rigorous set of procedures on the marketplace, including a time schedule. We separated the assets into packages for marketing. Final offers for the assets were due on a particular date. When the offers came in, they exceeded both our expectations and those of the appraiser who had opined to the public shareholders on the fairness of the structure of the transaction. We accepted the highest offer on each package and issued a press release.

A couple of days later I was in Baltimore with the CEO of the company. He took a telephone call, appeared stressed, and handed the telephone to me, stating, "Here, you better handle this!" The chief investment officer of one of the largest financial institutions in the world was on the line. They had not been the high bidder for any of the assets, but now they said that if we would change our procedures and reopen the bidding process, they would significantly improve their pricing on most of the packages, making it higher than any other offers received.

It was a telephone call I did not want—a possible pitfall on the journey. A higher offer would mean more money for the public shareholders, who were our ultimate clients. It would also mean a higher fee for Morgan Stanley, as we were paid a percentage of the sales price. On the other hand, there was risk to the reputation of the firm for fair dealing. The institutions we had already named would justifiably feel betrayed. But could I put the firm's reputation ahead of the shareholders' interests? There was also the issue of accomplishing a timely closure and avoiding the tax penalty. If we appeared indecisive and lacking in firm intent, it would be more difficult to push the prospective buyers to close within the one-year window to prevent a double tax on the shareholders. We had carefully orchestrated a controlled auction process. If we gave up that control, the market might not take our direction in the future.

I put my hand over the receiver and asked my client what he wanted to do. "You decide!" he replied. It was a telephone call my client and I wished had never happened. We had to make an almost split-second decision, balancing all the factors we could take in. He took very seriously his role as a fiduciary acting on behalf of the public shareholders. This was the largest real estate investment banking transaction up to that time, and we had very little precedent to go on. We wanted to do the right thing for all the affected parties, with little time to balance the risks. I felt I was called to put myself in the shoes of the public shareholder. Would I rather get a small amount more per share and risk paying a large tax, or would I prefer the certainty of closure at a "windfall" price. When acting as a moral agent, it is always important to know to whom you are ultimately responsible.

I was fortunate that my client was right there. We had to make an instant decision. We held a quick discussion. A key element was that we had worked closely together for the past nine months, under terrific time pressure, and we respected and trusted each other. Our sense of shared values and mutual trust empowered us to accept the risk of making the wrong choice and doing what we each felt intuitively was the right thing; we were responsible for each other. Others might have made a different decision. I also knew that, once the decision was made, he would move ahead to closure and not second guess me or duck his portion of the responsibility.

We concluded that the initially accepted offers were far higher than we had anticipated and, in our judgment, provided the shareholders with a price that was more than fair. I suggested we maintain the integrity of the process, reject the possible overbid, and inform the purchasers what we had done. I had about three minutes to make that decision. I never even asked the other institution how high they would go. My client and I had no misgivings. We each felt we had done the right thing by not reopening the deal, and we shifted into a closing mode. The shareholders had much to lose if we missed the date. We revealed to the highest bidder what we had done and did not use it to attempt to leverage up their pricing. This put us on strong ground to insist on their performance in the closing process, which is what occurred. It did not hurt our credibility in the real estate unit that, on completion of the Monumental assignment, we received the largest single fee in the then forty-year history of Morgan Stanley.

This transaction occurred in the mid-1970s, when Wall Street still played by the rules. Our actions reaffirmed that overall atmosphere and sustained it for at least a few years longer. Thirty years later, the investment banking world has changed such that it is likely that an investment banker would reopen the process. It also is likely that another investment bank would have attempted to break up the deal and bring in a buyer of their own. And yet, for most people, this goes against the grain on a personal level. We all feel more comfortable when we know what the rules are and that market participants are going to honor them. An organization or industry composed of participants with differing ethical sensitivities and values finds it difficult to sustain its culture in such a volatile environment. Once again, people are called on to decide what they are willing to lose for and where they take their stand. An abiding issue is how leading firms can take action to sustain professional standards when industry practices are incrementally deteriorating. Investment banks faced these challenges during and after financial deregulation. In more recent years public accounting firms, among others, have been unsuccessful in dealing with the issue.

Indications are that Americans dislike abandoning their authenticity in the workplace, believing that one should live honestly, even adventurously and eccentrically, but not leave one's character at home. Extended research by Kouzes and Posner reveals the top four characteristics people look for in leaders they will willingly follow: honesty, a focus on looking forward, competence, and the ability to inspire.[1] As noted in Chapter One, various studies performed by Peter Drucker and others have shown that the most important factors for individuals working in organizations are personal well-being, accomplishment, and integrity. Individuals like to feel they are part of a "good" and valued firm. Issues such as fairness, integrity, and empowerment are stronger drivers than either wealth or power in attracting and retaining productive long-term employees. Employees who identify with the vision and values of an organization experience a feeling of wholeness in their lives, and they are less likely to become obsessed with power and greed.

In reading, writing, and teaching about business ethics, I have developed a series of relationships with others in the field. One of those individuals is my friend Michael Josephson. Michael was an excellent law professor at Loyola University in Los Angeles. Along the way, he developed and sold a successful California Bar review course, and used a portion of the proceeds to establish a center for ethics in honor of his parents. The Joseph and Edna Josephson Institute of Ethics has become a nationally known resource for training in practical ethics. It is the initiator of the "Character Counts" movement, as well as a variety of programs for major corporations and public institutions.[2]

In his training sessions Michael typically has participants break out into small groups to discuss what it is they most value in a business experience. When the small groups report back to the full sessions, their findings are consistent, not only with one another but with the published literature. Michael lists these "Big Four" values as trust, integrity and character, fairness, and caring and compassion. These values may seem to overlap, as they are all getting at the empowerment of the individual, but it is useful for us to examine them separately. Josephson's "Big Four" resonate with me out of my personal organizational experience, both in business and in not-for-profits, and they reflect more than twenty years of his experience working with hundreds of groups of professionals.

TRUST IS KEY

Trust relationships are based on being truthful and loyal and keeping promises, including the "unimportant" informal promises. Trust allows no room for deceptive, devious, or tricky practices. But "telling the truth" is not always as simple as we would like it to be. One of the more penetrating analyses of truthfulness is contained in Sissela Bok's book on lying.[3] Bok's premise is that in the process of becoming socialized we become habitual liars. "Am I on time?" "Of course you are!" (Glancing at my wristwatch and grimacing) "How do I look?" "You look stunning." (Especially in that chartreuse and purple combination—we're late, it doesn't matter how you look.) We become so accustomed to telling half-truths that we no longer recognize when we are lying. A fairly recent film, *Liar, Liar!* illustrated the humor in and utter impossibility of a person who attempts to tell the truth at all times.

Bok suggests that we debase the truth so much, we need another word to describe it. She suggests the word *candor*, which implies that we are in such a close relationship with the other that we will seek to empathize with them and be as forthcoming and honest as possible at all times. She goes on to warn, however, that one can sustain only a limited number of such deep trust relationships. As our circle of candor relationships expands, we are tempted to begin trading off once again. Taking her position a step further, I would posit that, to live an ethical life, one must be supported by a cadre of such candor relationships with people with whom one can openly and safely share deep concerns and ambiguities.

Bok puts trust in an entirely new perspective. The issue is not when do I lie, but when do I stop lying? Know yourself. Recognize that you and I are constantly tempted to shade the truth in order to protect others or glorify ourselves. Be aware of such tendencies and keep your guard up. Where do I draw the line? Where do I dig in my heels and tell the truth, no matter the cost or risk of personal embarrassment? Put in this light, truth telling becomes a matter of self-discipline and habit.

In addition to "telling the truth," there are other ways, as managers or leaders, we sometimes unconsciously break trust with others. A corporate culture is made up of both explicit and implicit promises. If we are insensitive to the perceived informal promises or do not agree with them, we will have difficulty sustaining trust relationships. It is important to distinguish between manipulating values and aligning interests. The difference may seem subtle, but the result is either distrust and cynicism or empowered leadership. The balancing act requires covenantal leadership—understanding the implicit and explicit covenants of the organization and resonating with them. Public trust is a precious gift, and it should not be squandered. Thus there is a huge premium to be placed on wisdom and judgment in determining what is a "good" risk and what is a "bad" risk. Sometimes the answer does not become apparent for many years. Having a deep sense of the mission and purpose of the enterprise—a far deeper mission than pure greed and money making—along with a consensus among senior leaders about that mission is a great help in evaluating such decisions.

It turns out there are few real secrets in a business. Those must be guarded, and the regulations regarding confidentiality must be obeyed, but there is no need to conduct the business in a closed, secretive manner. Closed doors and furtive conversations breed suspicion, undermine trust, and provide the evildoers a place to hide. Questioning and dissent should be tolerated, and even encouraged. Good ideas need to be challenged, bad ideas even more so. Open discussion is an excellent technique for training. We need our relationships of candor, but they should not override the openness that creates trust.

A leader is positioned to establish and maintain deep trust relationships with key colleagues, customers, and other affected parties. An effective leader has a trusted group of individuals with whom he or she can safely share concerns and uncertainties, test new ideas, and just ask the question, "Do you think this is okay?" In the best of worlds, these people also fit Thornton Wilder's criteria: a couple of these trusted confidants are junior to the leader, a couple are peers, and a couple are superior in rank. With younger people, such discussions reinforce the fact that ethical questioning is a legitimate part of the business discussion. With honest peers you can gain some assurance that you are not off the track. With superiors you can begin to test the degree to which ethical inquiry is sincerely tolerated. Encouraging open inquiry helps define who you are and provides others the opportunity to become more comfortable dealing with ambiguous issues.

Throughout my career I tried to encourage people to raise issues of concern to them. I wanted them to be ethically aware and to know that it was always appropriate to raise ethical concerns in a business context. In most cases I could fairly easily assuage their anxiety, and I welcomed the opportunity to do so, giving my reasons. From time to time I could not come up with a good answer, and I was more than pleased to have their help in clarifying my own thinking. This sense and practice of mutual trust was of benefit to us all. In a trust environment people must know that they can count on their leaders to do the right thing or be open to challenge and questioning if they appear to others to be in error.

Such leaders will always look for opportunities to authenticate ethics as a logical and appropriate input in the rational business decision model. Some time ago a *Wall Street Journal* article described the reaction of PricewaterhouseCoopers to the accusation that it was overcharging clients for airfares to the extent of more than $50 million a year. According to the report, the internal reaction was to seek ways to justify not passing along transportation discounts.[4] No one ever seemed to ask the question, "Is this wrong?" In many organizations, it is made clear that one's career is in jeopardy if such questions are raised. Yet, ethics must be embedded into everyday corporate life if it is to be effective when the crisis comes. That is the lesson of Johnson & Johnson, as described in Chapter One.

A trusted leader will help choose which clients to take on and which to refuse. Taking on clients with value systems congruent with those of the firm will validate the process of values management, and the converse is true as well. A leader is thus continually challenged to make choices about which values to support and sustain, and which metrics to select to measure performance. Because all that needs to be known often cannot be known when the decision is made, a leader lives by his or her intuition. To be successful, a businessperson must be comfortable living in ambiguity, paradox, uncertainty, and risk. To achieve this is to reach a level of emotional maturity that is essential for all great leaders. Leaders always have to be willing to change the plan. This is when community trumps autonomy and self-will. A sign of emotional maturity is a willingness to change the plan with grace, rather than with impatience and frustration.

INTEGRITY AND CHARACTER AT THE CORE

There is always a tension between what we will adapt to and what we feel we must resist, especially when what we are resisting is power and pressure. How we live into that tension makes all the difference. Integrity means that one is willing to be accountable in all facets of one's life. There is a unity, or wholeness, to life. One does not have to "put on one's game face" when one goes to the office. Nor is there a false "goodness." One can play hardball when one has to. As in Bonhoeffer's life, the secular and the sacred are —integral. One becomes a person of action without losing one's basic values. A person of integrity is not arbitrary, closed, or prejudiced.

Character counts far more than self-promotion. My friend Michael Josephson has quoted Warren Buffet as stating, "In looking for people to hire, you look for three qualities: integrity, intelligence and energy. And if they don't have the first, the other two will kill you."[5]

Over the years, I had the good fortune to work with Hewlett Packard and to have many thoughtful conversations with Bill Hewlett. We talked of wealth, family, philanthropy, and personal values. I learned how Bill empowered younger folks, helping them up the ladder, just as he had chosen me to underwrite his offering—the young guy from Morgan Stanley—over the much older and experienced bankers (mostly CEOs) from other firms who also had sought the account.

In later years I served as an advisor to the finance committee of the William and Flora Hewlett Charitable Foundation. While many of the board members and staff trusted Bill's judgment and wisdom so completely that they could have become deferential to whatever Bill wanted to do, Bill was intent on not dominating the foundation but empowering his children and advisors to make good decisions without him.

Bill reinforced in me the need to have a deep caring for those who worked for and with me. He did not invent "management by walking around," but he was one of the great torchbearers for that skill. It was a joy to "walk around" the Hewlett Packard offices with him and see the love and respect his cheery countenance engendered in the employees. Bill talked with employees personally, taking an interest in their work. He modeled the truth that one can gain a level of success and power and yet remain true to one's personal values. With Bill there was no pretense. He exemplified openness, honesty, and integrity as well as anyone I have met. This was a powerful lesson for a young investment banker from Wall Street.

In contrast, in other leaders I saw self-importance and learned to view it as arrogance, a characteristic not useful in building long-term relationships either within or outside the firm. It is noteworthy that all the great religions attempt to draw one out of preoccupation with self and into relationship with others. The truly great partners, those to whom others deferred for wisdom and counsel, retained a sense of humility and integrity and an ability to listen attentively to the other person.

Unfortunately, in our day-to-day activities it is very easy to slip out of our principles into bad practices. One February in the early 1980s we were retained by the owner to sell the Aspen Ski Resort. We had never sold anything like it, since we were then developing our real estate investment banking business, and we had no idea how to value it. We could not afford to fail in such a high-visibility assignment, so we approached the risk of the unknown with a heightened degree of energy and focus. We knew our success depended on our ability to tolerate contingent living and become comfortable with the various types of risk we were habitually taking.

I called into my office a particularly intelligent and energetic young associate who was also an enthusiastic skier and assigned him the task of proceeding directly to Aspen for as long as it took to find out everything we needed to know about how to value the ski resort. Of course, he thought at first that I was joking. I gave him very little guidance in how I wanted him to carry out the assignment, but did caution him to be discreet, since the owner did not wish the operators to know the property was for sale.

The associate came back in a couple of weeks with a report that far exceeded our expectations. I called him into my office and inquired how he had obtained such detailed information. He was a British national, with a solid accent, and he told me that he introduced himself to the manager as a writer for a European ski magazine and said he wished to do a cover story on the resort.

In analyzing such a situation, one must consider who the affected parties are and what damage has been done. Clearly we had served our client's needs by not disclosing our assignment while gaining valuable information. We had not necessarily wasted the manager's time, as the asset was going to be sold in any case. Nevertheless, I had an intuitive feeling that it was inappropriate for employees of Morgan Stanley to be running around like spies, posing as someone else. I conveyed my discomfort to the associate, who continued to be ingenious and went on to have a highly successful career, but possibly with a deeper sense of ethical awareness. I know I became more sensitive as well—and more careful about the instructions I gave (or didn't give).

There can be a fine line between networking and spying. It would have been difficult to tell my associate in advance just what he might encounter on an assignment. What were the personalities of the managers of the resort? Would they be helpful to a young person who was trying to learn about their business? Would it have been possible to avoid any element of deception when we had promised the owner we would not tell anyone the asset was for sale? Should I put my people into situations in which an element of deception is unavoidable? We need to honor the needs of the client who is paying our fee—and we need to honor the integrity of the firm and the individual.

Ethics is contextual and experiential. I learned from my mistakes and from the multitude of situations to which I was exposed. I did not claim to know all the rules or have all the answers. I just tried to remain open, aware, and sensitive to the ethical issues as I encountered them, believing that integrity and the ability to trust that our leaders will always strive to do the right thing are the hallmarks of any successful organization.

DETERMINING FAIRNESS

We are often ambiguous about what "fairness" is, and yet without some agreed upon perception of what constitutes fairness, we cannot do business. Many times in my life I have been involved in determining "fairness." It comes up continually in raising children; it is often the cornerstone of discussions of wealth with certain clients. It was the foundation of the systems of rewards and punishments we devised at Morgan Stanley to motivate our professionals. As financial advisors, we were continually called on to render our opinion as to the fairness of valuations or of financial transactions. Fairness can be ambiguous and easily misinterpreted. One thing I know for certain: fairness is not equality. Equality is a simplistic parameter for achieving fairness, but in most cases it is not fair. Children are not equal in needs or aspirations. Professional employees are not equal in skills, motivation, or character.

There was widespread criticism within weeks of the 2001 World Trade Center attack when the American Red Cross had not distributed the half billion dollars of contributions to the victims. The only basis on which that could have been done quickly was to treat everyone equally—bus boys and window washers along with multimillionaire stock traders. The only fair way was to complete thousands of casework studies factoring in the variables of lifestyle, savings, foregone future income, financial awards from other sources, and family demographics. This required time, professional skills, and detailed analysis of each situation. Fairness is not easy. No matter how much care is taken, the results may not generally be accepted. There is often no set of rules to go by. Like ethics, fairness is essentially subjective and ambiguous. At times one must ignore rote rules and become creative.

Several years after I retired from Morgan Stanley I was invited to serve on the board of a newly formed public real estate investment trust. Six years later the founder and major owner determined it was in his best interest to make an offer to purchase the shares of the public shareholders and take the firm private. Another independent director and I were then asked to cochair a special committee to negotiate with the major owner on behalf of the public shareholders. We told him his offer did not meet our standards of fairness. It was, in our opinion, at the lowest possible range of fairness, and we felt he and the public would be best served if the offer were somewhat higher. Now this owner was a person of great wealth and power and success. We two independent directors knew we were the only representation the public shareholder had in the transaction, other than the potential for lawsuits after the offering was made.

The general counsel of the real estate investment trust attempted to obfuscate the issue and convince my fellow director and me that our role, as independents, was to balance the needs of the major shareholder with those of the public shareholder. We strongly disagreed. We felt such advice was biased in favor of the principal shareholder, and that the general counsel should have been representing the rights of the public shareholders. The principal owner was fully capable of protecting himself. Our role was purely to protect the public, and the difference is tremendous. If one is to present oneself as an independent outside director of a public company, it is important to be fully knowledgeable and committed to what that role should be. We spent a total of twenty hours in negotiations with the owner and his representatives during a series of meetings over several weeks. The negotiations continued until the last possible moment, with attempts on the owner's part to persuade our fellow directors that we were overstepping our responsibilities. Our position did prevail and the board was able to provide a higher price for the public, which the shareholders approved. The threatened lawsuits by the plaintiffs' bar alleging lack of fairness were withdrawn.

To consistently follow good practices, one must have a solid understanding of the business and of what constitutes good practice. One must have the intuition and sensitivity to discern a bad practice masked in the trappings of a good practice. One must have the courage to follow good practice even when it is not the norm. One must be willing to lose, as good practice is not always supported by the enterprise.

Fairness involves being open, consistent, and just. It is promise keeping. If an associate and I discuss a two- or three-year work plan and agree it will lead to promotion if successfully accomplished, the associate meets all the criteria, and I promote my niece instead, it is not fair; and I have destroyed the associate's trust, as well as that of all those with whom he or she is in relationship. However, if an associate has bought into a promotion-and-compensation system for several years and suddenly in a particular year does not receive what he or she wants, that is not necessarily an issue of fairness or ethics.

A leader intentionally chooses criteria for measuring performance. The specific criteria chosen will either align with the values of the performers or draw them into dysfunctional behavior. Above all, the criteria must be generally viewed as fair. Criteria that are not solely production-oriented and that include such factors as recruiting, training, teaching values, and good character will greatly enhance the empowerment of an organization.

Criteria must be viewed as relevant and integral to the values of the firm; otherwise a leader will become merely an enforcer of irrelevant and inhumane rules.

A reputation for fairness can quickly become an asset. As previously mentioned, Morgan Stanley was involved in the sale of seventeen regional malls for Monumental Properties Trust. The properties had to be sold within one year or the shareholders of the publicly held company would have to pay two levels of taxation. We knew it would take about four months to close the complicated sale once we had a committed buyer, so there was immense pressure to get out in the market and start selling. We were merging our investment banking practice with our newly acquired real estate business, and we insisted on due diligence and full disclosure in our private offering materials, even though it was not mandated by any regulatory agency (and probably not anticipated by the prospective buyers). The cleaner and more transparent our offering materials and financial projections, the better chance we felt we would have of a seamless and timely closing process. We spent four months on due diligence and preparation of detailed offering documents, constructing packages of shopping centers that we knew would fit beautifully with the existing portfolios of certain institutions, providing them with additional "portfolio value" and allowing them to pay a premium price. Thus we had solid offering materials and a well-constructed marketing strategy when we hit the market. The offering process went smoothly, and the closing process even better. One of the major purchasers informed us they audited our numbers. In the aggregate, across the package of shopping centers they had purchased, our initial year projections were within one half of one percent of the actual results attained. We had executed a complex assignment, and in the process we had considerably bolstered our reputation in the marketplace for fair dealing.

As a result of this and similar transactions, we rarely forwarded a client's financial projections to the marketplace without cross-checking and auditing them ourselves. We often caused the projections to be made more conservative before entering the market. On certain occasions, when the client would not change projections we felt to be unrealistic or risky, we refused to take on the business. It takes courage to insist on full disclosure, especially when operating in the private market where no rules and regulations require it. We tried to live by J. P. Morgan's credo: "We shall do only first-class business, and we shall do it in a first-class way." Clients then expected that standard of excellence from Morgan Stanley, and we were expected to live into it.

I attempted not to penalize my associates for making an honest error in judgment, especially when they were taking risks and trying something new. If I was responsible for putting them at risk, I felt I must share in their mistakes. I graded them severely, however, on their ability to extricate themselves from difficulties. An important role for a leader is to remain calm and somewhat detached from the day-to-day cacophony of the marketplace. Competition, both internally and externally, can become fierce.

I am reminded of Tolstoy's protagonist, the Russian General Bagration in *War and Peace*. In the great battle for Moscow his commanders are spread over the field, with little or no communication among them or with their commander. As Bagration sits mounted on his horse, behind the central battle lines, his commanders race to him pell-mell on horseback, eyeballs bulging, demanding instructions on what they must do to prevent disaster. Bagration has no idea what each of the commanders is confronting in their zones of battle. Rather than micromanage, he sits calmly, with a detached air, and, one by one, expresses complete confidence and trust in each of the commanders to assess their particular situation and do what is right. The commanders return to their units empowered and confident, and the Russians prevail over Napoleon.

CARING AND COMPASSION

Listing caring and compassion as a key business value often gets people's attention and surprises them, yet what it reflects is empowerment, which is well-supported as benefiting business. It is what caused General Bagration to win the battle. As scientific research was applied to the study of work, with time and motion studies and the famous Westinghouse studies, investigators found that their mere presence on the jobsite, no matter how they altered work conditions, created higher rates of productivity. This was so even when they deliberately made the working conditions inferior. When debriefing the workers themselves, they were advised that productivity went up because the workers suddenly felt someone was taking an interest in them and in their work. This made them feel important and empowered. Such were the beginnings of modern management theories of self-motivated teams, open structures, and flexible work hours as expressed by virtually all business writers starting with Peters and Waterman in their book *In Search of Excellence.* Perhaps no one has portrayed this better than Tracy Kidder in *The Soul of a New Machine,* which depicts a runaway project team at Data General inventing an unauthorized new computer after "working hours."[6]

Characteristics of an empowered organization include sharing credit with others, sharing information, running an open shop, promulgating promotion criteria and taking the mystery and apparent randomness out of the process, giving freely and not begrudgingly of yourself, and practicing random acts of kindness. It is not devaluing the other or being selfish and manipulative.

Although today some people may think of investment banking as the antithesis of caring and compassion, such was not always the case. In the early days at Morgan Stanley we associates all sat together in a bullpen. We were each on separate project teams, yet there were tasks to be performed that required cooperation, such as proofreading important documents aloud. Individuals would invariably drop what they were doing to help someone else, even though it was not their "deal," and they would be staying late into the evening as a result. There was an embedded norm of working together with a willing spirit, which reduced stress considerably.

In an organization founded on the principle of helping others such as United Way, one would expect caring and compassion to be at the forefront. Yet the contrast between assumed and actual values has been problematic for the organization. In recent years United Way organizations in Los Angeles and elsewhere have lost ground, raising far less money than previously. Several years ago I served on a task force to evaluate the United Way operation in Los Angeles. We discovered, among other things, a very high turnover rate of employees, in the range of 40 percent annually, and a lack of focus in information technology, for which several major projects had been initiated but not completed. Our analysis of the situation included the notion that a primary cause of turnover and lack of prioritization lies in the fact that United Way activities, both professional and volunteer, consist mainly of fundraising and administration, with little hands-on experience in helping others in need. Organizations such as the Red Cross, in which one is directly involved as a volunteer in bringing comfort and relief to others, seem to have less turnover and burnout. Participants find meaning in those organizations in which they can express their desire to be caring and compassionate to others.

Effective leaders create meaning in small gestures. In many cases, it is the myriad of small gestures of caring that create deep meaning in a corporate culture, rather than the broad pronouncements and policy statements. Such seemingly small acts of kindness can powerfully reinforce loyalty to a firm or an individual by showing that leaders authentically care about the values they espouse and about you as a person. A personal gesture Bob Baldwin, our CEO at Morgan Stanley, made when I took off on the second three months of my sabbatical program stands out in my mind. I had spent the first half of my sabbatical in Nepal—far away from my family—and now, after six months back at work, I was leaving my family again, this time to teach at Stanford Business School. My wife and I had planned to spend every other weekend together, either at Stanford or in Connecticut, plus a family vacation on the West Coast. Bob encouraged me to spend as much time with my family as possible. As he sent me on my way with his good wishes, he picked up an envelope from his desk and handed it to me. In it were three first-class round-trip air tickets between San Francisco and New York. It was a gracious gift, well beyond anything I might have anticipated, and it underlined in a powerful way how strongly he felt about my family situation. His gesture increased my connection to Morgan Stanley and helped reassure me regarding the anxiety I felt about being away from the firm for so long.

In a talk once at the seminary where I had spent a part of the sabbatical, I spoke at length about the many advantages of a virtuous organization—no rules, no rules enforcers, no rules interpreters, better spirit, deeper trust, less expense, higher-quality people, higher-quality clients, higher productivity, and greater profits. An older gentleman, who happened to be a theologian, challenged me. "That's well and good, McCoy, but you can't have virtue without sanctions!" As soon as he said it, I knew he was right. We are humans and thus prone to stray off the path of goodness. We need a system of rewards and punishments to keep us on course. It is the unusual person who does not respond to incentives, bonus systems, and promotions, as well as to admonishments and other forms of discipline, when they are fairly administered.

From my perspective, we need the equivalent of the Jewish law of the Old Testament together with the Christian love of the New Testament (which, of course, are to be found in many other religions as well). This is particularly true when one is encouraging others to take risks and deal in a highly competitive environment. Excessive behavior must be punished and bad practices discouraged as soon as they are discovered. When bad practice, distrust, and lack of cooperation run rampant, there is no fixed point from which one might restore an atmosphere of empowerment.

For me, this connects to the theory of "tight/loose" management that Peters and Waterman describe and advocate in their book *In Search of Excellence*.[7] Theirs is an empowered, self-motivated, "loose" organization structured around core "tight" principles of good practice and behavior.

An atmosphere of caring and compassion allows us to draw on our deep spiritual and religious values and incorporate them into our daily work lives without feelings of embarrassment or betrayal. We need to be comfortable being ourselves, being in open community with others, and being called to a deeper level of transcendence or compassion.

As the medieval theologian Meister Eckhart once stated, "You may call God love, you may call God goodness, but the best name for God is compassion."[8]

THE ISSUE now becomes, How do we incorporate these basic values into our daily lives and find tangible meaning from them? If we can be in open community with others and confide our deepest values without a sense of losing status, we can be open to learning and sharing the journey (growing together), and we can much more readily establish a set of agreed values in which we all deeply trust. In the next chapter we discuss how learning from our work can help us develop and sustain lasting values and the importance of leading a balanced life.

CHAPTER 5

Learning and Finding Meaning
Continuously

MY FATHER USED TO SAY he had a "divine dissatisfaction." This was his
way to define the restlessness that he felt over the way things were; it was
driven by his urge to make things better, whether in his personal life or in
his role in the American Red Cross. This "divine dissatisfaction" was, for
my father, the catalyst to revisit his vision. He recognized the rightness of
the angst we experience when we stray from our vision—from our deeply
ingrained understanding of who we are. This drives our lives, defines us for
ourselves and others, and grounds us when change and uncertainty cause
us to lose our center. In this chapter, we look at personal vision more carefully, along with the need to revisit it periodically.

PERSONAL VALUES AND VISION

A vision arises out of our deep sense of who we are; it shapes all that we
accomplish. It might be called an intuitive orientation toward what life
can be, and it is affected deeply by our ingrained values. It is the expression of one's values over the long term, as tempered by life experience.
It is how we define to ourselves who we are. When such values are integrated into daily living, our lives take on an integrity. Others begin to
perceive us as we perceive ourselves. The Belgian intradisciplinary philosopher Leo Apostel suggests we need to develop an integrated worldview
that connects us to all aspects of reality, taking into account as much as
possible all aspects of our experience.[1] The material used to construct
this worldview comes from our inner experience and our practical deal-
ings with our everyday life. Such a view is culture bound, and as culture
is constantly changing, it also must be renewed and revised to adapt to
changing circumstances.

Our vision sustains us through the bad times, when we fail to live out
our values. It is always there to guide us to a better future. We attain the
vision by being true to our values whenever we can. Having a life plan,

based on a vision, causes us to be more sensitive to our values and become more consistent in living them out, which is to live with integrity.

As we live out our values-based vision for ourselves, we are free to allow our worldview to become deeper and broader. The situation may change, but the vision remains true. A vision differs from a plan. A plan is a series of discrete steps allowing one to focus on and prioritize a particular objective.

My personal vision, like most people's, began to take shape in childhood. It is during this time that we incorporate into our psyche a mélange of rules such as "Share everything," "Play fair," "Don't hit people," or "Put things back where you found them." As we grow into adolescence, our needs become "I wants." I want a fast car, a beautiful girlfriend, lots of jazz CDs, and to travel to Nepal, Tibet, and other exotic places. As we attain greater depth of experience, we sort through our values and begin to recognize the real and lasting ones. We learn that the best relationships are based on trust and integrity; that real beauty is much greater than the visual; that possessions are not substitutes for deep fulfillment; and that our love can, like Dante's for Beatrice, grow into unimagined richness over time.

My parents' vision for me reflected their great love and hope for my life, and it was easy for me to buy into it. I wanted to form deep trust relationships with others, to be respected by others, to be self-sufficient and independent. I honored my father, and I longed to make him proud of me. He was an authentic World War II hero, having helped a train full of Jews escape into the Basque country of northern Spain, and he landed with the fifth wave of Marines on the first day at Iwo Jima. His leadership activities for the American Red Cross during World War II made him legendary in that organization. He had a keen sense of adventure. Time and time again, as a young man, I would ask myself, "What would my father do if he were in this situation?"

As I grew older, I began to realize my father was not perfect. Among other things, he loved good whiskey and he was attracted to interesting women. In later years he became disillusioned and burnt-out in his job. As my own sense of values became formed, I began to see things in his behavior that I wished to avoid in my life. His influence remained powerful, but in a different way. It does not hurt to realize that even our role models and mentors can have feet of clay. Such imperfections require discernment, but also can foster an even deeper affection and love for our mentors' basic humanity. We need to be critical and forgiving, and not disillusioned.

My own course did not always follow the straight and narrow, and it certainly was not obvious that I could become successful. Being tall, I could bluster my way into obscure bars at age sixteen to listen to the jazz music that I loved. On my way into Korea I found myself challenged to a knife fight by a longshoreman in a Yokohama bar, because I had offered to buy a drink for the wrong girl. My zest for seeing what was over the next cliff left me at one point hugging an ice ledge in Massachusetts with my dislocated shoulder dangling uselessly at my side. Thankfully I was not alone, but with a good friend who was able to rotate my shoulder back into place right there. Those trust relationships we develop can become even more important when we get in trouble or fail.

I was very fortunate to have parents who would always be there to support me and whose values I could assimilate. Although my father died when I was in my early thirties, my mother lived to ninety-three, and she never stopped loving me. Many do not have this. In such cases, we need to develop our own sources of heroes and a personal mythology out of our friendships, reading, and continual thoughtful inquiry into the nature of the world. We also need the imagination to reach for more. Obviously our choices as to who and which characteristics we desire to emulate and what we want to achieve will have a profound impact on the eventual outcome.

My father died eight years into my career at Morgan Stanley, just as I was selected for partnership. By then I had lived out his vision for me. Now I had to live out mine, and that required a transition time to reassess my goals and priorities. I had to take my own journey, not piggyback on his. The sabbatical several years later was a part of that transition, as were visits to monasteries, deeper involvement in church activities, and a renewed interest in teaching. As a result I added such goals as structured continuing education and growth in my areas of interest, and improving my teaching skills and ability to mentor others.

Fortunately we do not have to experience a personal loss such as a death or serious failure to nudge us into healthy reexamination of our vision and our goals. We do, however, have to be careful not to be lulled into complacency with the way things are or to drift into gradually accelerating bad practices. Operating without a functioning, well-adjusted moral compass is risky business. Instead, we need to find ways to routinely reorient ourselves and keep our focus. In a full life, the need for crucial, life-shaping decisions surrounds us.

After twenty years as a successful investment banker, there came for me a time to pause, reexamine my vision, and do some remedial work on the areas I had neglected. The continuing cycle of doing deals, annual budgets, and annual motivational personnel reviews became less exciting than it once had been. I was getting restless, yet I had no desire to leave investment banking or Morgan Stanley. Hence the six-month sabbatical to ponder the depths of my values in the wilds of the Himalayas, see if I could teach in the big leagues after my career in investment banking, and fill in the intellectual and spiritual gaps in my understanding of moral theology.

As I found, sustained personal values provide us with filters through which to evaluate and affirm—or perhaps negate—the world we have created for ourselves and allow us to make adjustments when necessary. When we are anchored in values and have a sense of who we are trying to be and become, we can continue to grow, learn, and find meaning in our lives.

To avoid burnout and frustration, the vision one has for a business career should be integrated within one's own view of oneself. One's personal vision must also be in sync with reality. A vision held by many at Morgan Stanley in the early 1960s, during my early business life, was one of wealth, privilege, connections, tradition, sophistication, and intelligence. I was weak in many of those areas, and had that vision been entirely accurate, I would have failed. I made it clear in the interview process who I was and what I had to offer, as well as who I was not. The fact that they wanted me for my energy and intelligence, and what little they could discern at that stage of my character, meant a great deal to me. I found the firm to be essentially a meritocracy in which one could receive the best on-the-job training in the business and prepare for what turned out to be unprecedented growth in the need for financial services. It was a good fit for me.

There are many whose personal values would make them uncomfortable with the rough-and-tumble competitiveness, advocacy, and compromises of an investment banker, a real estate broker, or a trial lawyer. Some are far more comfortable being full-time teachers or caregivers. Some feel they can integrate their lives by balancing a career with philanthropic endeavors. Some feel they can serve others even in the more freewheeling and competitive arenas. There is no right and wrong in this. The key is to know yourself and align your values with those of the profession and the firm with which you affiliate.

There can be many detours along the way. It would be unusual today for one to stay at the same firm as long as I did. The reasons I did include the continuing growth and success of the business, my personal growth and success in the firm, and the fact that my responsibilities and array of clients changed substantively three different times. I gained early success as a traditional corporate investment banker, then led the real estate business, and finally became a senior banker with administrative responsibilities for a geographical area. Throughout the years the mix of clients and the financial problems they trusted us to resolve for them varied considerably. Also, I fundamentally enjoyed a client service business.

We are not always perfect, however, nor do we always live up to our own goals for life. Money and power are very real motivating factors. There were times when I became emotional about compensation differentials that seem trivial to me now. Perhaps of greater importance was coming up on the short stick in the allocation of scarce resources. As the firm grew rapidly the various units were in constant struggle to attract the best professionals and the capital to finance our businesses. Competition for resources could become fierce, with winners and losers causing ill feeling and divisiveness within the enterprise. A longer view was required to sustain performance over the rough times. When we "young tigers" did not always have that vision, the wisdom of experienced senior leadership provided it, helping us to keep ambition and goals in focus.

In my business I competed every day with highly motivated, intelligent, creative individuals, both within the firm and in our competing firms. We also took risks with our capital, which occasionally resulted in significant losses to us personally as partners. Excellent performance was not enough. To survive, one had to learn to live with defeat, regenerate self-renewal, and get back into the game. As with financial risk, one needed to set limits to the downside, whether it be in time set aside for hiking, running, family activities, or intellectual activities. In addition to the intense relationships with my clients and cohorts at work, I maintained networks of running friends, hiking friends, and church-going friends with whom I could share my concerns objectively.

A strong personal vision helps one to develop a vision for leadership. It is not possible to have either a business plan or a leadership plan for oneself without self-knowledge of who you are and who you want to be. My vision of what might be possible sustained me during the long nights of my apprenticeship at the calculating machine or at the printers. In those early years, I could define my job as spending evenings and weekends in front of an electromagnetic Frieden calculating machine, filling up columns of accountancy paper. This was not precisely what I had envisioned—and yet I understood how it linked to my vision, how it was an essential part of the path that would get me there. Without the vision of ultimate success and my confidence in myself resulting from being a part of an organization that supported me, I could never have labored for three years on one project, or for seven years on the Irvine Ranch transaction.

Without a long-term vision I could never have sustained myself during the dark days of the early 1970s, when I was thrown into a new business and desperately struggling to understand it—even as I was in charge of it. Throughout, we all found our joy in the struggle, rather than in the success. Without my long-term vision and the organization's deep trust I could never have taken off six months at the peak of my career and done something entirely different, then come back to my position in the firm. Making this leap away was not easy; nor was the return. Many of my peers had thought I would not come back; and clients abhor a vacuum, so I had much work to accomplish upon returning to rebuild relationships. Through it, I retained a longer-term integrated vision of reorienting myself for six months, returning for ten years, and then taking early retirement to live out some of the new avenues I had opened up on the sabbatical. This vision helped me over the difficult reaches. Our vision is the sense about who we are and who we want to be, and living into it enables us to be free spirits in a sea of conformity and anxiety. It comes from the depth of our being, and it is nurtured over many years by life experience. We do not always know where it will lead, but we must learn to trust it, adjusting to contingencies and opportunities. Thereby we have the courage to make decisions and head into the unknown.

We can speak of layers of personal values. There is the layer of values learned in kindergarten. How do you build and sustain social relationships? One can also speak of aesthetic values. How do you cultivate your values in music, art, and literature? There are moral values. How do you relate to the increasing responsibilities of raising a family or running a business unit? Finally, there are also deep ethical, spiritual, or religious values. How do you sustain deep meaning in your life as you cope with frustration, failure, and death? We do not learn these values all at once. We enter seasons in life in which we are called on to take new responsibilities in our family, our career, or our roles as caring members of a community. There comes a time when we wish to integrate all these values into our daily lives, and not continue to compartmentalize them. This can be seen as a neverending journey to full maturity or integrity.

But if we become so complacent that we "know it all," we can lose our way. There have been too many cases of "last bad acts" occurring at the end of otherwise exemplary business careers, ranging from former Secretary of State Clark Clifford's involvement with an Arab bank subsequently connected with the Al Qaida movement to a former business school dean failing to exercise his duties in chairing the Enron audit committee. To avoid this trap, we need to continue to learn and grow throughout our careers and thereafter, as we are continually tested, learning from our failures and our successes, seeking out opportunities to both learn from and teach others.

As T. S. Eliot has written in "Little Gidding":[2]

> We shall not cease from exploration
> And the end of all our exploring
> Will be to arrive where we started
> And know the place for the first time.

Eliot, as always, is enigmatic. To me, what he is saying here is that a life of integrity is one in which life's experiences validate the essential truths that are learned at one's mother's knee (or perhaps in kindergarten).

FINDING MEANING ON THE JOB

Whatever your first job, if you have a vision for yourself to continue grow-ing and expanding, you need to be able to see how your entry-level position will take you to the next step. Especially in the dynamic, global world in which we live, we can never stop learning, whether from cohorts and men-tors or through teaching others (which itself is another form of learning). I was fortunate that for me, Morgan Stanley became yet another school, a university even, where learning never ceased.

My insurance broker is from a Hispanic family, and she has limited formal education, but she has considerable intelligence and energy. Her entry-level position in the brokerage firm was as a file clerk. Her boss be-came a mentor, observing that she was a lousy file clerk because she kept reading the files instead of filing them. She hungered for knowledge and skills, and she had the right boss. It helps a great deal to have a boss who takes an interest in you.

It may seem possible to scope out which entry-level jobs seem to lead somewhere, and which are dead ends—but it's not always so clear. The best organizations are always seeking high-potential employees. To make some money for graduate school, I drove a truck for Union Oil Company for several months after leaving the Army. It was an interim job that I hadn't expected to lead to anything beyond a paycheck. I did hang around the front office, and I was dating a secretary who worked there. Two years later, during my job search at Harvard Business School, the president of the oil company recommended me to their investment bankers, Dillon, Read, who offered me a job in New York City. That was a lesson for me in real-izing that we do not always know when or where we are being evaluated. It truly is best to try to behave always as if someone were looking.

At Harvard Business School we learned to speak and write accurately, organize our thoughts, and defend a position. My years at Morgan Stanley honed these skills still further. At an early stage we were expected to attend long, tedious, highly technical meetings with the lawyers or accountants, return to the firm, and give the partner in charge of the team a succinct and completely accurate summary of what had transpired. If we seemed uncertain or unclear, the partner would tear us apart. We were expected to check and double-check all of our statistical analyses (we were, after all, "statisticians"). We were held to a standard of complete accuracy. That was "the Morgan way." Every document or letter that left the firm was proofread by a team of two, one reading aloud to the other, sounding like Victor Borge as we recited the punctuation marks. We acquired lifetime habits of spotting typographical errors or miscalculations a mile away. We could perform mathematical calculations mentally, without a computer.

Such attention to detail, as archaic as it may sound in today's world, carries over into all areas of business. In theory, the availability of data on the Internet saves all the time we spent laboriously preparing spreadsheets. Such time might be spent on more detailed and thoughtful analysis. Yet in the detail we learned the subtle differences in accounting policies, and we paid attention to which firms were conservative in their financial accounting and which were more aggressive.

It seems to be normative behavior at present to tolerate misspelling and imprecision of thought in the content of e-mails. Speed and convenience have become more important than detailed accuracy. Yet in several court cases resulting from the corporate scandals of the early twenty-first century, such inaccuracies proved detrimental to some of the key players.

So as laborious as the Dickensonian apprenticeship was in the early days at Morgan Stanley, it paid dividends in a lifetime of attention to detail, which can make all the difference.

Learning from Transactions

Once we begin to establish who we are, our goals, and our plans for business and life, and to acquire personal skills and embedded values, we can determine how best to conduct ourselves in actually doing business. If we have an overall goal with intermediate steps, we can begin to create a context out of the drudgery and details of most entry-level positions. We should attempt to learn something from each assignment or transaction we work on, and from each person—whether senior leader, client, or cohort—to whom we are exposed.

No matter how well-educated we may be in a formal sense, there is much more to be learned before we can have serious impact in the business world. In my experience, intense on-the-job training in the early years is far more important than immediate financial rewards. Become known through experience as having sound judgment, honesty, and creativity; establish this as your reputation; and others will want to know what you have to say. The financial rewards will follow. Build a base of knowledge, and over the years it can turn into wisdom and judgment. One gains the requisite experience by being exposed to as many business situations and people as possible, even if it means, in the very early years, shadowing a senior person. My first assignment at Morgan Stanley involved sitting and listening to a partner discuss and negotiate the inclusion of property improvements in a railroad bond mortgage. I felt I had entered a new land where they spoke an unknown language and where nothing I had learned was relevant. A few years later I conducted such negotiations myself.

As a result of Morgan Stanley's wide-ranging business as a world-class leader in investment banking, I was continually exposed to new learning situations. I could envision my job as filling out countless spreadsheets, or I could also see my job as having the chance to learn about financing railroads or public utilities, or a start-up integrated aluminum business in Australia, or a chemical company in Germany, or a new kind of retailing in the United States. When I was given the responsibility to manage our real estate business eleven years after starting at the firm, I was suddenly immersed in the construction and marketing of regional shopping malls; the leasing of high-rise office buildings; the dynamics of room revenue and food and beverage revenue in convention hotels; the importance of architecture, transportation, location, design, and myriad other fascinating pieces of information. I was seeing the world through a new prism. Together, these new aspects of my knowledge base all contributed to making me a better businessperson. Given the changing world market, we're fortunate that business is a continual learning experience. This is how we grow and remain successful; it is also how we stay interested and avoid burnout.

My mentor John Gardner was ahead of his time in suggesting we change our perspective, or "repot," every ten years. I was able to so by changing responsibilities periodically within the same firm. I was not afraid to let go of all my established clients and relationships and try something new. It meant I had to work harder, but it also made life more interesting, even adventurous. With such a Kierkegaardian "rotation" out of everydayness, we can become intentional about changing parts of our life to retain that everyday freshness, so long as in doing so we retain our core values. What parts of your life would you like to change? Do you have the courage to do so? Are you prepared to take risks, to move out of your comfort zone and risk failure in the process?

Learning from Clients

A hallmark of banking practice is "know your client." One can best serve a client by listening carefully to his or her needs. Sometimes clients cannot articulate their needs, and a deeper level of knowledge is required to infer them. A basic premise is that we know our clients to be honest and trustworthy. The old adage "You are only as good as your client" remains true. J. P. Morgan's admonishment to "only do first-class business" was always before us. It is important to know the other side in negotiations as well. Patiently listening and being sensitive to the needs of others helps a great deal in framing arguments or in negotiating solutions.

I learned so much in other ways from my clients. I learned about the depth of friendship. I learned that it can be productive to consciously put adventure and spirituality and core values into your business life. It is good business in the long run to attempt to lead a life of complete integrity. It's not all about ego. A client is not an object you try to rip off and get as much out of as possible. A client is someone with whom there is always the potential to establish a long-term relationship and explore the depths of life.

Sometimes my clients complained that they were paying me to learn their business. I agreed with them, and I sopped up as much knowledge as I could. Learning their business was part of my job. The more I listened to my clients and attempted to understand their business, the better I could serve them. What they saw as "down time" actually made me better prepared to serve them. Over time an investment banker, lawyer, management consultant, or accountant gains a perspective on a variety of businesses that, if approached in a disciplined manner, can lead to a significant level of experience, and even wisdom.

One of the powerful aspects of a young person's beginning career in a professional service firm is the opportunity to relate to leaders a generation older. I have been most fortunate in that regard. One of the highlights of my life was my friendship with Harry Cunningham, CEO of Kresge prior to the company's name change to K-Mart. Harry started in the stockroom of a Kresge dime store in Washington, D.C., when he was nineteen years old, and retailing was in his blood. Over time, he created modern retailing through his vision, the K-Mart, which Sam Walton in his autobiography acknowledged as the model for Wal-Mart stores.

Harry loved to teach the retailing business to young people, and I was fortunate to be one of them. It was an opportunity available to anyone who was within Harry's compass and kept their eyes and ears open. As a young Morgan Stanley partner, I was responsible for escorting Harry on a two-week "road show" throughout the United States and Europe in connection with selling a large issue of Kresge common stock. With many clients, the two-week road show can become tedious: one hears the same speech three or four times a day for ten days and eats three meals a day with the same cast of characters, running out of things to talk about. With Harry, every minute was a joy. Every chance we had, we would sneak off and look at competitors' stores. That was all he wanted to do. When he saw that I was eager to go with him, we conspired to see how we could alter the time schedule to fit more in. I must have walked through thirty or forty Woolworths, J.C. Penneys, Sears, Montgomery Wards, and other stores with him. He would coach me on his basic rules of retailing and grade each store on how it complied. Employees must be courteous, helpful, and friendly. Eighty percent of the merchandise must be on the floor, on display, with only twenty percent back in the stockroom. Merchandise must be fresh and replenished promptly. If it isn't in the bins, you won't sell it. Merchandise must be tight on the racks, not loose. Harry would put his fingers in between garments to see how tight the rack was. Everything must be spotlessly clean, even the baseboards between the selling counters and the floor. Merchandise should be arranged so that the average-sized shopper could reconnoiter the entire store from any position. Merchandise must be repriced consistently, with every item properly priced. Harry invented, among other things, the "blue light" special. Throughout the store hours a blue light would go on, meaning some item had been repriced at a steep discount and was available in bins near the checkout counter, creating a sense of excitement for the shopper.

Harry knew the productivity of every K-Mart and Kresge store by store number, and he knew the name of each manager. He never let an opportunity to teach and reinforce his message go by. His masterstroke was to set a goal of eight inventory stock turns a year for each K-Mart. Thus the entire inventory for each store was, on average, sold out every forty-five days. In certain cases, the cost of the goods might not have to be paid for forty-five days. This meant that, literally, an item could be sold before the company had to pay for it. He had wallet cards made up for every employee, hammering away at "eight turns a year." He was a classic in setting a vision, relentlessly focusing and prioritizing, and genuinely loving his people. He died several years ago, but I cannot go into a retail store anywhere without unconsciously grading it on Harry's criteria.

Harry exemplified the great leaders we can only hope to become. He started with little formal education, but was devoted to learning and understanding the business from the bottom. He never lost his sense of humility or of where he had come from. He had an engaging personality. He trusted others, and he engendered trust in himself. When he eventually became CEO he had the courage to take a year off and reinvent not only his company but the entire retailing business. A major factor in his being able to do this was the fact that he always remained open to the needs and suggestions of employees, suppliers, and customers. He listened carefully to what the customers wanted and redesigned Kresge's merchandising strategy to meet their needs. He had a passion for detail and for doing it right. Like Bill Hewlett, he was always reaching out a welcoming and encouraging hand to young people coming along behind. He was one of the great ones: a great listener, a great learner, and a great teacher.

He did not become burdened by his lack of formal education. He had the courage to go against the grain and take that year off to study retailing. He treasured open, direct, transparent personal relationships, and he was a consummate builder of trust. He took personal risk in his job and in the individuals he trusted on faith. Without that formal education, what could possibly have sustained such autonomy and courage? Again, I would say a strong set of core values that focused Harry on the other—the consumer, the supplier, the employee—and not on himself.

Learning by Listening

Success in transactions can breed hubris, not necessarily the best trait for a manager of professionals. So one must keep an ear to the ground and be aware. One of the oldest—and still relevant—written guides to the art of managing people is the Rule of the Order of St. Benedict.[3] The first word and sentence of the Rule is "Listen!" There is an immense difference between doing deals and building a business. St. Benedict built a large number of hospitality-based communities that have lasted for over twelve hundred years. His Rule allowed groups of individuals to live together in harmony while living out their vision of obedience to God. And the lynchpin of that Rule was for everyone to Listen!—and listen hard, not only to the voice of God speaking from within but to all of the other members of the community.

A good listener becomes more and more rare in our wired age in which the desired fast pace of communication places ever-increasing importance on intuition, masses of data, and speed and presupposes a base of knowledge and experience. Fast responses, however, are not enough. We cannot live into our personal vision unless we are in relationship with others. I need to know how I am going to fit into your world, or the worlds of my friends, my employees, and my clients. I need to develop the emotional maturity to become sensitive to your needs, your values, and your goals if I am going to expect you to assist me in growing a business, serving customers, or creating a supportive and effective work environment. As Peter Drucker has written, we need the emotional maturity to deal with the anxiety caused by the fast pace of change we are all experiencing.

As much as I like to talk and tell stories, I've had to work at listening. Developing the skills and finding the time have often been a challenge for me. I place high value on accomplishing as much "work" as I can as efficiently as possible and then having time for other pursuits such as reading, hiking, and listening to jazz.

As a result of not always making enough time for listening, I have misjudged people and situations; this has led me to work harder and more conscientiously to hone my listening skills. It's all too easy to make serious mistakes by focusing on our own agenda and not slowing down to listen to the needs of others. The calls not made, the phone calls not returned, or the wrong people turned away can be haunting. Luckily for me, we are not always punished for our sins of omission.

As just one example, in the midst of the three years of trying to sell the Tishman office properties, when no one would look at office buildings in New York City, I was asked to chat with a man who had walked unannounced into our offices. He was a tall, burly, bearded gentleman, wearing a yarmulke. He was extremely cordial and soft spoken. He humbly stated he was a tile contractor from Toronto, and that he owned a few office buildings there. I mumbled a few pleasantries and escorted him to the door as soon as basic courtesy allowed, feeling hard-pressed by all the "important" things I had to do. A few weeks later I was startled to see his name listed in the financial press as the purchaser of the large Uris Brothers real estate portfolio in Manhattan. The Uris purchase was the beginning of an immense real estate empire. I could have sold him Tishman properties and saved both the Tishman family and Morgan Stanley an additional year of work. Just a few more questions on my part and a sincere interest in what my mysterious visitor was looking for could have made all the difference.

The extra effort to listen and stay alert to possibilities is never wasted. In one instance, a corporate finance partner regularly went through the lobby of a client company for meetings over the course of a year. Each time he walked beside a glass case that contained a model of the proposed new headquarters building, yet he never thought to tell me about the project or to suggest a meeting with his client. Had he listened more carefully to the excitement around the office about the new facility and not been so rushed, we might have shared in a profitable transaction, one whose significance he was then too preoccupied to fully notice.

A positive outcome of listening carefully to the other occurred when a young superstar banker in the firm, who was soon to give birth to her second child, told me she felt she could not sustain the pace at Morgan Stanley and raise her family. This was twenty-five years ago, before flex hours were widely accepted and when investment banking included few professional women. I asked her to define the type of workload she would be comfortable with, stating I would rehire her on her own terms and conditions. I arranged to allow her to work part-time for as long as she wished. This did not sit well with my superiors, who stated that she could never earn another promotion while working part-time. There were those who could not conceive of investment banking, especially at Morgan Stanley, as a part-time job. Three years later I enumerated her achievements to my seniors, without revealing her name, and asserted that her body of work was worthy of a promotion. They agreed. She received recognition for distinguished work and is currently co-CEO of one of the most powerful real estate firms in the world. Morgan Stanley benefited both from her continued work and from being regarded as a more enlightened employer of professional women.

Many years ago a highly successful businessman and world-class mountaineer was seated next to my wife at a dinner party. He talked the entire time. She could not get a word in. The next day he came to my office to discuss a real estate financing he was interested in. He opened our meeting by telling me what a wonderful conversationalist my wife was!

If a social scientist were monitoring your typical client business meeting, what percentage of the time would you be talking? Listening? Thinking? If you come home without the order, what have you learned about why you lost it? What have you learned from the potential client about how you could have gotten the order? What is the client looking for? What are the client's needs? How can you serve that client better next time?

Learning Continuously

It's important to become intentional about finding time in your busy life to grow intellectually. A focused program of reading, writing articles, public speaking, and teaching offers one way to accomplish this. It takes an aggressive posture to seek out new opportunities and accept new responsibilities when you're already busy. As you become a leader, you're likely to be concerned also with identifying new programs and opportunities for others in your firm and broadening your scope by bringing them along with you. It's also important that this work in both directions: ideally, the mutual learning, teaching, and growing should never stop.

Anyone entering a business or profession brings a certain set of requisite skills, usually gained in a school or university setting. That is a good starting point. Then the real education begins. As we continue to learn and gain wisdom and understanding, we become teachers, both formally and informally. Business is about teaching, coaching, and mentoring. In this world of fast changes, we need to educate our employees, our peers, our bosses, and our customers; and we need to be educated by them. We need to convey an understanding of our history, vision, attitudes, culture, and techniques. To sustain our interest, in a world of super-specialization, we need to grasp the greater role of our enterprise. To become a manager and, ultimately, a leader, we need to reintegrate the enterprise in our minds and achieve a sense of whole-task involvement.

Just as I learned investment banking on the job, I had to learn the real estate business while leading it. While still in my mid-thirties, I was given responsibility for managing a real estate finance firm we had purchased, Brooks Harvey & Co. The firm had a New York City office as well as branch offices in seven other cities; it was soon to have its own real estate investment trust, a real estate development firm, and a real estate joint venture with the largest real estate firm in Japan. My job was to integrate the firm into Morgan Stanley.

I soon discovered that Brooks Harvey had not been well run—at least not by any measure I knew. I had to create a list of assignments, a list of clients, and a pay roster; I also had to introduce business school recruiting, compensation systems, evaluation systems, training sessions, planning sessions, budgets, and a host of other customary business practices—all while learning the business and amid what would become the second-worst real estate recession in fifty years. The metaphor of a raw egg seemed most apt: I had to change the yolk without breaking the shell. We had to appear strong to the marketplace on the outside, but the inside had to be thoroughly changed and revitalized.

It was an intense real-life crash course in commercial real estate. I surrounded myself with the brightest I could attract from the corporate finance department at Morgan Stanley as well as the best from Brooks Harvey. I put myself on several of the major assignments, and I traveled with the most experienced real estate professionals and picked their brains at every possible occasion. Morgan Stanley's vision of professionalism had much to offer the real estate business in terms of integrity, techniques, and access, but we could not be just a bunch of financial analysts playing at real estate. We had to get inside the business. I had to understand Brooks Harvey's vision of the business and integrate it with Morgan Stanley's. I acted as player-coach, doing deals while building a business. Intense growth and learning were once again mandatory for me, even at mid-career.

Fortunately, within a few years, we not only led Wall Street in bringing investment banking skills to the real estate industry but demonstrated to the senior management of Morgan Stanley that our work product and approach to the business now measured up to firm standards, and so we merited a name change to Morgan Stanley Realty. We accomplished these changes in a variety of ways. We brought a handful of young investment bankers into Brooks Harvey to work side-by-side with the real estate professionals. We recruited from business schools directly into the real estate business, which had not been done before. We set up joint project teams when Morgan Stanley clients had real estate needs. We gradually expanded Morgan Stanley benefits, support services, computer skills, and other services to the real estate business. We spent considerable time explaining and teaching each side what the other had to offer, breaking down resistance to client sharing and cross-selling where we could. In this, and many other circumstances, I learned the many values of teaching.

Quick learning, focus, prioritization, and adjustment also became very important. What do I have to do to get us through the next day or week? How do we manage our cash? How do we complete the client assignments in-house? How do we build the business? How do I make my quarterly budget? On an intermediate-term basis, how do I build up my staff? How do I gain the confidence of Morgan Stanley? Whom do I promote? Which offices do I close? Whom do I get rid of? On a longer-term basis—well, I just had to survive to get to the long term. For the time being, those were the things I took a risk on not getting done at all. And I didn't.

Learning by Teaching

A leader is a teacher. A leader teaches employees, peers, colleagues, clients, and others, empowering them, training them, and giving them enough autonomy to learn from their mistakes. In an investment bank, a leader is always helping to convince others, including those within the enterprise, to use new products and new ideas. A good salesperson is a good teacher. A good salesperson listens hard to identify client needs and then teaches the prospective client how his or her products and ideas can meet those needs. Such a person does not thoughtlessly complete a call list hawking someone else's ideas. A good salesperson attempts to sustain a long-term relationship with a client based on trust and a genuine desire to serve.

I grew to enjoy the process of offering securities into the public markets. The give-and-take and the endless individual negotiations reminded me of the more primitive markets I had observed in Kuwait or Nepal. The contract we used with client firms and other investment banks came alive for me as I collected stories that exemplified how the various provisions were handled. Due to this interest and my pursuit of it, as a five-year associate I found myself called on to teach the elements of underwriting contracts to newly hired lawyers at Davis Polk & Wardwell. I was nervous about teaching lawyers from the top law schools something meaningful about contracts, but I responded positively to the invitation, seeing it as an opportunity to continue to grow. The potential of embarrassing myself was, for me, a great motivator. I made certain that I really understood those contracts before standing up before those young lawyers. Teaching others, especially those who are highly intelligent and motivated, is a great way to deepen your learning.

I learned this lesson again and again in later years, when I began teaching formally, including full-term courses on the management of financial institutions at graduate business schools at Stanford and UCLA as well as individual classes on business ethics at Notre Dame, USC, and elsewhere. I taught these classes primarily through discussion, which required that I have real depth of knowledge of the subjects. Initially, I was surprised at how much work it took to prepare for my four two-hour sessions a week at Stanford. Teaching at that level is a great learning experience. It is one thing to read a few books. It is an entirely different experience to read the books knowing you will soon be before a class, hoping to impart some lasting lessons.

I really learned about teaching from the military, in which there is considerable reliance on teaching one another. During my officer training I was taught to make out lesson plans and actually perform practice teaching assignments. Some of the practical field training in leadership in the Army was as effective as any leadership training I have experienced, including that at Harvard Business School.

A great joy for me has been developing a series of jazz lectures illustrated with cuts from CDs. I have researched, written, produced, and delivered these lectures for several local clubs, in the course of which I have greatly expanded my knowledge of this life-long hobby and developed meaningful relationships with members of the professional jazz community.

The combination of ongoing activities of practical engagement, teaching, reading, and writing on the subject mutually reinforce one another and have brought a depth of meaning to these aspects of my life.

In recent years, I have sought opportunities to pass on knowledge and information by teaching in more informal venues—my Protestant church, a Benedictine monastery, and a seminary summer school. The discipline of studying areas of interest to me, such as moral philosophy, theology, and spiritual literature, has helped me to maintain balance in my life. I actively work at bringing my organizational values from the business world into the church and the church's values into the business world. My hope is that my efforts might help to break down institutional walls that obstruct learning, valuing, and growing.

Over the years I have put together "mini" courses on Protestant theologians Dietrich Bonhoeffer, Paul Tillich, and Karl Barth, as well as on spiritual literature including T. S. Eliot's *Four Quartets*, Dante's *Divine Comedy*, the novels of Charles Williams (a friend of C. S. Lewis and T. S. Eliot), the short stories of Flannery O' Connor, the novels and essays of Walker Percy, and the mysteries and theology of Dorothy Sayers. I enjoy the ongoing inquiry, making connections among the subjects and making them meaningful in a business-related discussion. In addition, I find all these areas of research and teaching useful in my ongoing business activities. Many individuals appreciate the opportunity to have a serious literary or theological or values-based discussion, rather than skimming along the surface realities. I find it a way to explore and discover the deeper and more interesting facets of others. Once people connect at a deeper level, it is more likely that a trust relationship will develop. A deeper sense of values and a series of trust relationships with others helps one over the disappointments and rough spots in business and helps provide a deeper vision of what can be accomplished both professionally and personally. It also helps in that *constant* struggle for balance.

What areas would you enjoy studying, mastering, and teaching? Are you willing to take the risk of committing to teach something that will be brand new to you? Might this not be another method of breaking out of "everydayness"?

CHAPTER 6

Aligning Individual and Corporate Values

BEING A PART OF ANY ORGANIZATION, including a business firm, is a bit like being a piece of a puzzle. Are you enough of a fit to make it through the interview process? What if, in trying to meet the demands of the position, you realize that the shape of the position is not congruent with the shape you perceive in yourself? Can you reshape yourself? Should you? Some aspects of character and personality are easily changed; others are not. How much can you adapt without losing your self? Without endangering your integrity?

As discussed in the earlier chapters, to address these questions, you first have to know yourself. You have to know how your personality and character have been formed by past experiences. You need to be intentional about how you adapt to the new culture and still claim your identity. The changes required can be great, or they can be minor and seemingly superficial. It is important to understand this process of acculturation and to be proactive about when to go along and when to retain your own unique personality.

When I was first interviewing at Harvard Business School, Morgan Stanley was considered to be one of the elite jobs one could have. As the day of the on-campus screening interview approached, I thought about how I would handle it. I had already determined how I wanted to be known—as honest, restless, curious, and perhaps a bit unusual. I really had no other option; that was how I viewed myself. Sometimes I have been too honest, even blunt. I wanted to be certain that Morgan Stanley understood who I was, so there would be no misunderstanding resulting in a mis-hire. I am not afraid to face the truth, and I believe "you shall know the truth and the truth shall set you free." I wanted to live out my journey authentically and not try to become someone I was not.

My on-campus interview was with a senior partner, who portrayed to me a sense of seriousness, gravitas, even intimidation. He asked me to tell him a bit about myself, so I told a couple of family stories. I was proud of my father and grandfather, and hoped their strong genes might have been passed along to me. I told of my grandfather, who had completed the eighth grade, run away from home to enlist in the Spanish American War, and ended up a general in the Army. I told of my father, who flunked out of college his freshman year, drove to California to become a movie stunt man, ended up directing all American Red Cross aid to England and France in 1940–41, and was eventually knighted.

My stories were greeted with silence. Was he impressed? Puzzled? Did he find my stories interesting or unbelievable? I found the silence uncomfortable, so half-way through the interview I suggested that, if he had no further questions, we adjourn to the lounge and observe John Glenn on the initial manned space flight. So we spent the last fifteen minutes of my interview watching television—and I was invited to come to New York for further interviews.

I was operating in the dark. I did not at the time understand whether the man was shy (why would Morgan Stanley send a shy man to conduct interviews at Harvard Business School?), or if it was some form of stress interview. I was lucky that the man I had drawn to see had come from a background similar to mine and became interested in promoting my cause at Morgan Stanley. Part of what I was doing was improvising, living by my wits, and part was trying to be transparent about who I felt I was. My hiring process continued in this unconventional way. I made sure my interviewers at Morgan Stanley knew who I was and where I came from. They could decide whether I would fit in or not. On my trips to New York for further interviews I looked around at my potential fellow employees and saw that they appeared to be more in the groove for what I imagined a Morgan banker might be. Even so, I was willing to give it a shot; luckily, the company was also willing to take a chance on me.

As a further mark of my "eccentricity," I took the entire summer off, becoming the last of Morgan Stanley's new employees to arrive for work after Labor Day. I had worked hard in Korea, then at driving an oil truck for five months, and then at Harvard Business School. I had been married for just the final year at Harvard, and I felt my wife and I needed ten weeks off to reorient for the long pull ahead. Just as with the sabbatical twenty years later, I saw it as a natural break point and a time to stop and take stock of things and spend quality time with my wife and my parents.

I knew that I would be at a disadvantage in the socialization process at Morgan Stanley, where the typical young professional appeared to have attended a well-known private prep school, an Ivy League college, and Harvard Business School. Some of these professionals had known for most of their lives that they would become investment bankers; I had first heard the term only eighteen months before.

Some adaptations are easy and beneficial. They concern such details as dress, speech patterns, and social customs. I suspect regional differences were greater and were given more weight forty-five years ago. Suddenly my jackets seemed too long and my cuff links too flashy. Early in my career I was confronted on the corner of Wall Street and Broadway by a founding partner and told in no uncertain terms never to go outdoors again without a hat. I promptly set off for Brooks Brothers. On the great day when a senior partner invited me to lunch with him at his private club, I was dismayed when he pointed out that I had just eaten his salad. Thus I learned the tradition of "salad on the left, beverage on the right" a bit belatedly. Being left-handed as well as socially dysfunctional, when I was finally allowed to rub elbows with people in the partners' dining room, I had all I could do to keep from dribbling creamed spinach from the large serving platters onto my newly acquired but already shiny cheap Ivy League suit.

Social graces that had appeared overly stylized to me in the fraternity house or in the Army took on more importance in the rarified air of Morgan Stanley. Lack of good manners can undermine your credibility when you are trying to convince an important person to respect your opinion and use your services. The partners apparently saw that I had potential, and they took the time to coach me as to how a Morgan partner might behave. A short eight years later I was one; and over the years, much to my amusement, I came to be regarded by some who did not know me well as a "blue blood." We must guard against becoming so socialized that we forget where we came from.

In my early days at Morgan Stanley I felt as if we were working in a banking house described by Charles Dickens. The total head count of the enterprise, including all the support staff, was only 140, yet a few of the senior partners did not even bother to learn our names until we had established our credibility. All this was counter to my Southern California upbringing of openness and friendliness, yet I determined not to take it personally.

One particular partner's indifference to our names had become a joke among the new hires. One day I came bounding up the internal staircase from the library, where I had been perusing old deal files, and met this partner face to face. "Have you seen . . . ah . . . ah . . . Buzzzz McCoy?" he asked, exaggerating my first name for effect. "Yes, sir!" I replied. "He was down at the bottom of the stairs just a second ago." I raced out onto Wall Street amidst the laughter of my peers.

I didn't know what had gotten into me. I could have been fired. I am sure a part of me wanted to curry favor with my peers. But also part of me was rebelling at his continuing attitude of indifference to us as individuals. He was upsetting my personal vision for myself and my job. Although I would not recommend my approach, I must admit it was effective in a limited way. He invited me to see Bobby Short with him (and called me "Jack" throughout the evening). I wish I could say the partner knew me well enough to realize that I would particularly enjoy Bobby Short, but it seemed he was merely fulfilling his own interests.

Baiting him had been a high-risk decision on my part—and an immature one. In asserting my independence and attempting to keep my center, I had read one man's weakness with name recognition and recall as a corporate value of all the senior partners. That was wrong. Most of the partners with whom I had the closest contact as a junior associate took an interest in me and proved to be able mentors and teachers, providing me with some of the most powerful learning experiences of my life. As I learned, uncovering the true foundational values of an organization demands much more concentrated study.

LEARN THE VALUES

The socialization process in a new business situation, or even a new client situation, involves sensitivity to what is going on around us. Not all the signals will be explicit, and it's easy to misread a situation. It takes self-discipline to be intentionally discerning about a new culture. Time is a key factor in adaptation, and it's important not to rush it. But if after a reasonable period our values and those of the new enterprise don't match, we need to be wary.

It was particularly difficult, in the "old" Morgan Stanley, for a young person to discern whether he or she was doing well. There were no formal assessments of performance, either following a major assignment or on an annual basis. One had to become adept at reading the tea leaves and alert to minute differentials in annual bonus payments or in the character or prestige of the assignments. It would be all too easy to overanalyze the situation and become depressed or less confident for the wrong reasons. My own goal became one of learning as much as possible and of establishing my credibility, slowly and methodically, one-on-one, with as many people in the firm as I could. This involved not only good work habits and productivity but also the beginning of sound instincts and good judgment. I learned who the good mentors were and which of the partners were inaccessible to us as juniors or were to be avoided as much as possible given their lack of patience, poor teaching skills, and impossible demands.

In firms such as Morgan Stanley, one does not become a partner because it is owed to you. Partnership, rather, is the validation of work already being performed at that level. Toward the end of my apprenticeship process, I was given responsibilities that exceeded those of some of the partners on the assignment team. This clearly required a high level of tact and diplomacy, but was a strong signal to me that the mesh was working.

Matching up the deep intuitive sense of who you are with the culture of a firm is experiential. It can happen quickly, or it can evolve over a long period of time. It is a classic case of a fast no and a slow yes. An obviously negative series of events such as occurred at Enron or Tyco, for example, can become formative and determinative early in a career. Deep trust is built up over a long series of events, as you see how the organization responds to stress, crises, and the previously unknown. Such trust is not built in a straight line; there are diversions and setbacks along the way. One must, over time, develop through experience a level of trust that gets one over the pitfalls but is not so ingrained that it accepts the hard-to-perceive invidious incrementalism of bad practices. What is important is that we consciously adapt gradually to our environment. We must always be on guard against destructive adaptations in our values, our honesty, and our sense of who we are. We must be willing to take the responsibility of becoming ourselves one of the cornerstones of the enterprise, with all that that means.

There were a few times when I was disappointed that my personal values did not seem congruent with those of the firm. When such events occurred I spoke up, and I was usually heard. When I was not heard and the firm took a decision I did not agree with, I tried to learn from it, and I moved ahead to the next deal or the next decision, hoping we would do it better the next time. Sometimes I felt the firm had taken the wrong decision. Other times I was just not being flexible enough myself. I never gave up, even when the firm did not appear to live up to my expectations for it.

The greater game was more important than winning each and every time. One is balancing short-term decisions with longer-term decisions. Occasionally we have to compromise our principles to be influential in shaping the decisions that remain. In many professions, including investment banking, we are continually making trade-offs and compromising. If we make each and every decision cosmic, we will soon lose influence and respect among our colleagues. If we slide through every trade-off without taking a stand, we will lose our self-respect and our sense of who we are. We must be able to bend and not break. The elegance and the creativity of ethical living lie in the existential decision of when to have the courage to take a stand and stop trading off.

The section that follows outlines some methods for determining a corporate culture. Using them, or similar techniques, you can become your own "organizational cultural anthropologist." The issue then becomes, What do you do with this information? How much should you change your own values to align them with those of the enterprise? Do you have any influence in changing the values of the enterprise itself? Can a mutual tinkering be accomplished? How long do you go along with an atmosphere that is dysfunctional from your point of view? Where do you draw the line? Are you unemployable? Are you in the wrong industry or profession, given your personal ethical sensitivities? Are there areas outside of work in which you can achieve the satisfaction you may not be achieving in the workplace? Finding that balance in your life is crucial to long-term success and happiness.

LOOKING FOR CLUES TO THE CULTURE

We can become intentional about analyzing a firm's culture, using both objective and subjective clues. Objective clues include the CEO's message in recent years' annual reports, press releases, data deemed important enough to put on the firm's Website, senior officers' public speaking files, statements of corporate purpose, goals, codes of behavior, and the like. A review of Internet data regarding current and past years' litigation and regulatory compliance will give an idea of how close to the line the firm likes to play the game. A very important clue, not always available, is printed employee evaluation forms for salary reviews and promotions. What does it take to get ahead? Are the criteria solely production driven, or is there emphasis on character, recruiting, training others, mentoring, and, most important, ethical behavior?

Subjective clues to implicit values are far more important than the printed material, and harder to come by. They can be derived from an examination of the culture of the organization. By culture I refer to the myths, legends, stories, styles, commitments, attitudes, and reward-and-punishment systems that make up the fabric of the organization and which the individuals in it use as their signals as to what is or is not correct behavior—that is to say, the cumulative transmission of corporate experience. An understanding of the implicit values of an organization is indispensable for individuals at all levels, from the entry level through the position of CEO. Employees must be able to ascertain whether or not there is a good fit between their values and those of their employers. The CEO must, implicitly or explicitly, encompass the understanding and management of the corporate value system.

Examples of subjective clues to corporate values include the following:

How does the organization obtain and hold new business?

What criteria are used to turn business down?

What criteria are used for advancing employees? To what extent are these criteria consistent with printed forms and policies?

To what extent do younger employees believe in the basic fairness of the formal performance evaluation and feedback system? Is there a formalized program of upward feedback?

Is there evidence to support a general atmosphere of openness? Does the system tolerate internal conflict?

To what extent does the system tolerate a sincere inquiry from a junior employee about whether a particular action or policy is right or wrong?

What evidence is there of capacity for growth, change of goals, and change of values?

To what extent are activities in support of minorities, the church, or social justice tolerated? To what extent are they supported?

If the organization is a multinational, what are the policies and attitudes toward third-world countries?

What are the basic attitude and style toward the law and regulatory authorities? How close to the line is the game played?

In informal bull sessions, who are the heroes? For what values are they admired?

To what extent are the traditional values maintained and supported when the corporation is under stress (for example, a raid, threatening litigation, major competition, declining earnings, government policy change, and so on)?

A high level of correlation and consistency between the subjective and the objective value systems is a good indication of the basic character and integrity of the organization. Integration into the planning process of basic societal values (social justice, third-world problems, minority rights, individual values) is a fairly good indication that the organization is committed to change to meet future needs and markets. It is also a measure of the basic integrity of the enterprise.

Hearing—and Finding—the Stories

In my experience, much of the culture is shared through stories, and in the choices of which stories to tell and when to tell them. The senior partners at Morgan Stanley were more than generous with their time and could spin great yarns about the deals they had worked on. "War stories" can be just that, but they can also be great learning experiences when placed in context. They commence a bonding of the neophyte with the culture of the firm and help instill good practices. They reveal the range of the organization. How does it make money? How does it attract customers? When things were slow, I would roam the library, reading about the history of previous transactions or perusing the memos describing senior partners' visits with European central bankers.

Selecting an investment banker for assistance is not a casual decision. Neither is deciding which clients to take on. Indeed, this decision is a fundamental issue relating to good and bad practices. In the real estate side of the business, we rarely received easy assignments, and we needed to assess the probability of their successful completion. Most of our assignments had a degree of complexity or risk that made them difficult. The firm was typically paid only for success. We also had to assess the character of our clients in a way that was more fundamental than in corporate finance. Many of our clients were entrepreneurs who ran their own private firms. We had to assure ourselves of their character and ability to carry off their projects. The New York Stock Exchange motto of "Know your customer" was especially apt for those of us in the real estate unit. On occasion, we even hired private investigators to check out potential clients. We needed to be alert for the occasional developer who would run out of funds or otherwise drop a project in midstream. In such cases, we would hang on to a bundle of rights, entitlements, and architectural designs; a couple of leases; and a mortgage commitment. We would try to find another developer to insert into the transaction who would then become our client. Reinforcement of good practices in the informality of day-to-day operations is important and effective.

One day I discovered a real gem. It was the "declination book" that contained one-page memos describing each transaction the firm had turned down since its inception, and the reasons why. It was a wonderful learning tool, yet none of us juniors had been pointed to it, or even knew it existed. I mentioned to a partner that I had discovered it and was looking through it, in case there might be a problem. He raised no objection, so I read it from cover to cover.

From it I learned that Morgan Stanley turned down more business transactions than it accepted. Usually the dollar volume of rejected transactions was considerably less than those undertaken by the firm's larger clients. The focus was on quality, with the understanding that you can only be as good as your clients. Lack of seasoning was another issue. To take a company public we wanted to see a solid five-year record of consistent and improving performance. I learned that industries differed in their acceptance of their investment banker's working with competitors. The oil industry favored the banker who had as much knowledge of their business as possible, so we had a wide array of oil company clients. However, I also learned that some companies let it be known that they would not favor our banking their competitors.

At that time, Morgan Stanley considered itself the ultimate arbiter of Wall Street. Its sponsorship of securities was felt by some firms to be the highest mark of good standing in the financial community. Of course, not everyone agreed. The business was intensely competitive, with all the other investment banks seeking to convince potential clients that they were just as good as us, if not better. One mark of Morgan Stanley's dominance in this period was that the firm would not share the management of an issue of securities with any other firm, even though every other firm on Wall Street would do so.

Although the general reputation of the firm was one of conservatism, it turned out that Morgan Stanley had done a number of risky transactions. The partners took pride in the story of the firm's financing of Northspan Uranium, a Canadian uranium producer. The Atomic Energy Commission wished the company to secure permanent capital to supply the United States nuclear projects, but little could be told about the business because it was all classified information. Morgan Stanley was given the assignment and received secret briefings on the business, but it could not discuss the information with other members of the underwriting syndicate nor disclose them fully to the SEC in the public-offering prospectus. Morgan Stanley's reputation was such that all of Wall Street relied on its assurances, without full disclosure.

The large volume of rejected business was the implementation of a sharply focused and disciplined corporate vision. Morgan Stanley wished to serve the largest and most important corporations and was prepared to dedicate to its clients a depth of resources for financial analysis and the pricing of their securities, including the combined wisdom and judgment of the partnership as a whole. Following financial deregulation, the firm's vision underwent drastic changes, and we all struggled hard for business just like everyone else. The culture inside the firm changed from emphasis on absolutely perfect execution of transactions for a fairly stable client base to a far more aggressive one of seeking new business, expanding the product line, and opening new markets. We all needed to adapt quickly to the changes while holding on to the values of the past.

Learning in the Assignments

Looking into the past was an excellent, though rather passive, way to get inside the rich corporate culture at Morgan Stanley. There were other more personally demanding ways as well. I labored for several of my early years on an assignment with the J. I. Case Company, a premier manufacturer of farm tractors and implements. I watched with envy as my peers worked on financings for large, important companies. In reflecting on my investment banking career, however, I realize how fortunate I was to have gotten this assignment at an early stage. It was clearly a "nonglamorous" job, headquartered in Racine, Wisconsin, but it became one of my important learning experiences. It was on that assignment that I actually became a part of forming Morgan Stanley's culture.

J. P. Morgan had been the company's banker, and five years previously Morgan Stanley had managed a public offering of convertible subordinated debentures (bonds convertible into common stock of the company). The company had been taken over by a corporate raider who undertook several extremely intelligent steps, such as adding construction equipment to the product line and setting up a sales finance subsidiary. He also pumped up the sales, deceiving himself that sales to wholesale dealers (not sales to farmers) were final sales. As a result he booked healthy profits while his inventories were rusting in the yards of Case dealers. As transparent as this now seems, others—including Chrysler—were later to make the same mistake.

The company was as good as bankrupt, although the banks had not as yet pulled the plug. The raider protested that all he needed was a little more time. The senior partners of Morgan Stanley decided they had to step in to protect the members of the public who had purchased the convertible debentures that Morgan Stanley had underwritten. This was a step not called for by law or practice, and it became a hallmark of Morgan Stanley that they took it. Moving in on a client company to protect the bondholders to whom one had sold securities required courage and raised important ethical questions: Who is the client here? When do you blow the whistle on a client firm's CEO who still believes his plans will work?

A senior partner was called on to do the job. He became the *de facto* CEO of Case for several months. The first thing he did was to find a permanent CEO. The next steps were to slow down and sort out production and refinance the business. I was assigned to the team as the junior statistician. What was so intriguing about this assignment was that everything was upside down. Unlike our high-credit clients, Case was functionally bankrupt. Instead of performing the routinized dance of high-grade finance and S.E.C. filings, we were left with a blank canvas to fill in. Every line of the indenture that specified the rights of the bondholders had to be examined to see how much flexibility we had. Instead of negotiating the last two one-hundredths of a percentage of interest rate with the banks, we had to show them a vision (and a vision was all it was) that would persuade them to stay in the credit line. There were 101 banks in the credit line, a huge mistake, and two of the smallest ones, including a Mormon bank in Salt Lake City, threatened to put the company into bankruptcy, even though Chase and First National City Bank were willing to stay in and give us a chance. Without Morgan Stanley's extracurricular involvement, the company would have been a goner. We expanded the finance company to carry a larger portion of the debt, renegotiated other layers of debt, and brought in an equity investor, Kern County Land Company. I became intimately knowledgeable about the rights of bond holders and how they were tested *in extremis*. I learned, early on, that finance could be highly creative and need not be performed in a conservative, traditional manner.

The Case assignment proved to be fundamental in my career. The partner involved ultimately became the initial CEO of Morgan Stanley when we incorporated, and we had a strong working relationship. As a result of my depth of knowledge of the company, as a five-year associate, I was sent out to Racine with a partner from Davis Polk & Wardwell and no one else from Morgan Stanley to write my first registration statement, a major responsibility. Kern County Land organized a new board of directors for Case, including George Shultz and Bill Hewlett. I remained friends with those gentlemen and other officers of the Case Company for the next forty years. Part of the great adventure of a career in investment banking is that you never know where assignments will lead. At any time the phone can ring, and you are off to Tokyo, Melbourne, or Racine—and, who knows, Racine may be the best destination.

The financial community was impressed with Morgan Stanley's commitment to the Case bondholders and its willingness to commit resources to seeing the company through its financial reorganization. In fact, for many years afterward, certain new clients would report that one of their reasons for selecting Morgan Stanley was the way they saw the firm live out its ethic in the Case situation. We learn from everyone—fellow employees, clients, and potential clients—by observing and interpreting what is going on around us. This works in both directions: employees, clients, and potential clients also learn from us, so we should always behave as we wish to be remembered.

A few years later, Kern County Land Company, the savior we had found for J. I. Case, was itself raided. This was in the mid-1960s, and surprise corporate raids were not yet a part of the Wall Street culture. In this case, Armand Hammer, the notorious leader of Occidental Petroleum, pulled what became known as the first "Saturday night special" on the senior officers of Kern County. I found myself in San Francisco as the junior member of a Morgan Stanley team sent to defend against the raid. The senior managers of our client company were so distraught and angry about the situation that they lost their capacity to provide the necessary leadership for what was to become the most important decision in the company's history. In my naivete I was surprised to see senior leaders become so distressed and break down under the pressures of the situation. A hallmark of true leaders is a certain detachment from the day-to-day crisis; this detachment comes from an embedded inner core of values that can sustain the leaders through the stress and disappointments of the job.

It is difficult to fend off a corporate raid. In most cases, the company "trades" to another, more attractive, perhaps more benign, suitor termed a "white knight." In this case, three powerful CEOs, representing Union Oil Company, Pure Oil Company, and Tenneco, came on three separate days into the offices we were using and made half-billion-dollar bids for Kern County. All the offers were subject to review and discussion by their separate executive committees and boards of directors, but the three CEOs were operating in a highly entrepreneurial fashion, assuming they had *carte blanche* to commit their firms to the transaction. Thus, as a young analyst, I had a revealing lesson in how corporate governance really worked.

TESTING:
ARE YOU PREPARED TO LIVE THE VALUES?

We learn by the crucible of personal challenges. Six months after I became partner we were all summoned to a special partners' meeting at which we discussed the fact that American Express had offered to purchase Morgan Stanley for $100 million. We juniors each had a one percent interest in the firm, so we felt we would each receive a million dollars. Our full-year compensation the previous year had been $35,000, so this was not an immaterial sum to us. We were asked to make a choice between current wealth and preserving the culture and future of Morgan Stanley. The vote was taken in inverse order of seniority. I voted second. All the younger partners voted against the transaction. Only four partners out of thirty-three voted for it. Harry Morgan, a founding partner and grandson of J. P. Morgan, made a magnificent speech about "not selling his birthright for a mess of pottage!" This vote was taken in December 1970, only five years before financial deregulation on Wall Street changed the environment in which we lived. The business became more competitive and challenging, and we had rough times and uncharted waters ahead. That vote bonded the younger partners in an implicit pledge to hold rather than sell, deal with the changes we knew were coming, and become a powerful survivor in our industry. In choosing this course we held our egos in check for the most part, resisted the star system so prevalent in certain other firms, and dedicated our individual successes to the enhancement of the name and image of the firm above all else. I have always seen this event as a milestone during my time at the firm. The offer, which was attractive at the time, forced us to focus and act on our vision for the business.

In later years I was given the opportunity to serve on an operating committee that ran the various businesses of Morgan Stanley, and this provided me with insights into the firm as a whole. That group, with a few additions, was called on in 1985 to do the work in preparation for taking Morgan Stanley public in 1986. The offering would constitute a windfall for the then shareholders, since we bought and sold the stock among ourselves at book value and the public offering would be at a multiple of book value. In addition, though this was not necessarily predictable, the stock moved up rapidly in the after-market trading.

There remained to be resolved significant issues of equity that could have a major impact on the firm after the offering. Those of us who had been partners or managing directors for fifteen years or more were deemed by the younger partners to have built up an inequitably high stake in the firm in relation to their positions. As a result of their protests we voted a voluntary recapitalization, each of us giving about a quarter of our stake in the business to the younger partners, making the bet that if we kept them motivated we would all become winners over time. This proved to be the case. Those of us who had voted against the American Express offer were called on once again to forgo current profit for future gain, and we did.

Another issue was what to do about the older partners who had devoted their lives to the firm and then retired at book value. We opted to go with the future and not look backward. When Goldman Sachs went public many years later, they chose a different course, giving a share of the windfall to the retired partners. But they gave only a small share to retired partners, some of whom were resentful at the amount received. There is no "correct" answer to these deeply personal ethical issues. Such major events cause firms to choose whether or not to live out their perceived value system.

We were particularly worried about the reaction of our recently retired leader, Bob Baldwin, who had been paid out at book value. At the meeting at which all the partners voted to favor the younger partners but not the retired ones, Baldwin stood up and said he had something to say. A nervous hush fell over the room. He strode purposefully to the front of the room, turned around, made an imaginary golf putt and stated, "Well, boys, it's all in the rub of the green." Then he sat down. Bob Baldwin's handling of our decision was one of the most gracious gestures I have ever seen in the business world, and it revealed more than anything else his deep sense of who he is. Rather than risking damage to the firm to gain a personal share in the proceeds, he held to his vision of putting the firm ahead of any individual partner. His behavior was far different from that of many current CEOs and their feelings of entitlement to large compensation packages.

There are times in business when we are called on to make highly complex and hard ethical decisions. If we were to reach backward as well as forward with our public offering windfall, where would we draw the line? How far back would we go? Would we consider the widows of former partners? I felt uncomfortable about what we had done with respect to the more senior partners, but I also felt we had been generous in what we had given up to the younger partners. As it turned out, the stock price rose to levels such that, in retrospect, we could have been even more generous, but we did not know at the time that this would happen.

The issue was particularly close to me, since I had seen the other side. After my father's death three weeks before his sixty-fifth birthday, the American Red Cross paid us a settlement on his pension plan. But because he hadn't yet reached sixty-five, the Red Cross cut off any future medical benefits for my mother. My mother and father combined had served that organization for ninety-five years. Despite numerous entreaties, the national organization held firm, unwilling to change a policy that affected thousands of employees. Such decisions can make organizations appear to be arbitrary and inhumane, but when you are on the firing line, making such decisions, it can become quite difficult.

As Paul Tillich has written, it takes courage to make the hard choices. The challenge becomes even greater in larger organizations with vast numbers of stakeholders. Such decisions cannot be as individually humane as in a smaller private firm. There is a need for limits, rules, and laws, in part because of the public scrutiny: decisions cannot appear to be arbitrary. Thus the larger the organization and the more impact it has on the world, the greater are the challenges in behaving ethically.

A key to success in an organization is developing an appropriate level of ethical sensitivity or awareness. If you "blow the whistle" every week, or every month, you are probably in the wrong business. On the other hand, if you coast through a career without ever seeing an ethical issue, you are probably ethically unconscious and a danger to the organization and yourself.

It is necessary, from time to time, to test your personal values against those of the organization. These recalibrations can become important for one's peace of mind so long as they do not become disruptive. (If they do, there is obviously a still deeper problem.) Timing and tactfulness become issues when one is going against the grain.

In the early 1970s I brought in a $1.5 million fee for liquidating Tishman Realty. This was a tremendous advice fee at the time. It had taken three years of very hard work, and the transaction had been featured throughout the financial press, so I fully expected to be treated as a hero. Instead, and much to my surprise, one of the senior partners stated in a partners' meeting that such a fee was unconscionable in a situation in which the firm had taken no financial risk. Instead of being a hero, I was being accused of breaking the rules! This was a result I hadn't even considered.

His point of view was indicative of the range of ethical sensibilities, even in an investment bank. It was also indicative of the culture of that older generation's partnership, in which such issues could be freely discussed. The senior partner's deep core values demanded that he raise these issues. What he was doing at that early stage was cautioning us all about the dangers of greed. Perhaps, over the long term, we should have listened more carefully. And yet, as many of us argued, an essential aspect of successful business is risk taking. In investment banking, that is part of what aligns us with the interests of the client who is expected to pay large fees. Any serious professional should be expected to take risks from time to time and to push the envelope. We were straddling a cultural change that was moving from the traditional offerings of securities to a broadened role that included reorganizing and liquidating businesses.

The Tishman transaction did indeed involve risks that needed to be factored in. We had to execute the transaction in the midst of a recession that bankrupted the city of New York and plunged its commercial office market to the lowest depths since the Great Depression. We moved markets and convinced investors to take risks they had not been prepared to take. We exposed the firm's name in the financial media. As it turned out, the articles written about the transaction were laudatory. They would not have been if we had failed. So we had taken on a high level of public exposure and reputational risk, which could have cost the firm far more in the long run than the Tishman fee. The client's reaction was expressed by Bob Tishman in a note to me stating that it was the highest fee he had ever paid—and it was worth every penny.

CULTURE SHIFTS

It is very difficult to change a culture. You need sufficient stature and reputation to get away with taking the risk to affect appropriate change. It is obviously not advisable to set forth tilting at windmills unless you have first established your credibility and even moral authority within the firm. Then you must decide when and how to expend that credibility. It is helpful if you can pick battles you know you can win.

Sometimes the very best practice is contrary to what is deemed on the surface good practice. It can take courage to go against the grain and do what one intuitively feels is the correct thing. A friend of mine on the West Coast was trying to open up his law firm to women law graduates back in the 1960s. He was sent from Los Angeles to Stanford Law School to scout for possible prospects, to be interviewed later by a senior partner. Almost half of the best prospects he found were women, so he rewrote each of their resumes, changing everything to the masculine case including their names and athletic interests, to disguise their gender before circulating the resumes to the partner. The partner read the resumes and approved of my friend's selections. At the on-campus interviews he was very surprised to find his first candidate a highly qualified woman. He approved the selection, then groused "There aren't any more women, are there?" giving the impression there would be an exception made for the candidate he had just interviewed. Of course, there were several more women, and as a result of the day's interviews, the senior partner had invited five women to Los Angeles for further discussions. My friend had to stay up all night changing their resumes back to the original condition. Several were hired, and from that time women professionals were accepted within the firm. Such subversive tactics are obviously risky. And you had better be right. My friend led his firm into new territory. At Morgan Stanley, several of the younger partners also led the firm into new territory, at times through behavior that might be considered aggressive, or even subversive.

New Territory

There are times when one has to stand up and be counted. It sometimes takes courage to prevail in the marketplace and hold to your principles. It takes judgment to know when to take a stand and cease trading off, and courage to go against the grain.

My strongest desire for Brooks Harvey (see Chapter Five) was to have it regarded in the marketplace with the same degree of respect as was accorded to Morgan Stanley. We had accomplished this in part by creating Morgan Stanley Realty, but many of the mainline real estate practitioners still regarded the business as the old Brooks Harvey with a Morgan Stanley wrapper. This served us well at certain places, where Brooks Harvey remained respected, but other individuals sought to take advantage of any possible ambiguity.

We sold a motel chain for Standard Oil of Ohio (SOHIO) to Harold Helmsley, a powerful New York City real estate operator, who was very familiar with the old Brooks Harvey organization. Someone at SOHIO transferred the obligation to pay our fee to the acquirer as a part of the purchase price. Harry Helmsley agreed to this so long as SOHIO was in the picture, but after he acquired the property, he refused to pay the fee, although he had contracted to do so at the closing. Morgan Stanley was not willing to go after SOHIO, as they had been acquired by British Petroleum and they were our stake in the Alaskan Pipeline financing. So I was left with our team having done all the work and with no fee. It looked even worse to the folks at Brooks Harvey, because it was a Morgan Stanley transaction that created the difficulty.

I announced that I was going to sue Harry Helmsley. I was tired of having Brooks Harvey pushed around, and I thought it was outrageous that one of the most prominent real estate personalities in New York thought he could get away with it. I had too much psychic income invested in the real estate operation, and I was not going to tolerate Helmsley's obvious disdain for us.

Morgan Stanley was uncomfortable with my approach, but I was determined to take a stand. We hired Davis Polk & Wardwell and filed suit. As was his custom, Harry settled for five-sixths of the fee before the case was docketed in the courts. As a result of this action, the real estate group became known as an organization that would not allow itself to be cheated out of a fee, even by one of the most "outstanding" players in the real estate business.

Changing the Values

The most difficult task for a leader who has ingrained and rewarded a value system that has been accepted by an organization is to change that value system. For those who have bought in and become "owners" of the previous value system, such a change appears initially to be deceitful and unethical, yet it may be in the best long-term interest for the survival and success of the enterprise.

In the case of Morgan Stanley, the firm survived for many years as the preeminent firm on Wall Street, a leader in the statistical tables of new issues of equity and debt securities, the bankers' banker. It had a superb corporate finance department and the best client list on Wall Street, including such luminaries as Standard Oil Company of New Jersey, I.B.M., Du Pont, and the Commonwealth Government of Australia. The emphasis was on maintaining client relationships by performing "only first-class business, and that in a first-class way." There was zero tolerance for mistakes, which made us all quite cautious. Taking on a new client was a momentous matter, a decision for the senior partners only, and the issue might have to be discussed with certain existing clients as well. Needless to say, in those years we did not "cold call." In fact, there was little or no expectation that an associate would bring in any new business; to become a partner, one would simply be perfect and keep one's nose quite clean.

The firm distributed securities as a wholesaler, through several hundred broker-dealers around the world. The firm did not trade securities or make markets. In the 1970s, with financial deregulation imminent, the new leader of the firm, Bob Baldwin, began to work with the younger partners, including my peer group, to transform the firm into what became a modern securities house. We commenced making markets in government bonds, corporate bonds, and common stock; set up a common stock research capability; established real estate and merger businesses; expanded internationally; got up to speed on computers; and became far more aggressive as a firm in soliciting new business. We incorporated the business and began to build up our capital base. We adopted new measures for performance, including measuring the profitability of individual clients and business units. We became individually accountable for client profitability and, as unit leaders, for business unit productivity.

All this required a change in the internal culture of the firm. We needed to become more aggressive, competitive, and client oriented. We needed to begin to perceive purchasers of securities as clients as well. We had to do all this while retaining the core culture of high integrity and excellence. Seniors who had thrived on excellent transaction execution skills were dismayed when the rewards were reoriented toward those who could "cold call," bring in new business, and run a new unit.

While we may not have been fully aware of our situation, we literally were fighting for our survival. Some seven hundred broker-dealers, including some of our major competitors, either went out of business or were absorbed by others during the period of deregulation. In 1962 I had joined a private firm of 140 employees and $7 million in capital. When I retired twenty-seven years later, the firm had 6,700 employees and almost $3 billion in capital. It was far more powerful in an absolute sense than it had ever been, but it was no longer preeminent in an industry that had consolidated into a couple of dozen large, well-capitalized, and powerful firms. The business had been completely transformed.

One of the great challenges for any organization that grows as rapidly as Morgan Stanley did is how to sustain and promulgate its core values. We changed the culture through a number of techniques. Baldwin had a strong personality, and he provided excellent leadership for the changing times, especially for a smaller firm, through the force of his own personal leadership. We instituted annual planning cycles, with individual business plans for each unit. We became proficient first at projecting annual expenses and ultimately in predicting annual revenues by product line as well. Annual evaluations, bonuses, and promotions were used to instill goals both financial and nonfinancial that reinforced the strategies we were pursuing. The individual performance reviews and goal-setting sessions, while time-consuming and often exhausting, proved an effective tool for coaching and instilling new behavior patterns. When we lost momentum we resorted to more draconian measures such as reducing compensation, withholding resources, limiting promotions within a nonconforming unit, and the like. Thus we managed through both virtue and sanctions.

Aside from addressing any obvious ethical indiscretions or inattention to client needs, we also had to remain on guard against the almost invisible growth of bad practices that eat away at the personal and corporate values on which a reputation is built and also undermine the disciplines and virtues of an entire profession. This required constant screening, filtering, detection, discussion, and review. Bad practices are insidious, like a virus; they grow incrementally and can take over an organization unless they are checked. Checking them takes courage, since it means going against what some perceive to be good. Many times good people are lured by small steps into practices that, on clear examination, they would never have engaged in. Less often, those who have full knowledge of what they are doing deceptively lead individuals in business organizations into bad practices.

We tried harder to become sensitive to the needs, problems, and even addictions of individuals; the intra-office relationships; the maintenance of professional standards and practices; and the behavior of the industry and society in general. As partners in charge of units, we all worked hard at building teamwork and discouraging ego, pretense, and arrogance. When hours were long and resources were short, there could be heightened competition for support, resulting in emotional confrontations. Although our work environment was stressful, we attempted to make it as pleasant as possible for everyone, including secretaries and clerical staff. Periodic celebrations triggered by successes, milestones, or just the time of the year helped develop a feeling of community.

Yet try as hard as we might, we were not always effective in checking the mistakes, or intentional violations, of our people. When the insider trading scandals finally caught up with us and a couple of our junior analysts were implicated with young bankers and lawyers from other firms in a scheme to share inside information on pending mergers and trade illegally, we called all of our investment bankers into an auditorium. We announced that the following morning the firm would be on the front pages of the *New York Times* and the *Wall Street Journal*, because two of our employees were to be indicted for insider trading violations. Among the group of a couple of hundred bankers, including many hardened veterans, there was scarcely a dry eye. They viewed the indictments as a betrayal of the basic nature of the firm they had worked so hard for, and they felt they had been personally violated. Something extremely important to them—their vision of what Morgan Stanley stood for—had been taken from them. One can imagine the same occurring at Arthur Anderson during 2002. When culture and values are made meaningful, they run deep.

We asked ourselves, How could this have happened? Surely it was a downside to rapid growth in personnel. Had we failed to transmit our values to the new employees? Was there any ambiguity in what our standards called for? Were we somehow encouraging unconstrained risk taking? We might have relied too much on culture and virtue and not enough on sanctions. One result of the scandal was that we locked the doors to the merger area (making them even more a separate fiefdom) and had each employee sign a statement saying, in effect, that he or she knew insider trading was a violation of firm policy and that we would enforce penalties to the fullest extent of the law.

We were trying to hold onto a vision of who we thought we were in a financial world that had grown increasingly larger, more volatile, and complex. Changing a vision and a culture is the most difficult thing a leader can do. There will always be mistakes, as we are dealing with human nature in all of its weaknesses. As leaders we need to play to the strengths in human nature and always reinforce the deeper values that sustain us.

Vision and Values

Vision can create a reason for radical change in an organizational culture. Vision becomes far more difficult to change than a plan. Sustaining a live and dynamic vision is as great a challenge as having a creative vision to begin with. Vision can be shaped by fearlessly addressing such questions as, What are our core values? How do we sustain them? Who are our customers? What are their needs? How can we best serve them? What business are we really in?

Although most of the examples in this book are from investment banking and big business, the principles are applicable whatever the venue. Vision is needed, no matter what the type of organization, whether not-for-profit, public, or private. In all cases, including family businesses, the stakeholders must be considered.

It would seem apparent that publicly held firms require a vision that includes their responsibilities to shareholders. At a minimum such responsibilities include transparent and fair reporting of financial data, fair employment practices, good business practices, stewardship of corporate assets (including human capital), compliance with the spirit of the law and regulations, and fair compensation practices. Being a public company and enjoying a stock exchange listing in the U.S. market economy is a privilege, not an entitlement. Yet in too many firms the duties and responsibilities of being public are seen as a series of obstacles to get around. In recent years a number of real estate firms have gone public, most often in the form of real estate investment trusts. For many but not all of these entrepreneurs, the transition from private ownership, under which they dominated their firm, to public ownership, with its expanded fiduciary duties, has been problematic. It is difficult for some to change their vision from that of a sole-proprietor-deals person to that of custodian of public assets. They failed to include in their vision the inherent aspects of a public company. Indeed, what they had was a plan, not a vision.

Ironically, while some public companies are seeking out loopholes to get around their responsibilities, many privately owned family businesses are more disciplined than they are required to be in trying to live out their governance responsibilities to other family shareholders as if they were publicly held. They feel that living by these stricter standards creates a higher level of professionalism and trust. I happen to serve on the boards of several such private family businesses that feel it is appropriate to behave as if they were public stewards, including having outside, independent directors.

In one case, in which I chair the compensation committee of a family-owned resort hotel company, the CEO was willing to change his million-dollar-a-year-plus "guaranteed" compensation to an incentive-based package in which his "guarantee" was $400,000 a year with all the remainder tied to performance of agreed upon short-term and long-term objectives. There was no explicit pressure from the other owners to do so, although they wished the fairness of the compensation system to be validated by independent outsiders. A couple of the outside directors made the suggestion that the compensation be more performance-based, and the CEO readily agreed to it. The CEO had formed the independent compensation committee, as he had a vision of what appropriate corporate stewardship should be, and he abided by it. He felt his compensation should not be guaranteed but should be risk-adjusted and aligned with the return from the business to the shareholders. The family shareholders felt reassured that his compensation level was fair, knowing that it had been negotiated by experienced independent parties and that it was in line with industry standards. A higher level of trust had been created among the ownership family.

All too often, vision and values are not woven together. Much as one might expect a not-for-profit business to have a better grasp of the vision of the enterprise than a for-profit business, this is not a given. Not-for-profits, including even churches, can gradually slip into bad practices and lose sight of their basic vision. Many urban churches are failing. There appears to be a great proliferation of charities, none of which wants to go out of business. Charities formed for a specific purpose, such as eliminating a particular disease, find their mission substantially accomplished and engage in mission creep to remain in business and support their staffs. Many charities suffer from poor leadership and a lack of planning, poor budgeting, lack of fiscal responsibility, and even bad employment practices. There can be a limited antibusiness vision in a not-for-profit. Such flawed vision greatly reduces the effectiveness of the organization.

Several years ago I became associated with a not-for-profit outdoors hiking and mountaineering organization that embarked on an ill-conceived capital campaign. It was running current operating deficits, borrowing money from the banks to pay current expenses, and suffering from an outmoded and ineffective governance system. The organization's managers made the easy calls, raised 20 percent of their goal, and stopped dead in the water. Because I had experience in fundraising for charities as well as general business experience, they asked for my assistance in straightening things out and relaunching the campaign.

I suggested strongly that they cancel the campaign, rebudget their operating expenses, prove to potential donors they could run an efficient organization, improve their governance system, and gain a better focus on their mission and the goals of the campaign. They had to imagine what the vision of like-minded major potential donors might be and align their vision with that. It takes a crisis to change a vision, and a multiple-year capital campaign can be viewed as just such a self-imposed event. In this case, they followed my suggestions and subsequently completed a successful $11 million campaign.

For any organization, conviction about a long-term vision that can capture the interests of a large group of constituent supporters is paramount. That vision must also connect to the embedded values.

Our personal values are derived from our culture. The culture of the United States reflects deep values of independence, fairness, concern for others, the "frontier" community spirit, and an unparalleled philanthropic bent. To the extent that we are informed by our culture, our values are shaped, and our personal values help shape the institutions to which we commit ourselves. We live in a symbiotic relationship with all the organizations to which we devote our energy. We help shape and preserve our culture and our institutions, including our place of work, at the same time as they are informing and reinforcing our own values on an ongoing basis.

As individuals who benefit greatly from the opportunities created by our open, free-market economy we have a responsibility to see that our actions sustain or even add to the positive aspects of our culture and do not provide a stimulus for an otherwise adverse incrementalism of bad practices. An excellent leader, anchored in a deep personal value system, becomes a reference point who sustains values even in what can become an environment of flux and chaos.

PART THREE

Maintaining Balance and Renewing Continuously

BACK IN 1982, when I first wrote about my encounter with the sadhu, it was with the purpose of presenting an ambiguous situation. I reported the experience in as much detail as I could remember, and I shaped it to the needs of a good classroom discussion. Over the years, I've heard a wide variety of responses to the story, all of which are, naturally, colored by people's experiences in the world. The simple answer is to say that younger people are more likely to see the issue as black-and-white; older ones tend to see shades of gray—and it's more complex than that.

People have varying attitudes toward and beliefs about life and death and the efforts properly expended to preserve life. These attitudes and beliefs vary from culture to culture and from age to age. One who has experienced combat or high-altitude trauma may react differently from one who has not. The reactions of others to stress situations can condition our own response. In my case I also had been conditioned for more than twenty years in an environment that continually traded off risk and reward and lived by the utilitarian model.

Some people suggest that the sadhu may not have wanted our help at all—he may have been intentionally bringing on his own death as a way to holiness, or *nirvana*. Why else would he have taken the dangerous way over the pass instead of the caravan route through the gorge? Hindu businesspeople have told me that in trying to assist the sadhu, we were being typically arrogant Westerners, imposing our cultural values on the world and ignoring the beliefs of others when they are different from our own.

I've learned that each year a few Nepali porters are left to freeze to death along the pass outside the tents of the unthinking tourists who hired them. A few years ago a French group left one of their own, a young woman, to die there.[1] The difficult pass seems to demonstrate a perverse version of Gresham's law of currency: the bad practices of previous travelers have driven out the values that new travelers might have followed if they were at home. Perhaps that helps to explain why our porters behaved as they did and why it was so difficult for Stephen or anyone else to establish a different approach on the spot. Bad practices, once ingrained, take a major effort of will and courage to root out.

The fact was, we had no plan for dealing with the contingency of the sadhu. An ethical dilemma had come on us unexpectedly; we had to decide how much to sacrifice ourselves to take care of a stranger. And given the constraints of our trek, we had to make a group decision, not an individual one.

Pasang, our Sherpa sirdar, was focused on his responsibility for bringing us up the mountain safe and sound. His livelihood and status in the Sherpa ethnic group depended on our safe return. We were weak, our party was split, the porters were well on their way to the top with all our gear and food, and a storm would have separated us irrevocably from our logistical base. Stephen felt he had to do everything he could do to save the sadhu's life, in accordance with his Christian ethic of compassion and of saving the one lost sheep. My utilitarian response led me to the goal of doing the greatest good for the greatest number. Give a burst of aid to minimize the sadhu's exposure, then continue on our way.

There it was: a true ethical dilemma requiring a decision between hard choices—and we could not unite our multicultural group in the little time we had. The sadhu could not (or would not) speak. We had no chance to develop any kind of relationship with him. It is difficult to create a context when no community has been formed. Perhaps a previously bonded group of climbers, one more steeped in the earlier mountaineering culture, might have reacted differently.

Consider how this small slice of culture has changed over time. When the British mountaineers were scouting for routes up Mt. Everest in the 1920s and 1930s, climbers typically ascended as roped teams. The rope was a protective and a psychologically unifying force. Roped teams went to great lengths to rescue their companions, often to their own peril or death. This mountaineering ethic persisted well into the later part of the twentieth century.

In more recent years "free" climbing became popular: one climbed alone and was not encumbered with the ethic or responsibility of caring for others.

"Free" climbing can be said to represent glorification of the individual rather than the group. It is a classic trade-off between freedom and responsibility. How much will we sacrifice for the other? Does it make a difference if we have a relationship with the other or if the other is unknown to us?

My friend Carlos Buhler, a world-class mountaineer, was climbing in the Himalayas with one of his best friends, also an experienced climber. They utilized a mechanical ascender to reach the summit slope of an 8,000-meter peak. Attaining the summit was more difficult and time-consuming than they had expected. It was late in the day, and they had to hasten back to the fixed rope to avoid a night at that altitude and almost certain death. Even if they survived the night, the frostbite they would certainly have suffered would have prevented them from descending the mechanical apparatus. There were no other people on the mountain, and the only way to safety was back down the rope they had climbed up. Carlos's friend began to stagger, a sign of cerebral edema, a critical phase of high-altitude sickness during which the brain cells begin to deteriorate. Carlos went back up the slope after him twice to direct him to the rope, but his friend had become disoriented and insisted the escape route was in a different direction. Carlos could not get him to return to the rope. Carlos himself was tiring rapidly and needed to conserve enough energy to descend the summit slope. He made a third attempt to rescue his friend, but he failed. As dusk fell Carlos had to decide whether to stay on the mountain overnight with his friend, where they would both surely die, or descend the rope alone. Carlos chose to descend alone. He later visited his friend's family, giving them the details of their son's death, and they ultimately understood and accepted his decision.

In the comfort of a mountaineering hut or one's study it might seem fairly easy to come up with hard and fast rules about never abandoning a friend on a slope. But what if it means certain suicide? Ethics informs us that having rules does not allow us the freedom to escape the existential anguish of having to make hard choices.

The facts are that being on a peak like Everest is very risky, and a large percentage of those attempting such climbs die. Everyone on the mountain should know of the risk, accept that risk, and deal with the consequences. Yet in today's culture, paid guides take amateurs up peaks they could never ascend on their own. The going rate on Mt. Everest is about $65,000 a person. A paid guide may have three or four, or more, clients on a given climb. The guide's future financial success depends on how many of his clients he can get to the top. Because oxygen cylinders are often required to prevent acute mountain sickness, Sherpas preposition the cylinders on the mountain. Some climbers denied the use of oxygen belonging to a professionally guided party have died within reach of these cylinders. How do we balance responsibility to one's own group, to oneself, and to the stranger? Does paying you to be my leader create a different or a greater moral context? Does it prevent the paid leader from expending the group's resources to aid others not in the group?

Climbing Everest is, for most, a once-in-a-lifetime experience. Should one be expected to give up that opportunity to go to the aid of another who has also accepted that risk and happens to be unlucky? How much responsibility do others have for us when we intentionally put ourselves at risk? Has the focus on the individual created a culture of irresponsibility? Is it proper for us to deny the risk and impose an entitlement to receive care, placing ourselves ahead of all the others? Where do we discover the balance in this?

Such changes in values over time are of particular interest to students of organizational behavior. How do values change? Who changes them? How are the changes transmitted? How do we ensure that the changes are for the better, that good practice is reinforced and bad practice rooted out?

I often am asked how time has changed my perceptions of the events and choices of the sadhu. Faced with similar circumstances today, what would I do? Putting aside the realities of twenty-five years of aging and worn-out knees, would I respond differently? I had multiple stakeholders in my safe return home, including a spouse, three young children, an aging mother, friends, and business partners. The stakeholders have changed and fewer people are now dependent upon my survival. But the question remains: How much additional risk do I assume to care for the stranger and to what extent am I trading off against my stakeholders? In a way, Carlos's case may have been less ambiguous than mine, although some might state contextually that there is a higher obligation to a friend than to a stranger. In a deep theological sense, the stranger always counts. That is part of the meaning of the sadhu; in some ways he is always with us.

The basic question remains: When do we take a stand? When do we allow a "sadhu," an unknown stranger, to intrude into our daily lives? To change our sense of values? Few of us can afford the time or effort to take care of every needy person we encounter. How much must we give of ourselves? And how do we prepare our organizations and institutions so they will respond appropriately in a crisis? How do we influence them if we do not agree with their points of view? How do we maintain balance and integrity over the long haul, in business, and in the world? These are the questions we take up in these final chapters.

How do we develop and sustain our ethical balance over time? We cannot quit our jobs over every ethical dilemma, but if we continually ignore our sense of values, who do we become? Where do we draw the line, or, as is often heard in these times, "Which ditch *are* we willing to die in?" For each of us, the answer is a bit different. How we act in response to that question defines better than anything else who we are, just as, in a collective sense, our acts define our institutions. In effect, the sadhu is always there, ready to remind us of the tensions between our own goals and the claims of strangers.

In Chapter Seven we talk about the contextual nature of ethics and the trade-offs between right versus right, truth versus loyalty, individual versus community, short term versus long term, and justice versus mercy. In the balance of the book we discuss such things as the improvisational nature of ethics and ethics in a changing world environment.

CHAPTER 7

Ethics as Contextual:
Renewal as a Continuing Process

THE SADHU CASE may not be as exotic as it first appears. In Manhattan thousands of people each day head in and out of Grand Central Station walking past a homeless person living over a steam tunnel grate in front of the Yale Club. Few seem to notice his plight, keeping their eyes focused straight ahead, intent on their personal mission. In Los Angeles we have become acculturated not to stop and assist anyone having automobile difficulty on the freeways. If we even think about deviating from our "free climbing" mode, we have instant triggers to which we innately react. Is the person in difficulty a vulnerable-appearing child or a muscular man wearing his baseball cap backwards? Most of us are neither as kind nor as free of prejudice as we would like to think we are. We are much more willing to assist someone we know or who resembles us in appearance—and if providing help would not inconvenience us unduly.

One of the beautiful things about the Red Cross movement is that it is primarily strangers helping strangers. It becomes safe to help the stranger, any stranger, when we are a part of a community that encourages and supports such activities.

EVALUATING THE TOUGH CHOICES
Right Versus Right
In his book *Defining Moments*, Harvard Business School ethics professor Joe Badaracco discusses how difficult it is to stay ethical and stay pure.[1] He quotes Jean-Paul Sartre's "Dirty Hands," in *No Exit and Other Plays*. The veteran leader of an underground unit of the Communist party speaks to a younger member, saying, "How you cling to your purity, young man! How afraid are you to soil your hands! All right, stay pure! What good will it do? Why did you join us? Purity is an idea for a yogi or a monk. . . . To do nothing, to remain motionless, arms at your side, wearing kid gloves. Well, I have dirty hands. Right up to the elbows. I've

plunged them in filth and blood. But what do you hope? Do you think you can govern innocently?"[2]

Badaracco suggests that dirty hands are the inevitable lot of successful men and women with real power and responsibility in life. Positions of power carry complicated responsibilities, and on some occasions these responsibilities conflict with each other or with one's personal values. All of these choices have strong moral claims, and it is not possible to meet every claim. As Badaracco says, "These are not the ethical issues of right and wrong that we learn about as children. They are conflicts of right versus right."[3] I would suggest wrong versus wrong conflicts also have strong moral claims, as Bonhoeffer discovered when faced with the choice of going along with the Holocaust or participating in the schemes to assassinate Hitler.

From a theological or eschatological point of view, one might imagine being asked at the Last Judgement, "Where are your wounds?"

In his book *How Good People Make Tough Choices*, Rushworth Kidder urges us to work at becoming ethically fit.[4] This requires us to be engaged with the tough issues with both our passion and our intellect. Like Joe Badaracco he describes the tough issues as good versus good. Rushworth describes four classic ethical trade-offs—truth versus loyalty, individual versus community, short term versus long term, and justice versus mercy—described more fully in the following sections.

Truth Versus Loyalty

One of my trusted younger partners came into my office and announced he was quitting Morgan Stanley. I happened to be on a small committee planning to take the firm public at what we anticipated would be a premium over our cost in the stock. If he left before that happened, he would lose a considerable amount of money. I was sworn to secrecy, occupying a classic "insider" position of trust within the firm. Was my greater loyalty to the firm or to telling the truth to a trusted protégé? While I am normally a firm believer that "the truth shall set you free," in this case I could not default to the full truth. I remained loyal to the firm and attempted to convince him to stay without telling him of the windfall. Fortunately, I prevailed, and to this day he says it was the best financial decision he ever made (although ironically the resources ultimately allowed him to retire early anyway and go on to study theology), and he thanks me for convincing him. Nevertheless I lost a bit of my purity on that one.

But I might have lost more. What if I had misread this situation? Imagine if, knowing of our relationship, my protégé's peers had put him up to a fishing expedition to find out what, if anything, was going on with the firm. My encouraging him to stay might then have been read in an entirely different light, potentially at my expense or even hindering the "process" of the public offering.

Similarly ambiguous situations occur with some frequency. For example, let us say you are about to announce layoffs in a couple of weeks to avoid bankruptcy, and one of the individuals on the confidential termination list tells you he is closing on a new home tomorrow. What should you do? What do you do when a long-standing friend is clearly breaking a company policy? Your first instinct may to talk with your friend and attempt to convince the friend to change his ways. What if you fail? What if it gets worse? At what point, if ever, do you blow the whistle and turn your (former) friend in?

Issues can become even more complex when we are trading off loyalty to an individual against loyalty to the larger community.

Individual Versus Community

The balance between the needs of the individual and those of the community raises the issue of the sadhu once again. To what extent do you sacrifice the community for the individual? What right has the individual to disproportionately affect the welfare of the community? The entire health care system in the United States remains confused about this. By far the greatest portion of health care resources is spent on prolonging the lives of terminally ill patients. If we were to give up extreme treatment at the end of life and focus on palliative care (making the dying patient more comfortable) we could resolve the health care financial crisis. Economists call the reason we don't take this step the "fallacy of composition." In the aggregate we would all vote for a rational solution; we just would not want to give up extreme health care measures for our own parent, spouse, child, or grandchild, assuming that was their desire.

Recently a hospital in our area had as a patient a premature baby suffering from a variety of terminal ailments. It was certain the baby would never leave the hospital and would ultimately die there, and the parents admitted so. But the parents insisted on keeping the baby alive as long as possible, although they had no financial resources to cover the great expense. This was their first child, and they had had a hard time having the child. The father would hold the baby in his arms and claim the baby was responsive to his presence. The medical staff disagreed. Some nurses on the floor suffered moral distress and refused to treat the baby any longer, as they felt the child was suffering from the various treatments and should be allowed to die in peace. Other specialists favored keeping the baby alive so they could continue their research.

Standardized end-of-life protocols state guidelines for such cases under which withdrawal of life support might be indicated when there is no chance the patient will ever leave the intensive care unit or when all of the physical strength of the patient is expended on sustaining life and there remains no quality of life beyond that.

Cases like this produce multiple stakeholders with conflicting interests, some stating that the baby has a right to die; others that the baby has a right to live. Sorting through such issues requires an exquisite degree of ethical sensitivity.

No one can claim to have the "right" answer. It is hard for all of us to make sacrifices in the known situation in the short term to balance ambiguous and depersonalized long-term benefits.

How do we evolve procedures for rationing spare body parts such as hearts, kidneys, and livers? Do they go to the youngest? The most talented (by what definition)? The wealthiest? Those with a sibling ready to donate a kidney? Is triage ethical? Or is everyone entitled to the same level of care? How do we ration scarce resources fairly?

Short Term Versus Long Term

The balance of the short term versus the long term is an issue faced by many public companies. Augustine and others have defined time as being only in the present. Yet, if we lock ourselves into the present we give up hope for a better future. As a manager, do I focus on current stock price (and my options) or on the creation of long-term value? How do I find the balance? Am I a better partner for Morgan Stanley by selling every real estate product we come up with to Trammell Crow or by telling him that some of the products are probably not suitable for him and attempting to build a longer-term relationship? Who benefits most from that longer-term relationship—Morgan Stanley or me? How do I balance these interests?

If all of my competitors in the chemical business are dumping their residues into a river, why should I be the only firm in the industry to pioneer environmentalism and increase costs to my disadvantage? How do I change an industry norm? Am I willing to risk going out of business to do so?

Here is another case in which having a long-term plan, or vision, for one's life, as well as for one's business, makes it easier to sustain short-term losses in order to attain deeply ingrained goals.

Justice Versus Mercy

Justice involves a clear definition of the rules and of the reward-and-punishment system that enforces the rules. Justice means the rules are administered fairly and consistently, and not in an arbitrary fashion. If we do not punish malefactors, we can never root out bad practices, and they will grow. Strict enforcement of the rules can take the heart out of an organization, turning it from an empowered system to a command-and-control system. It can frighten people. Tempering justice with mercy can help align a just enforcement of the rules within a trust organization. Insider trading can have an ambiguous appearance and be said to be a state of mind. One can infer intent from circumstantial evidence, but sometimes one can never be certain criminal intent is present. How does one differentiate among the surface results of laziness, ineptitude, unconscious going along with incremental bad practices, well-intentioned pushing the limits of the regulations, or criminal intent? Jurors in the corporate scandal cases involving Frank Quattrone; Martha Stewart; and executives of Tyco, Enron, and others were asked to make these judgments. Guidelines are vague, yet the differences among no penalty, civil penalty, and criminal penalty are huge.

In the case on insider trading that I often use in my business ethics classes, I attempt to create as much ambiguity as possible. A young stock trader has made a telephone call to a friend in another firm. Our trader's firm is working on a confidential merger deal. A few hours later the other trader's firm buys a large amount of stock of the target company. The stock runs up rapidly, so the deal is probably off. On the surface, it looks like our trader tipped off the other firm, an illegal act. Yet our trader denies the charge strongly, and no one heard him say anything suspicious on the telephone. (In these cases an innocuous statement such as "I'm going to Nepal this summer" can be the trigger of the tip.) What do I as manager of the trading desk do?

Experienced managers typically solve the issue by firing the young trader in a manner that makes an example of him and demonstrates the tough zero defects policy of the firm toward insider trading. Others raise issues of unfairness, lack of proof, the impact of the termination on the young person's business career, or the possibility that the trader had been poorly or improperly trained and supervised.

It isn't always easy to perceive a "right" answer, and the first approach is an easy way out. I would be troubled if a firm did not support individuals expressing both points of view. Organizations need to support dissenting views on the tough ethical calls, including calls for mercy. If those calls are ignored, it is easy for a firm to become hardened and inwardly oriented and lose contact with its stakeholders, including valuable employees.

Ethics is something deeper than complying with the law. We need the law to keep us honest and provide a level playing field, but true ethics involves some form of compassion. Ethics is not "What do I have to do?" but rather "What can I do?" Spontaneous nonmandated acts of generosity are what build long-term trust and loyalty and move our businesses onto the "most admired" and "companies I would most like to work for" lists.

FINDING ANSWERS RIGHT FOR THE
TIME, THE PLACE, AND THE PERSON

Bad practices in business grow incrementally; at times they are barely detectable. We look back in shock at what we have done or been a part of. Bad practices can include activities such as false accounting, kickbacks, falsified documents, improper sexual behavior, price fixing, and insider trading.

A friend of mine in Connecticut, an elder in our church and an upstanding citizen, was promoted to senior vice president for marketing in a major container board firm. Container board, used in packaging, is basically a commodity product. The most obvious way to differentiate the product is by cutting price. A method that has evolved over time to avoid ruinous price cutting and loss of profitability is to "rationalize" the marketplace by sharing price information among competitors and fixing prices. When my friend arrived in his new position in the 1970s, he discovered that price sharing had become an industry practice among senior executives of competitors.

While such behavior is tolerated in certain countries, it is illegal in the United States. We have decided as a society to restrain competition within certain rules and to impose criminal penalties on those who violate them. In some cases firms slip into noncompliance through a series of increasingly bad practices over a period of years, and no one has the ethical sensitivity or courage to speak out against them. A pernicious aspect of enforcement is that the government comes after price fixing episodically. It is a perverse game of musical chairs, and companies can usually get away with it for a couple of decades. The executive periodically caught out is hammered, but by that time the practice has become accepted behavior, and little reform takes place. My good friend spent six months in a federal prison, losing both his job and his reputation.

We need to ask what he could have done differently. Certainly going to a superior and asking, "Isn't this illegal?" might have been a wise step. Unfortunately, however, such openness is not always practical. Lax government enforcement and the fact that "everyone else is doing it" allowed bad and illegal practice to become ingrained. My friend was active in his church, and there were several individuals there who would have counseled him on his dilemma. Sharing the anxiety of ethical decisions with trusted peers is one of the best practices. He was probably too embarrassed to do so. He knew the right thing to do and probably was lulled into complacency regarding the degree of risk he was taking. For him, completing the journey expeditiously became so important that he ignored the warning signs along the way.

There are times in our lives when we must be willing to risk everything to take a stand. My friend's failure to do so and his decision to go along with past practices, not rock the boat, and take the easy way out cost him his reputation and his career. He was not a bad person; far from it, I would say. As but one reflection of this, he spent part of his time in prison helping others and was instrumental in enabling an innocent man to gain his freedom via the legal system.

Knowing when and where to draw the line and risk all is the creative and courageous aspect of attempting to live out an ethical life. Constant self-examination and self-questioning—asking "Is this right?"—are essential to avoid falling into the trap into which my friend fell, and other, similarly treacherous traps. Having goals and a sense of who we are helps us to recognize the hazard and take the high road. So does a strategy that includes fallback options. The goals of the enterprise must be worthy of us, and we must know where to set the limits.

Staying Alert to Moral Tests

In describing the nuances in ethical decision making we might make distinctions between moral uncertainty, moral dilemma, and moral distress.

Moral uncertainty is when we begin to feel uncomfortable in a situation and start questioning the behavior involved. We are not sure if there is an ethical issue or not, but we want to talk with someone about it. A great degree of ethical sensitivity needs to be part of our being to allow such disturbing thoughts to interrupt our agendas. An environment that permits and supports such questioning is essential if ethical behavior is to be encouraged.

A moral dilemma occurs when one sees conflicting but morally justified courses of action and is in a quandary about which one to choose. The classic moral dilemmas are being forced to choose between two morally good choices or between two morally bad choices.

Moral distress comes about when someone believes he or she knows what to do and cannot do it because of time pressure, lack of supervisory support, institutional policies, or legal limits. Ethics can cause us to wish to do what is required beyond the law, or even against the law. As Plato has written, "Good people do not need laws to tell them to act responsibly, while bad people will find a way around the laws."[5]

One can only imagine the moral distress Dietrich Bonhoeffer went through in deciding to commit himself to a cabal to assassinate the ruler, even if it was Adolf Hitler. The propriety of his joining that plot is questioned to this day in certain parts of the German church and society.

Considering the Questions

Bonhoeffer was in his mid-thirties when he was called upon to make momentous life-changing ethical decisions. He was, then, approximately the age of the students I have taught over the past seventeen years. As a part of a business ethics module in the graduate real estate program at the University of Southern California, I ask each student to prepare a written description of an ethical situation they have encountered in their previous work experience. I have received now six or seven hundred student stories, and I find that most of them can be classified into a handful of generic types, most of which describe the balance between aggressive behavior and crossing the line into unethical activity.

When does networking become spying? It is common for retailers or single-family home developers to "shop" the competition. Is it proper for me to send someone out to pose as a land buyer to obtain data regarding the value of commercial land in a location I'm not familiar with? Wouldn't it be better to call someone directly, tell them what I want, and offer to pay for their services or to provide them with market judgments in return?

Is hard bargaining contextual? One might behave differently toward a sophisticated counter party than toward an unsophisticated one. Two bond traders, one from an investment bank and one from an insurance company, might engage in hard bargaining on the telephone all week and go out for drinks on Friday afternoon. They are playing out a ritualistic game that each understands; they are improvising within guidelines they both know well. Behavior that is entirely appropriate between the two of them would be entirely inappropriate should they utilize the same techniques to sell bonds to an occasional, less sophisticated investor.

When does hard bargaining become lying? How do we draw the line between aggressive puffery and misrepresentation? When do we start telling the truth? There will always be a range of opinions on the rate of inflation in rental rates or expenses or in the ultimate financial success of a given asset. Am I better off being known in the marketplace as someone whose opinions always have to be adjusted downward or as someone whose financial projections can be trusted?

When is it appropriate to confront an issue? If I go to my boss once a week with an ethical concern, the firm's values and mine are not in alignment. It may be that my values are too rigid for the culture I find myself in, or it may be that the organization is engaged in highly unethical practices. Either way it is time for some soul searching and a trusted cadre of friends with whom one can share their concerns. On the other hand, if I never have an ethical concern, it is probably time to reassess my core values.

Can I disobey a bad rule? Rules do exist for a reason. Yet the reason for a particular rule may have disappeared, and the rule stays on. It is important to understand the context of the rule and to discuss the fairness of it with others prior to taking on the responsibility of deeming it "bad" on your own. Changing the rule in concert with others trumps breaking it unilaterally.

What is enough effort? To return to the sadhu story as symbolic of one's efforts for others, how much should I do for the sadhu? What must I do, to meet my own standards? Can one ever do enough? In a way, the Christian response is that we can never stop trying, and we can never do enough. Practically speaking, however, we do have to draw a line and move on. For each of us, it is where we draw that line that defines our character.

DOING THE RIGHT THING

One can drift into ethical issues through sloppy practice, but at times the issues are staring you right in the face and the pressure is on from the beginning. Under a consent decree with the Department of Labor, in the early 1980s a labor union organization was forced to take on an outside advisor to run its affairs. The organization had about $1.2 billion worth of assets, of which two-thirds was real estate. We had a shot at the initial assignment, but Morgan Stanley decided to turn it down because of the unsavory nature of the client. When the contract came up for renewal, we saw it as an opportunity to grow our new initiative in asset management. So we got the overall assignment as "named fiduciary," taking over the responsibilities of the previous advisor to the fund.

The real estate investments were not of institutional quality, and many had been made for idiosyncratic reasons. The real estate included investments in dog-racing tracks, motels filled with prostitutes, churches, third-tier casinos in Las Vegas, and partnerships with known members of organized crime. There were layers of complexities and personalities underlying certain assets that were not apparent on the surface. We did our best to apply our technique of triage to the portfolio, organizing ourselves to focus on those areas on which we could have the most significant impact. William Saxbe, former U.S. senator and attorney general, had been appointed by the Department of Labor as the "watchdog" over the fund. He warned me that I could expect to be contacted by virtually anybody, including congressmen or senators, to put pressure on Morgan Stanley to back off if we got too close to something somebody didn't like.

The first crunch came when we had to decide whether or not to extend a loan on a third-rate casino in Las Vegas. One of my associates and I traveled to Las Vegas to inform the putative owner of the casino that Morgan Stanley would not "cooperate" in extending a $12 million loan that was due in a few weeks. Heretofore the fund and its previous advisor had deferred and extended the loan. Senator Saxbe continued to warn of undue pressures that might be put on us, but he encouraged us to do our job. We knew this first confrontation with a mob-related loan would set the pattern for our work.

Our "client" was a middle-aged man from the Bronx, about five feet four inches tall, wearing a shiny gabardine suit. His office, on the second floor of the casino, was unlike any I had seen. He was seated behind a huge desk of aluminum tubing and glass, establishing his power. On the wall behind him was a life-size photograph of Albert Einstein. The walls of the room were covered with about a dozen television sets, monitoring the pit bosses.

I sat sideways on a sofa, facing him. My female associate sat across from me, conservatively dressed, hands folded in her lap. We did not know what to expect, but we had coached ourselves going in to be unrelenting in our refusal to extend the loan, no matter the circumstances. To flinch now, the first time out, would be to ruin our effectiveness throughout the assignment. The client inquired politely if Morgan Stanley would not cooperate, as everyone had in the past. I looked him straight in the eye and stated that we would cooperate in any way we could be useful to him, but we would not extend the loan. We repeated this dialogue three times. I never blinked. He never threatened me. My associate said nothing.

We walked out, not knowing what to expect. What happened? Absolutely nothing. Perhaps the government had finally worn them down. Neither my associate nor I—nor to my knowledge, anyone at Morgan Stanley—ever received an improper telephone call or request from the fund or any of its supporters over the time we worked off all the bad assets. Obviously, had we appeared to be less than resolute, there would have been no end of pressure exerted on us. Doing the right thing may not always appear to be the easy solution, but over the long term it well may be.

In this case knowing what to do was not difficult, and once we had taken our stand, performing at that level was not difficult either. The hard part would have been if we had appeared to be unsure of ourselves or flexible, in which case we would have had to deal with unrelenting pressure from the other side. Unlike my friend at the container board company, we were also fortunate in that behaving ethically was completely aligned with the interests of our company.

We obviously were improvising in that loan extension negotiation. I had absolutely no idea what was going to happen going in. The "owner" might have threatened us, sworn at us, offered us cocktails, or even mentioned our children's names in order to frighten us. I had to be prepared to react to an unknown multiplicity of scenarios. But through it all, I had a major theme to improvise around, and that always gave me the direction. The theme was: "No!"

ETHICS IN ACTION:
IMPROVISING IN THE WORLD

Thus ethics, like fairness, is contextual. Once an ethical sensitivity is a part of one's being, ethics becomes intuitive. How does one strike just the right balance? Often there is little time for reflection. Ethical thinkers are catalysts: they act and they shape the world. Rushworth Kidder makes the point that ethical decision making might well be described as "intelligence functioning at intuitional velocity."[6]

I often think of practicing ethics as similar to an accomplished jazz pianist improvising. Even the best cannot keep the jazz going indefinitely. They need a key, a chord structure, harmony, tempo, rhythm, tone, and some sort of melody or connecting theme that gives them a place to come home to. They need to practice for hours on end. They also need rest, renewal, and a cleansing of the spirit.

The same can be said for attempting to live out an ethical life. We need the tenacity and even courage to shape our own reality. We need to develop a hopeful approach to life so that we can turn failure into advantage. We need to make time for our physical, emotional, and spiritual renewal and well-being. We need to develop that deep awareness of our core values that can only be attained out of our own intimate, internal search for meaning in our lives. To live with integrity is to live out our beliefs. What are those beliefs that we are willing to lose for? We need proactively to develop those habits, activities, routines, and disciplines that can sustain us in confronting the tough choices we will have to make over the long haul.

FINDING THE FORTITUDE
TO SHAPE YOUR REALITY

It takes courage to live an examined life, to make choices, and to risk error. Living creatively means finding meaning in seemingly unrelated activities, making connections, and affirming oneself beyond the surface level. It means having the fortitude to shape one's own reality and not let it be shaped by others' desires for money or power or fame.

Such deep introspection takes time and a willingness to be alone, reading, walking, thinking, meditating, and trying to figure out just who it is you were meant to be. As always, there is the tension between a desire to be alone and a desire to be in community. The results of such introspection become valuable and real only when expressed through communities of others. Without community one can become too self-preoccupied, and depression can set in.

One of the toughest times in my life was the period between my return from service in the military in Korea and my beginning at Harvard Business School. During this five-month period I had little in the way of community to sustain me. I had held important responsibilities in Korea. Now suddenly I was back at the oil company operating as a plantman once again as in college, saving money for graduate school, living with my parents, reverting to a life I thought I had outgrown. Moreover, I suffered from what became known subsequently as Peace Corps reentry depression. I had become attuned to the pace of life in the Korean village where I had served for thirteen months in support of the South Korean Army. Tolerating the waste and frivolity of southern California's consumer society was hard for me, and I fell into the deepest depression of my life. I felt alienated from society at large. My friends were all scattered and not there to sustain me. I was doing backbreaking work in 110-degree temperatures with a man I considered certifiably crazy. The days were, for me, straight out of Dante's *Inferno*. The path was not clear; I had no Virgil to guide me.

The main resource that kept me going was the deep hope that if I could successfully complete the program at Harvard I might find a position that would allow me to grow and create meaning in my life.

At Harvard I began to develop a new circle of friends and quickly became too busy to fall back into that self-absorbed depression. I also met the woman who was to become my wife for thirty-one years—and traded in the depression for the joy of romance. That period of self-absorption and self-investigation was not all negative, however. I had identified holes in my life—lack of relationships, commitments, spirituality—and I was determined to fill them. And with a sense of optimism and hope I went—in just ten short years—from feeling I was in Dante's *Inferno* to becoming a general partner of Morgan Stanley.

But making partner is not the whole story. As a long-term investment banker and a fundraiser for volunteer organizations, I sometimes half-jokingly say that the key to my success has been a high tolerance for rejection. At Morgan Stanley we competed day in and day out with a long list of well-qualified and highly competitive firms such as First Boston Corporation; Goldman, Sachs; Drexel; Lehman Brothers; Merrill Lynch; or Salomon Brothers. A good baseball batting average was considered successful, which meant that you lost two or three pieces of business for every one you won. The same ratio is true for any kind of "cold calling," including volunteer fundraising. This was the environment I lived in for almost thirty years.

How do you sustain resilience in the face of such disappointments over so many years? In part, by having a realistic set of expectations about the nature of the business you're in. It also helps to take a longer-term perspective and focus on building relationships, a business unit, a career, and a life, rather than just swinging for the fences in an endless parade of deals. And a constant supply of optimism helps.

OPTIMISM IN THE FACE OF FAILURE

Only through risk taking and the ever-present risk of failure can we grow and improve. Even the best of baseball hitters fall into slumps, and the best adopt a proactive approach, taking extra coaching and practice to get through it. We must learn to cope effectively with adversity. A successful investment banker inevitably acquires a sense of optimism. A market-making, trading, risk-taking firm loses substantial sums on occasion. It's important not to dwell on the disaster but always to look ahead, learn what you can from the situation, conduct a forensic examination, and then focus on the next trade. A leader rises above hard times and turns failure into advantage.

It takes moral stature to be a leader and, when all else seems to be failing, to do the right thing or to take the risk of doing the wrong thing. A deeply centered person is connected to the world through genuine respect for others, listening and questioning. Such a person purposely surrenders a part of his or her autonomy to others and in turn is sustained by the broad range of communities in which he or she participates, both within and outside the business community.

Above all, a leader is a person of principle. As Kouzes and Posner state in *The Leadership Challenge*, "The most striking similarity we've found . . . is that the list (of leaders) is populated by people with strong beliefs about matters of principle. They all have, or had, unwavering commitment to a clear set of values. They all are, or were, passionate about their causes."[7]

Many biographies of leaders are a testament to the fact that surviving a stressful childhood can produce a leader better able to deal with adversity. Having the self-discipline and the longer-term orientation to deal with setbacks and keep moving forward are powerful attributes of a successful leader. No one makes it to the top in a straight line. The path is often obscure, and there are many pitfalls on the way. Becoming successful at intensive competition at a young age in athletics or other areas can help one develop similar characteristics.

We all know that Churchill and Roosevelt struggled at different times in their lives. John F. Kennedy suffered excruciating back pain from World War II combat injuries. Bob Dole overcame his war injury handicap in a successful career. We are continually surprised to learn of "famous" personalities afflicted with depression or mental disease. One of the great leaders at Morgan Stanley dealt successfully with the ravages of polio all his life. Great leaders find meaning in setbacks. They are realists, cool under pressure. They accept responsibility for failure and identify action steps to adjust to the new situation. They have developed strong trust relationships in the organization with people who come to their aid when required. They have acquired an orientation toward life that enables them to survive and even thrive after setbacks.

We may proactively engage in such a reorientation without necessarily going through the stress. Various forms of self renewal—including physical, emotional, and spiritual renewal—can be useful in gaining balance and a fresh perspective.

Our physical well-being has a great deal to do with our approach to life and our emotional maturity. I have always followed the philosophy of "work hard, play hard." Jogging and running were important to my life for over forty years. In the early 1960s, long before joggers were part of the cityscape, I regularly ran around the reservoir in Central Park in Manhattan, attracting stares from pedestrians as I ran the city streets over and back from our apartment. Business trips provided unique opportunities for jogging in such places as the Santa Monica Mountains in Los Angeles, around the zoo in Milan, alongside Lake Geneva, on the towpath by the Seine in Paris, and through innumerable city streets. A twenty-minute run in the dark might provide all that I would see of Paris or Frankfurt. My neighbor Jim Fixx, who wrote two best-sellers on the joys of jogging and running, became a close friend. Our runs together became times of complete openness and transparency, and we shared our dreams and anxieties with one another. Such deep friendships can become a major resource in gaining a "second opinion" on ethical dilemmas one may be facing.

The culmination was my completion of the New York Marathon in 1977 at age forty. Running gave me energy, fast exercise, a feeling of well-being and accomplishment, and several friendships. In addition, it gave me a mental edge.

On the solitary runs, I would often zone out, playing over and over in my mind negotiating points for an important meeting that day. It's possible to get so caught up in the contemplative role playing that you lose track of where you are, even to the point of getting lost in a strange city! I'm convinced that the physical and mental well-being and the deep "rehearsals" while running and jogging allowed me to function at a higher level in the business world. Cramming in a daily thirty-minute run on an extended business trip several time zones away, with daily flights and too many rich meals, kept me less stressed and preserved a balance in my life, such that I could still cling to a bit of "my" time and space.

EMOTIONAL RENEWAL

There is much down time in any business life, especially in the daily commute as well as on most business trips. The secret is to become intentional and use those bits of time well. Non-business reading, whether it is fiction or an unrelated nonfiction topic, can be a useful antidote to the often tedious nature of business reading and meeting content. It helps keep your mind and spirit alive to plunge into something entirely different and absorbing, even if only for a few moments. This practice allows you to come back to the task at hand refreshed and renewed. My own reading has always been eclectic, including such diverse topics as mountaineering, music, philosophy, theology, organizational theory, business biographies, history, and fiction. I always carry a book in my briefcase to pick up as a reward once I complete my "homework" reading. These days we have access also to books on tape, business CDs and videos, and laptops on airplanes. I find books on tape extremely valuable on car trips, and my freeway commutes are filled with the calming sounds of jazz from my CDs.

Business reading can be beneficial. I have gained from almost everything I have read by Peter Drucker, and I still find Peters and Waterman's *In Search of Excellence* extremely valuable. Gardner's mentoring and his *Excellence* and *Self-Renewal* had a profound impact on my decisions to take a sabbatical and to retire early from Morgan Stanley. Another particularly valuable book for me was George Vaillent's *Adaptation to Life*. It is important to hear other voices and learn from their experiences. Reading can be an adventure into new growth, and it can help us achieve a richer interior life, as well as reinforcing decision-making skills.

My interest in Bonhoeffer, for example, and my extensive reading of books by or about him, have broadened my life and interests; I am continually learning and making connections among ideas and interests. Bonhoeffer led me to an interest in Karl Barth and to Paul Tillich (author of *The Courage to Be*). A theologian friend interested me in T. S. Eliot's *Four Quartets*, along with the spiritual novels of Charles Williams; these in turn led me to Dante and *The Divine Comedy*. My current journey is with Flannery O'Connor and Walker Percy, Christian existentialism, Søren Kierkegaard, and the world of semiotics. I am also constructing mini-courses on Dorothy Sayers and Iris Murdoch. I can make connections among all these individuals, whether they are theologians or literary figures. Each points to the need for strong relationships between the deep interior life of ethics; spirituality and religion; and the challenges of the everyday, secular, modern world.

One needn't branch as far from the world of business as theology for renewal and perspective. Doing the same activities in a different environment, for a different purpose and with different people, can also become a form of relaxation and self-renewal. Putting myself on the line in the classroom, whether at a graduate business school or in a church or a monastery, forces me to clarify my own thinking and allows me to become more confident in pressing for the importance of values and integrity in the business world. Volunteering and philanthropic activities in which I use my business expertise also provides benefits. Such service opens a window on new communities, new ways of seeing the world and its needs—especially important for those in fast-paced, high-pressure jobs—and a new array of problems and contingencies. It is refreshing and renewing to work hard at something entirely different with a new cross-section of people.

I was able to balance volunteer activities with my work in interesting ways. In each case I advised the firm on what I was doing and worked to fit it into my schedule. Volunteering is no substitute for carrying out your business responsibilities effectively, but it can mesh nicely. To fulfill my role as president of a West Coast–based volunteer organization required sixteen trips to California over five years. I enjoyed coming back "home," and I began to look for creative ways to tie Morgan Stanley's interests to my own. Morgan Stanley at that time had no office in the West, and it seemed to me we should become more aggressive in soliciting business there. I volunteered to make calls in conjunction with each of the California trips, as an additional responsibility. Bob Baldwin, our leader, supported my idea, and he provided me with a young banker to do the follow-up work. I was able to combine the corporate calls with my real estate calls, so it only cost me an extra few days of work a year. The activity also fit with my personal objective of remaining involved in corporate finance.

This was a classic example of alignment of interests and flexibility. The firm was still small enough that I could engage in activities outside my immediate area. I was able to revitalize my strong interest in corporate finance, meet my real estate responsibilities, and perform volunteer work in the area where I had grown up. I was working a bit harder, but I was empowered, as I was doing things I had initiated; I also had terrific staff support from corporate finance. I had no qualms about charging my expenses back to the firm, as I was always adding value to our business on the West Coast.

Nothing succeeds better than a consistent calling program over several years. As a result of taking advantage of my trips out West we picked up a number of important West Coast clients, including Hewlett Packard, Times Mirror, Getty Oil, and several others. In a different context, I saw the work on the national Presbyterian Church Board of Pensions as providing me with a look at the investment process from a fresh perspective, adding a layer to my business experience as well.

Within Morgan Stanley itself, I was given the additional responsibility of running our charitable foundation for three years. Until that time, the foundation had been mainly a repository to cover charitable dinner solicitations by important clients of the firm. I suggested we send such solicitations back to the business units, where they would be considered as client maintenance expense, and turn the foundation into a proactive philanthropic organization complete with a specific field of interest and a business plan. After discussion with Bob Baldwin and others we made the foundation a vehicle for supporting educational and social service programs in the communities in which we had offices and for encouraging and supporting volunteerism on the part of our employees.

My secretary-assistant at that time had developed a keen interest in the foundation, and she ultimately was promoted to a mid-level professional rank and became the administrative head of the foundation. The foundation became a focal point for encouraging volunteerism. The firm made such activity valid by providing financial support to charities where employees were willing to spend their time. This was a signal that the firm supported its employees' having balanced lives and giving back to society. Not all employees took advantage of it, and such activities are never a substitute for professional dedication and excellence. All of these nuances, including the treatment of women and minorities, can add up to what makes a firm a "good place to work." On the margin, they may result in attracting employees and clients with similar core beliefs.

In more recent years volunteer activities have allowed me to continue to practice my professional skills. I have served on the Los Angeles Philharmonic board for twenty years and have chaired our summer efforts at the Hollywood Bowl. This provides exposure to a diverse group of individuals interested in music and opens a window on how to balance artistic excellence and financial success. In that capacity for several years I was responsible for coalescing a team of architects, contractors, Los Angeles County officials, and others in a project to rebuild our performance shell. The project included environmental issues, construction management, and artistic issues. I also became part of a team to negotiate a new thirty-year lease of the facility from Los Angeles County, bringing my real estate skills to bear.

Volunteering also can open up a new window on the world. A friend invited me to join the citizens' advisory board to the UCLA Medical Center, a major teaching and research hospital. Subsequently I became chair of that board's ethics committee, and I became immersed in complex issues relating to health care and health care finances as well as organizational issues and the teaching of ethics to medical students.

We cannot expect all philanthropic activities to have "payback." In many of my activities, including fundraising and activities at our local church, the payback is simply the satisfaction of helping others. There is always, however, the payback of new friendships, shared experiences, professional and personal enrichment, and the chance to make a significant difference in people's lives.

I enjoy finding and making connections among multiple constituencies, and I appear to have adapted well into the multitasking world of the present. How can we bring our talents and skills to useful purpose in different types of organizations? How can we use our experience to leverage ourselves into additional interesting challenges? It seems to me this is another way of exploring Kierkegaard's notion of rotating out of everydayness and making one's life more meaningful.

THE SPIRITUAL AND THE SACRED

Having a spiritual perspective can elevate your view of the world and of the people around you. It allows you to do ordinary things with an appreciation of their enormous value. Spirituality teaches us how to see the larger meaning and the richness of life. To become whole, we need the introspection as well as the "reality." We must find a balance between materialism and spirituality. I found my own spiritual underpinning essential in my attempt to live in balance.

Spirituality draws us out of ourselves and helps us focus on the other, including the divine other. If spirituality can help us focus less intensely on our personal needs and more on the needs and desires of others, it can be an important factor in our emotional maturity and success. It cannot always tell us the right thing to do, but it can provide us with the inner detachment to slow down and search for the right answer. It also can give us the courage to move ahead when the answer is ambiguous and the path potentially dangerous. It makes a great difference to our outlook if we see life as a gift rather than as an entitlement.

I do not view myself as unusually religious or spiritual, but I was "churched" as a child, and church is a deeply engrained aspect of my week and of my daily living. I do not feel particularly evangelical, and I am a bewildering—even to myself—mélange of liberal and conservative religious views. The organized church is not perfect, but I find it can provide wonderful opportunities to serve, teach, give, grow, and develop a community in which we can express our concerns and doubts in safety.

In my beginning days on Wall Street I particularly enjoyed attending an early Wednesday morning men's breakfast and chapel service at my church in Manhattan. I was the youngest person there, and I was struck by the presence of the senior law partners and corporate executives who came in early to help prepare the food and join in the worship service. We shared a meal together and then gathered in the chapel for a short service of prayer, psalm reading, and meditation. I learned from these successful men that it is appropriate to make connections between your spiritual life and your professional life, and that being religious is not something one needs to be embarrassed about. When I later saw some of these men in a business setting downtown, I felt a completely different relationship with them. A combination of fellowship and praying together with older men who were successful Wall Street lawyers and bankers gave me a different perspective on what my professional life might become. They became for me role models, opening up different possibilities for the future.

Sometimes on the commuter train from Connecticut I would perform a fairly quick "triage" on the newspapers and then pray quietly while the other passengers were engrossed in their conversations or reading. This time to quiet down and center myself was, for me, a good trade-off. I could always catch up on the details when I arrived at the office. It was more important for me to be there for the others. I did not pray to invoke divine forces to my side to allow me to prevail over others, but rather to provide me with the clarity and strength to be the best I could be. Instead of arriving in the office stressful and anxious about my "to do" list, I would sometimes arrive in a relative state of serenity. Commuting along the freeways in Los Angeles in later years presents a far greater challenge, but even in that situation one can quiet down by listening to music or the right spoken word.

Developing an inner calmness, even a sense of detachment, can help one deal positively with the chaos and confusion of an active business life. Prayer, or deep contemplation, may become a form of refuge from what can easily become a dehumanizing routine. Whatever the circumstance, one can develop a habit of prayer or contemplation by fixing on a particular habitual time and place to do so and making it a part of the daily routine and not something exotic.

Through my reading of Bonhoeffer and others I became interested in Benedictine monasticism, and I visited Weston Priory in Vermont to experience it firsthand for a few days. I was enthralled that a fifteen-hundred-year-old tradition of praying the psalms and living the Benedictine Rule was being maintained in the midst of our secular society. I established a relationship with St. Andrew's Priory in southern California when I moved there, becoming over the years an oblate and teaching several courses there. For me as a non-Catholic, it is a hospitable and accessible source of deep renewal and spiritual growth.

Bonhoeffer became a touchstone for me. I am drawn to what he termed "religionless religion" or "stealth religion," in which individuals attempt to act out their religious faith in all that they do without appearing to be particularly religious. Their faith is a unifying, transparent fabric underlying their lives. It fits them well and it is never ostentatious. For such people, life becomes a spiritual quest, and they are always seeking out ways of quietly putting their faith into practice. If we are proactively attempting to live out our faith, we are less likely to become guilty of price fixing, insider trading, or breaking trust with the public. Knowing we are accepted by the Other as we are can give us the courage to stand up against injustice or improper behavior. The workplace becomes the place where we live out our spiritual awareness.

Practicing our faith at work does not mean we need to give up our worldliness. Don't confuse the issue. Be an authentic businessperson. Rely on your faith for renewal and support. Depend on it to help create a context and to shape a corporate culture. Build trust; be fair; take time out for others. The issue becomes, Where do we stop trading off? There will always be competitors who will cut corners and engage in practices that make other market participants uncomfortable.

No rational decision-making system is perfect. In the true ethical dilemma, we are thrown back to our own inner resources; we have to hope they are adequate for the task. A personal faith helps us to set our priorities and to live with the consequences of our actions. Then we can confidently balance our intuition with our rational nature. As Paul Tillich has suggested, we must live out of the depths of our being.[8]

Let us move on now to see how we can, practically speaking, put all this into practice.

CHAPTER 8

Organizational and Business Ethics: Developing Ethical Sensitivity

MY GOAL IN THIS BOOK and in many of the intellectual pursuits of my life is to increase ethical awareness and sensitivity in myself and others. When we are not rooted in the depths of the Dantean fourth level, we can unconsciously walk right through an ethical dilemma and not allow the ambiguity and nuances of the crisis to affect us. This is a part of the lesson of "The Parable of the Sadhu." However, when we do not get what we want out of a given situation, we may jump to the conclusion that the process is not ethical, when it may be that the process is very fair but we are just poor losers. We allow hurt feelings or disappointments to confuse us. Like learning a new language, it takes practice and discipline to recognize ethical issues.

Creating an ethical sensitivity causes one to listen to points of view one might have previously shut out. This can be true of a variety of issues, including those related to environmentalism, feminism, disabled employees, or employment practices. Having the imagination and self-confidence to seek out other points of view can prevent costly errors in judgment. It becomes important to construct a group of parties affected by a corporate decision—stakeholders—as broadly as possible. If we allow ourselves to become isolated moral agents, we are almost certain to commit immoral acts. We find our morality in community, removing our ego and letting in the world.

The true spirit-crushing ethical dilemmas occur when one is caught between two opposing powerful ethical issues. To be human and to act out one's own life, one must make a choice. To refuse to choose is to lack integrity. This is the stuff of great drama and great literature.

Ethics is often presented as, How do you want to be remembered? There are plenty of cases in which individuals have felt that they have been "good enough" and are now "entitled" to get something back. Basically good people often make thoughtless or bad decisions because ethics is not always allowed as input or is overridden by expediency or greed. In a theological sense, we can never be "good enough." We can never attain closure on what it means to become a "good" person. "The Parable of the Sadhu" raises this issue as well. How do I attain closure? When have I done enough? When do I get off the hook? The fourth-level response is: never.

In resolving true ethical choices, be certain to understand why you chose the path you chose and why you rejected the path you rejected. Loyalty is perhaps a weak ethical standard, and the preservation of human life may be the strongest. You must be tough enough to make a decision when you have sought out divergent points of view and all that needs to be known cannot be known. You must at times answer questions that have no established solutions. Many issues are jumbled amidst ambiguity and paradox; the ambiguity of many dilemmas cries out for a polyphonous response. Stop, gather your community of peers, and come up with as many options as possible for consideration.

Perhaps, if one has "perfect moral pitch"(as Hannah Arendt said of William Shawn, editor of the *New Yorker*), the decisions come more easily. But for the rest of us, each day and each issue bring a time to practice. We are each moral agents, with great potential for good, yet we often give up our agency to others without thinking. A standard psychology experiment has a student apply electric shock to another student who appears to be a poor or slow learner. The current is not really connected, but the student applying the shock does not know this. On many occasions the student being tested will knowingly intend to inflict pain on another student. During the debriefing, the student will say he or she is "only following orders."

Johnson & Johnson has each new employee read an ethical training guide, which states that "Every day you make decisions that reveal your personal values. . . . Good decisions will build and strengthen relationships of trust, enhance economic performance and sustain our corporate reputation. . . . Perhaps the facts are ambiguous, the consequences difficult to predict or the ethical values at odds with each other."[1]

The training guide then lists some examples, as follows:

Do you tell a customer the whole truth when it might cause you to lose a sale or your job?

How do you deal with legal limitations on marketing or labeling when your competitors seem to be ignoring them?

In managing others, how do you handle the high-producing associate who abuses clerical help, stretches the truth, or ignores company policies she thinks are foolish?

The Johnson & Johnson manual then goes on to describe obstacles to ethical decision making:

Complacency: It can't happen here. In any organization of significant size unethical behavior by someone is inevitable. Unethical behavior is just one more systemic risk that must be managed.

Self-Delusion: Our self-image is so important that we tend to exaggerate our virtues and minimize our faults. We tend to judge ourselves by our best intentions. Others are likely to judge us by our worst acts.

Rationalizations: I've got it coming. Minor percs. It's for a good cause. If it's legal, it must be OK. Everyone is doing it. Safety in numbers: Everyone's doing it. I was just doing it for you.

Survival mentality: No job is worth sacrificing your honor. This portion of the manual includes the following statement: "If you are unwilling to lose, you have to be willing to do whatever it takes to win."[2]

For me, this final statement reinforces the notion that being ethical is not about winning all the time. If you are completely unconstrained, there is nothing you won't do to get ahead. Thus the statement serves as a warning to new employees of Johnson & Johnson, and elsewhere, that there is danger ahead. Ethics is about how you will react to the unknown, the unexplored, the stranger.

I wish we had had available to us a Johnson & Johnson–style ethics manual when I began at Morgan Stanley. We had to work our ethics out for ourselves, on the job, reacting to situations. Investment banks are fraught with conflicts of interest. There are conflicts between pure securities research and investment banking, between money management and investment banking, between trading activities for the firm's own account and trading as an agent on behalf of a client, between a firm's private investment account and its client business. It's how one manages these and a host of other conflicts that matters.

Some individuals are so uncomfortable with conflicts that they simply wish them away, finding it difficult even to acknowledge and disclose them. In my experience, when operating in a business in which there are plenty of conflicts, it is of paramount importance to be sensitive to them, identify them, discuss them, proactively manage them, and promptly disclose them. When properly managed and disclosed, with the priorities always oriented toward the client, conflicts can become tolerable. At Morgan Stanley, we did not always get it right, but I never felt constrained about bringing up an issue for discussion.

There is no reason to have securities researchers, who opine on the merits of a company's common stock, involved in investment banking, in which one is asked to sell or independently value in a merger, for example, the same security. Prior to the tech boom of the early 1990s firms either did not participate in both issuing new securities and evaluating them for the public, or they built a firewall between these two separate businesses. Investment bankers became sloppy in the 1990s and blurred the distinction between the two businesses, using security analysts' implied high ratings for an issuer's securities to gain new investment banking business. That is a management issue that should never rise to the surface. It is certainly appropriate for a new client to assure itself that there is professional and competent coverage of its securities in the after market, but promising positive coverage in return for investment banking business is clearly unethical. When a firm refuses to accede to an improper request, a client may withdraw business. That is the risk, but I know of no better solution. To tolerably manage such a conflict, either the firewall must work or the investment bank can retain truly independent third-party common stock research, a solution that is being implemented at some firms presently.

APPROACHING RISK ETHICALLY

Being ethical does not mean conforming always to existing practice or avoiding risk. Our assignment to workout IDS Realty Trust, one of the largest public real estate investment trusts (REIT) of the 1970s, provides an example of risk taking and of not following the expected pattern. The

REIT had about 150 separate loans and investments. The industry was in the midst of the real estate recession of the early 1970s, and the management of the IDS trust appeared to be out of touch with the marketplace and the resulting chaos and confusion.

We performed triage on the loans and investments, organizing them into three categories. In the first layer were those from which cash flow could be preserved or achieved in the short term, within six months. In the second category were those for which action could safely be deferred six months without loss of value. In the third category were those for which it made no sense to expend time and energy. We then established action steps with respect to the first two categories.

As a result, we knew we had enough cash flow to service approximately $200 million of outstanding junior debt or $100 million of outstanding senior debt, but not both. The obvious investment banking answer was to deal with the senior debt and defer the subordinated debt. The issue went deeper than that, however. The senior debt was all held by one lender, a New York City money center bank, a highly sophisticated real estate lender. The subordinated debt had been sold in small pieces by the IDS salesforce to individuals, primarily in the Grain Belt, which was the main customer base for IDS Financial. Thus, there were two good reasons for favoring the subordinated debt. Doing so would preserve the customer base for IDS, an extremely important long-term asset. Also, we believed that if we went to court, a judge in Minnesota would have been far more likely to favor the individual investors over the big New York bank.

There was plenty of reason to favor the bank as well. They held a legal contract telling them they were the senior lender. To treat them otherwise was to violate the contracts previously entered into and fly in the face of both conventional finance and the traditional Morgan Stanley approach. I favored at least trying to persuade the bank that it was in their best interest to step aside and defer their debt in favor of the individual creditors, mentioning the possibility of a class action lawsuit on the part of the individual bondholders if they did not comply. This process became known as a "cram down" of the senior lender. My client, the chief financial officer of IDS Realty, agreed with the traditional approach of favoring the senior debt. When I made my final client presentation, the owners of IDS,

Alleghany Corporation, agreed with me. A delegation went to visit with the New York bank, and they saw the wisdom in our tactic. The subordinated debt was serviced. My client, the chief financial officer, was in trouble with his principle shareholders for stubbornly holding on to his traditional approach.

For me, this is an example of a situation in which the surface reality was not the true reality. One had to look behind the law of the loan contract to the new reality. The true reality was deeper and more complex, as well as being ambiguous. When there was not enough money to satisfy all the creditors, who got it? The New York City banks who had a first call in their loan agreement or the public bondholders who would go to their local courts for protection, if necessary? Protecting the individual bondholders was determined to be a higher good than protecting the New York City banks.

If a firm has established market leadership and a good reputation, it can lead the market to accept new types of financial instruments or even new ways of valuing existing securities or assets. Morgan Stanley enjoyed such a reputation, but along with it came a sense of responsibility to use its market leadership wisely. Public trust is a precious gift, and it should not be squandered.

When I took over the management of Morgan Stanley's real estate business in the midst of the recession of the early 1970s, we were losing money. I had to construct quickly a vision for the future and perform immediate triage, all the while learning the business.

As one aspect of this business, we had raised institutional funds for a private real estate investment trust. I was covering pension fund clients throughout the United States, Europe, Japan, and the Middle East who had invested with us, raising a second round of financing. Partway through, I realized that the initial investments we had made were going sour. I called off the second offering, having already raised most of the funds we thought we required, and turned to the task of finding out what had gone wrong.

Having recognized the problem, I felt it was my responsibility to tell my boss, my partners, and our clients that we had made mistakes. In time we learned that ours was just a small part of an industry-wide problem, one that no one else in our industry was yet admitting. My sense of honesty

compelled me to be the first out of the box, an unenviable position. I insisted finally, over virtually everyone's objections, that we close branch offices,
terminate professionals, slim down, straighten out our problems, respond
to the market, and then rebuild the business. This was a difficult time, to
say the least. Morgan Stanley was growing rapidly, and internal resources,
and even time to stop and think, were limited. I was fortunate to have a
handful of trusted friends with whom I could discuss my concerns, including
some of those who reported to me in the firm and people outside the firm. I
was pretty much left to my own devices, however, and I had to find within
myself the courage to stick to my guns and hold a vision of a better future.
And that future did arrive: in the late 1970s we became the most powerful
real estate finance unit on Wall Street.

I have been asked how, in my mid to late thirties, I had acquired the
self-confidence, even courage, to take such a big stand. The fact is, I did not
feel courageous at the time: I was scared. For many months my boss, Bob
Baldwin, the CEO of Morgan Stanley, had been telephoning me at home
every Sunday evening to tell me all the things I had done wrong that week
and what he expected of me the following week. I came to dread the calls,
yet I did not always agree with his conclusions and I managed to retain my
sense of independence.

It was always possible that I could be fired, but I had attained a high
level of credibility, one on one, throughout the firm for honesty, judgment,
and competence. I had started to acquire a set of outside mentors in the
real estate business who advised me and supported my business decisions.
I had recruited a fine set of younger men and women into the real estate
unit, and I trusted their loyalty and judgment as well. Throughout the crisis
of the early 1970s I retained, for the most part, a sense of detachment fed
by outside reading, jogging, and hiking friends unrelated to the business
world, and a growing interior life that was pointing me also on a spiritual
journey. Though I had not as yet studied Dante, I was being drawn into
what he termed the deep fourth level.

These days when someone asks how to know when to take a stand, I
refer him or her to the Dantean fourth level, stressing that it need not be
purely religious, but that a deep understanding of ourselves and the world
in which we live can sustain our moral compass when the world around us

appears to be going crazy. Sometimes we have to retrace our steps or take detours on our journey.

In a situation such as the one I faced in the early 1970s, there are no clear-cut answers. One must gather as much market intelligence as possible and make a determination about where the market is heading. One must face up to the weaknesses in one's own organization. One must build upon the strengths in place. One must have a positive vision for the future in order to lead the team out of Egypt and into the desert of change and anxiety. One must share the vision and the risk with those on the team who are the "keepers"—the future. One must also be confident we will reach the other side. All this requires courage, resilience, faith, and a state of mind that does not need the reassurance of a quick fix or short-term praise. It helps a great deal if one has cultivated that deep level of Stoic philosophy and faith that can sustain one over the sometimes lengthy rough spots. Having the right vision is immensely important.

What sustains the courage of a leader to get through the ambiguous rough spots where the outcome is never clear, and allows him or her to be a source of hope for the others? It is the clarity of the vision sharpened by years of trial and error and by mistakes and successes, and tempered by a sustained grounding in the transcendent.

OVERCOMING THE CHALLENGES

Time and again throughout the past forty years I have encountered either personally, in the press, or in my reading individuals so taken in by their own hubris that they attempted to stifle dissent and the free expression of ideas. The examples range all the way from Marc Rjoitman at J. I. Case in the early 1960s to Ken Lay of Enron in the twenty-first century. As a result of their excessive behavior and ego drive they voided the legitimate checks and balances of independent directors, accountants, or lawyers. Failing to allow the outside world into their interior worlds of power and wealth, they became imprisoned in their own self-created illusions of reality, to their own peril. The self-delusion of such leaders can trap their organizations into complacency so that, without a mooring in the depths, the incrementalism of bad practices is allowed to persist. Complacency, for example, caused the bishops of the state church in Germany to swear allegiance to Adolf Hitler and to mandate the appearance of the swastika on all church altars. It also led U.S. military police in Iraq to torture Iraqi prisoners without regard for the Geneva Convention, public opinion, or common decency. The fact that they also took digital photos of themselves while conducting the torture underscores the depth of bad practices and lack of common sense—a classic example of your ethics being defined by what you do when you think no one is looking. This activity represents a classic lack of leadership, of setting the standards. It also demonstrates again the "tragedy of the commons." If the MPs were contemplating their actions, it was "No one will ever know what we are doing here in Iraq at 3:30 A.M., and it won't make any difference anyway."

In its beginning first-year ethics course, Harvard Business School asks the question, "Our system survives on a moral culture that nourishes and values the virtues on which its existence depends. What responsibility do we have as individuals and organizations to contribute positively to this culture?"

We do not think of our individual actions as having cosmic possibilities. To do so would be seen to be taking ourselves far too seriously. Yet in the broader view, our days are filled with small, mundane, everyday acts of grace or of ugliness that, in an accumulative sense, can indeed become cosmic for us and those around us.

The former CEO of J.C. Penney, Richard Siebert, liked to tell little stories focusing on the impact of senior management on the organization. "What message would you convey," he would ask, "if you are racing out of your office, a briefcase in each hand, heading for LaGuardia, and you yell back over your shoulder to your secretary, 'Get my niece a job!' or 'Don't put that in the board minutes!' or 'I don't care what you call it. Call it overhead expense!'"

He would conclude that the seemingly "little" acts of the CEO, heard and reported by all, have far more weight on the firm than do printed speeches, codes, or warnings.

An integral part of leadership is the acceptance of the role as ethical arbiter and exemplar. This is not accomplished by wearing our heart on our sleeve but rather by becoming someone consistent, someone who can be counted on to live out ethics responsibly in the common, everyday acts of life as well as in the cosmic decisions. Leadership is also accomplished through openness—sharing information and being a guide to those behind you who are also seeking to get ahead.

In the "old" Morgan Stanley, everything to do with compensation was mysterious. No one was supposed to know what anyone else was getting. There were no evaluations or suggestions for improvement. One simply showed up for several years, did the work, and, through a sublime annunciation, was suddenly made a general partner of the firm. The culture of cloaked decisions was so prevalent that we nearly lost one of the great leaders due to a misunderstanding. He had been hired for one year. At the end of the year he cleaned out his desk and walked out. No one had said a word of encouragement to him. Fortunately, he was called back and rehired.

Not much had changed by the time the group of us later known as the "young Turks" became partners. We instituted annual performance reviews, gradations in the bonus payments, and a far more open discussion of what was required to progress in the firm. This process became refined over the years. By the time I was running Brooks Harvey, I had three-hour in-depth interviews annually with each of my key players, setting goals, offering suggestions for improvement, and explaining in detail what had to happen for them to take the next step forward. In some cases these annual interviews occurred over a decade or longer, and a deep level of trust was established. They delivered the goods, and so did I. The goods were not limited to dollar revenue production; I insisted on criteria such as training, character, and a strong sense of values as well.

The firm embarked on a rapid growth mode in the mid-1970s, adding many lines of business in addition to real estate, including mergers and acquisitions, government bond trading, corporate bond trading, equity research and trading, and international activities. Each unit required modified compensation systems. We tinkered with them almost every year, never getting the system quite right. Initially we established separate bonus pools for securities sales and trading. This had the unfortunate outcome of paying bonuses to salesmen for building up large inventories of securities that the traders had to sell at a loss. After a year or two we linked the two activities into a common pool.

The major lesson was about avoiding bonus payouts based strictly on production. We derived bonus pools related to the overall productivity of business units, but the managers were given an override to allocate the pools based on other criteria, such as skills at recruiting, training, compliance, and character. Bonus pools based purely on production are an abrogation of management's responsibility to develop and maintain standards, limits, and leadership. Managers who do not use incentive compensation to generate and reward good practices and character contribute to the destruction of the basic integrity of the enterprise. Managers must not leave control of the firm to those who are focused purely on making money for themselves and not on the mission of the overall enterprise.

Getting compensation right is one of management's toughest jobs, especially in a growing and changing firm that is adding new businesses and expanding geographically. When one continually fine-tunes the system to produce desired results and accommodate changes in the business, employees can begin to question the fairness of the system. A balance must be achieved between fairness and consistency and producing the desired results. This is what makes designing effective compensation systems so difficult, but it is one of leadership's most important jobs, and it must be managed effectively and continually. It is where the rubber meets the road.

When one designs compensation systems to emphasize character and values as well as production, some very high producers will receive less compensation than they would receive in a firm in which compensation is solely production driven. A decision must be made whether to adjust compensation to meet the high producer's demands or to let him or her go to a competitor and lose one of your highest producers. Such decisions signal the true character of the firm, and they are tracked closely by everyone.

The evaluation systems that underlie compensation decisions also become an effective management tool. Starting in the late 1970s, as I was continuing to learn on the job at Brooks Harvey, I had begun to wonder why we were not using our evaluation sessions more productively. We spent hours ranking the performance of our professionals and tied these evaluations to promotions and bonuses. But after all the good news was handed out, we stopped. I came up with the notion of eliminating the bottom-performing 10 percent each year as well. Many in the company saw this as unusual. All of our people were good. They had been through an intensive recruiting process, and we had expended great effort in training them. I thought we should become more proactive and asked how we could ever get better if we did not continually prune away at the bottom. Over time, we took steps in this direction within the real estate group. To temper justice with mercy, I gave those being let go plenty of time in the termination process and helped them secure other employment.

Ethics becomes complex in these cases. I had always felt it poor practice on the part of the older partners to let individuals who obviously were not going to make it hang around for several years before being told they would not become partners. For me, a sign of leadership is to make the tough decision, face up to the termination, and then assist the individuals in finding a position where they could grow and meet their potential. Individuals who made it in and out of the top business schools and survived our recruiting process were highly talented. Some of them just did not have an inclination for investment banking. Sometimes it took a few years for them and for us to figure that out. Individuals lacking the energy and enthusiasm for our work were not desirable as members of project teams, so by making these decisions, I was also raising the productivity, morale, and well-being of the organization.

Our emphasis on rewarding good performance and penalizing poor performance may appear inconsistent with the more modern approach to the empowerment of individuals. It would be ideal to work in a "perfect" organization, in which everyone is empowered to be their best and there is no need for rules, rewards, or punishments. It is reputed that a better class of employees and customers are attracted to a "virtuous" firm. Such an organization is cheaper to run than a command-and-control organization. Such an organization is more fun to work for, and turnover and dissatisfaction tend to be lower.

I accept all this, up to a point. We are all human beings, however, and we respond strongly to rewards and punishments. The large cash bonuses and the promotion to general partner at a firm like Morgan Stanley were powerful incentives to me, both financially and psychologically. The choice of which projects and which partners I was assigned to created large incentives as well. Obviously, the potential denial of large cash bonuses, promotions, and "good" assignments was also a strong motivator.

Everything in my experience indicates the need for virtue as well as rewards and punishments. Managers must be "tight-loose." We may have a "loose," "virtuous" organization on the surface, but beneath the surface we need to be rigid about certain things, such as ethical behavior and how we treat one another.

Rather than operating as a constraint, the rules, or law-based culture, operate as a minimum. The "virtuous" organization calls us to do much better than what the rules require. In the military we need tough discipline to maintain fire control and minimize loss of life. There are no rules, however, stating that combat soldiers have to teach English to occupied civilians or share their rations with them. There are no rules stating that a fully employed surgical nurse has to volunteer to open up a Red Cross relief shelter in a high school gym at 3:00 A.M.

Rules-based leadership follows Dante's third level. If we are to act at our very best, out of Dante's fourth level, there must be support and leadership. We must learn to trust others and allow them to make their mistakes, which they will. We must be willing to go in new, unexplored directions. We must have the self-confidence and trust in others to let go and not try to control everything, and to live with the consequences.

MANAGING WITH ETHICS IN MIND

As a manager of people, whether in a team or a business unit, one is looked upon as an arbiter of correct behavior. I soon recognized that my actions had a significant impact on others, and the result was a lifelong interest in business ethics. One defining responsibility of those who rise to management positions is their ability to build trust relationships within the enterprise as well as with key clients. Trust is not just following the rules; it is following the spirit that created the rules. Trust is established quite often in those unexpected defining moments when decisions must be made almost by instinct, since all the facts cannot be known.

In one situation, we had set up a real estate development firm to make investments for the partners of Morgan Stanley. One of the investments was a condominium project in Florida. We financed it with a bank loan. The loan was guaranteed by the partners of Morgan Stanley, who wanted to become released from the guarantee to reduce their personal liability.

There was a provision that once a certain number of condominiums had been sold, we were off the guarantee. When the time came for the release, we were short about a dozen sales. The condominiums were moderately priced at about $150,000 each. My associate urged me strongly to have a dozen Morgan Stanley partners each purchase a condominium. They could purchase on terms, with only a 20 percent down payment, and Morgan Stanley could be released from the guarantee. The partners could sell out their units as the real estate market improved.

I refused. My premise was that the spirit of the bank condition was that there be a viable third-party, independent market judgment for the project. By buying down the condominiums, we would, in effect, be rigging the market. Even though the bank was agreeable and was pleased to carry the loan, I did not let it go through. It simply did not fit my image of what Morgan Stanley stood for. We remained exposed on the guarantee until the project sold out. I'm sure some of my partners saw me as a roadblock, not as an ethicist. I, in effect, made their ethical decision for them. This was not universally regarded as a favor; but I could be comfortable that this was at least one time we would not be written up in the *Wall Street Journal*. As usual, I reported what I had done to Bob Baldwin, my boss, and he concurred with my decision.

ALIGNING ETHICS, PRACTICES, AND STANDARDS

It is unusual when one's personal standards are completely aligned with those of the firm as well as the industry or profession of which the firm is a part. Once again, an individual must decide where and when to take a stand. One determinant is practicality—the art of the doable. Don't underestimate the doable. As Vaclav Havel has written, "Politics can be not only the art of the possible . . . it can even be the art of the impossible, namely, the art of improving ourselves and the world. . . ."[3] Had we stopped at the unknown or the apparently impossible, civilization and politics would still be outside our reach. Clearly it is more difficult to change industry standards than to change a firm's practices, but both are possible.

In the old Morgan partnership a large number of partners, including me, were opposed to the firm sponsoring unfriendly takeovers of companies. This is a case of establishing and maintaining industry standards. At what price will a firm not "go along"? Most of our competitors soon began mounting raids on behalf of their clients, and a number of our important client corporations defected to other investment banks when we refused to help them. At some point the trade-offs become too great.

We finally succumbed, and the financial press, because of the influence and prestige of Morgan Stanley, claimed that unfriendly raids were thus made "legitimate." In later years, having opened the door, Morgan Stanley made similar decisions about such matters as financing savings and loans that were stretching the legality of their charters and about issuing "junk" bonds. It requires extraordinary leadership and a keen ethical ear to manage survival and growth in an era of deregulation and intense competition.

The issue becomes, Where do we stop trading off? There will always be competitors who will cut corners and engage in practices that make other market participants uncomfortable. The nineteenth-century financial theorem, Gresham's Law, states that abased currency tends to drive out good currency. Likewise, the cynic might state that bad practices tend to drive out good practices. Yet public trust is vitally important to an enterprise, an industry, and an economy. Indeed, the United States is looked upon by the entire world as the model for free-market capitalism. What responsibility does each of the market participants have for making the system a little bit better instead of a little bit worse? How do we ever get better if we always seek the lowest common denominator? What price are we willing to pay to get a little bit better?

Again, assuming we deeply care about being "good" in the first place, how do we do so? It seems to me that we each have a series of filters:

- Our personal intuitive sense of right and wrong
- Our interpretation of how the law informs our behavior
- Our sensitivity to what the public expects of us and how to retain public trust beyond what the law requires
- The extent to which we allow ourselves to become informed about the deep religious and spiritual truths of our culture

A person who is informed at all four levels and brings all four into play in daily life and work can be said to have integrity. Everything is aligned. These are the individuals to whom we turn for judgments during a crisis.

These are the individuals on whom we can depend. They live out their deep beliefs.

In some ways a good manager has much in common with your rabbi, pastor, or favorite grammar school teacher: their lessons carry forward. For me, one such individual was Charlie Shaw, an important real estate developer from Chicago, whom I counted as one of my favorite clients and friends. We were in a trust relationship for thirty years, and we shared many adventures together. The worst real estate recession since the Great Depression crept up on the business community in the early 1970s. The indicators were not as compelling as they would be today, now that there is far greater transparency of information about the real estate markets. I was then building our real estate business, and I received an inquiry from the Agnelli family in Milan, the owners of Fiat. They were interested in investing in U.S. real estate development and wanted Morgan Stanley to select a partner for them. We were concerned that such a partner should have the highest degree of integrity and reliability. I recommended Charlie Shaw. Ultimately the Agnelli family deposited $10 million, a substantial sum at the time, in the Chase Manhattan Bank to fund a joint venture with Charlie.

A few months later, Charlie came in to see me. He was concerned. He saw the deals the large bank-sponsored real estate investment trusts were making, and they did not make sense to him. He felt the market had become excessively speculative, and he was uncomfortable investing someone else's money in it. He had not drawn down any of the funds and asked me how bad it would look if we simply gave the money back, taking out no fees for ourselves. I replied that we would either look like heroes or extremely foolish, depending on how the markets resolved themselves, but that I was prepared to ride with his instincts. We gave the money back. Many large real estate firms subsequently went bankrupt during the recession. It takes courage to do the right thing, especially when you are not sure what the right thing is.

Charlie suffered the most in terms of foregone fees and services. Because we owned real estate investments in our investment fund, my hands-on knowledge of the property markets was running ahead of the financial press and my partners' knowledge at the time. For my partners, this decision was just one more indication of my independent, idiosyncratic behavior. The Agnellis appeared to be pleased. Each Christmas thereafter for ten years they sent me a monogrammed silver piece and a case of fine Italian wine. Ethics does not always pay so well.

Twenty years later, the real estate recession of the early 1990s was the worst one yet. Once again our professional knowledge of the property markets ran ahead of the financial press, and even the behavior of the large commercial banks. I gave a (poorly attended) speech to a major real estate trade association, the Urban Land Institute, warning of the danger signs. Six months later we were in the thick of it.

By then I had retired from Morgan Stanley, but I found myself counseling friends who were under incredible pressure from their lenders. Many of the financial institutions were under almost intolerable stress from government regulators, bond-rating agencies, common stock analysts, and the like, and they were overwhelmed with the burden of myriad distressed real estate projects. They had to make difficult decisions under extreme time constraints. An unattractive aspect of the situation was that real estate developers who hid assets overseas, gave fraudulent information, or were just the most ornery and difficult to work with often gained the most flexibility from the banks, while those who told the complete truth were often eaten alive. As usual, there were unexpected windfalls, and in many cases the wrong folks were punished. As I suggested earlier, ethics is not about always winning; it sometimes is about what you are willing to lose for.

Despite the discontinuities in the markets one excellent development out of this period was the expanded development of public markets for real estate debt and equity securities, with the resultant greater disclosure and transparency that greatly expanded the market for real estate finance.

Back in the early 1980s, Morgan Stanley had expanded its merger business, and we had commenced trading all types of securities. We decided it was time to enter the risk arbitrage business (trading in the equity securities of companies that have announced or might be anticipated to announce a merger). This involved setting up a trading desk to trade in merger takeover candidates—usually, but not always, after the merger was announced. Even when a merger is announced, there are remaining contingencies such as shareholder votes, accounting opinions, tax rulings, government clearances, and the like that can put pressure on the common stock, providing for trading opportunities. The even riskier part of the business is trading companies that might be attractive merger candidates but for which there is no announced transaction. We obviously saw profit opportunities in this business. More important, however, for us as a major player in the merger business was to be active in the trading markets in order to make market judgments for our clients in the merger business.

The firm recruited a gentleman from outside the firm, bringing him in as a partner to run this new business. At the end of the first year, the profits far exceeded our expectations. Even though this was several years prior to the insider trading scandals on Wall Street, we were suspicious as to how this person could do so well without resorting to improper behavior. The practice of taping telephone calls off the trading desks had not yet developed, and we had absolutely no proof of impropriety. Senior management discussed the issue at some length, weighing the risks of an improper termination, a lawsuit, and potentially destroying a career on mere speculation against the risk of a scandal at Morgan Stanley. Without all the necessary information, we terminated the gentleman at the end of the year. He immediately went to work for one of the individuals who became most deeply implicated in the insider trading scandals that occurred later.

Insider trading is essentially a state of mind; there is often little objective proof of the event. Messages to outsiders can be coded or highly ambiguous. We had to act on subjective opinions and emotions rather than hard facts.

LIVING INTO THE ETHIC

A leader accepts the role responsibly. Business affects the livelihoods of a wide range of stakeholders, including the families of all the main parties. We are looked upon as the standard of free market economics throughout the world. What we do will influence the behavior of firms all over the globe. Business is not just a game in which the players are manipulated. Our behavior in business needs to become integrated with our behavior in the rest of our lives. Are we rewarding the correct values? Are we serving our customers? Are we utilizing the correct metrics to measure performance? Are we encouraging excessive behavior? Are we informally encouraging a value system that we do not support ourselves? Do we feel deep in our being that some of the things we are doing are wrong? Do we need to put on a "game face" in order to come into the office and pretend we are someone we're not?

These are the kinds of questions we must continually ask ourselves if we are to avoid the incrementalism of bad practices, move toward the ideal, and become the kind of leaders we were intended to be.

CHAPTER 9

Changing Mores Through Time

AS OBSERVED PREVIOUSLY, society's view of appropriate behavior fluctuates, as society moves through long-range patterns of greater conservatism or greater liberalism. Forty years ago a typical business meeting might have consisted of an all-male group of conservatively attired Anglo-American men, each smoking a cigarette. Today an important discussion limited to such a group would appear offensive on a number of grounds to all but the most insensitive.

Because society's degree of tolerance for behaviors and practices changes over time, being ethical requires more than obeying the law. It also requires us to be sensitive to what limits society will tolerate. Individuals in the insider trading scandals went to prison denying they had broken any law. What they did not understand was that they had broken trust with the public. Laws can become vague or imprecise or can be interpreted differently by different judges or juries. Bad guys can attempt to take advantage of such inefficiencies in the system. Aggressive prosecutors can use the law to advantage in their careers. Laws imposed for a quite different purpose (for example, to prevent racketeering or tax evasion) can be purposefully misapplied to white-collar crime in order to "shake down" targets of inquiry. We need the ethical sensitivity and awareness to know what is "right" or "wrong" irrespective of the law.

KNOWING WHAT'S RIGHT AND WHAT'S RIGHT FOR THE TIME

Successful organizations change their view on what behavior is appropriate over time. Cultures and ethical standards must be modified and tested against new developments and the changing behavior of competitors and society at large. To a certain degree, then, ethics is contextual, although it is contextual around a set of core values.

This was certainly the case in my experience at Morgan Stanley. In the early 1960s a number of the older partners viewed it as unethical to offer new shares of common stock in a public offering to the public at large before offering them first to existing shareholders. They believed that each existing shareholder had a "right" to maintain his or her pro rata investment in the company by means of a right of first refusal on the new shares offered. Such a right might have been a part of the corporation's original charter, to prevent ownership by original investors from being diluted by subsequent offerings of common stock. This position required the firm to go through a laborious seventeen-day subscription period (as I did with Detroit Edison, discussed in Chapter Three), allowing existing shareholders time to make their decision, during which the firm's capital was at risk, rather than attempting to sell all the shares in a single day. By the 1970s, with the coming of increasing volatility in the marketplace, financial deregulation, and huge growth in the business, this standard was abandoned as impractical. The risk of a fixed-price under-writing for two-and-a-half weeks was too great for the investment banks to tolerate and too expensive for the issuing corporations to pay for.

In the late 1950s and early 1960s a practice evolved of placing newly issued securities, mostly debt securities, directly with insurance companies and other financial institutions rather than offering them broadly to the public at large. Such private placements tend to have more highly structured security arrangements with one or a handful of investors, but the terms are relatively easier to renegotiate, if necessary, especially as compared to deal-ing with a large number of public bondholders. In addition, as the pricing is negotiated directly, there is no capital risk to the investment bankers, thus reducing the cost of the transaction considerably. Nevertheless, several of our senior partners felt this practice was unethical, as the pricing of the securities was controlled by two or three institutions and not as a result of a public offering process that might more efficiently clear the market. The predominant view on Wall Street, and within our firm, was that the pri-vate placement process, on balance, added to the efficiency of the markets rather than detracting from it.

There is almost always resistance to change, and the ensuing dialogue can be therapeutic. We should always be able to convince others that the changes we are making are valid and ethical. Doing so can help us avoid pitfalls along the way.

Is insider trading a state of mind, as financial journalists have written? Consider that in 1964, an outside director of Texas Gulf Sulphur Corporation learned the company had discovered a large copper deposit in Canada. Before the announcement was made public, he called the trading desk at his firm and suggested they purchase the stock for their pension fund clients. Eight years later, the Supreme Court ruled that this conversation did not represent a violation of the insider trading rules, as the individual had not profited personally from the leak. Yet, in more recent times, overheard conversations at a beauty parlor or on an elevator that have led an individual to purchase shares of stock have resulted in jail sentences.

SUDDEN OR CYCLICAL SHIFTS

Public attitude, represented through legislators and judges, can swing widely over time. If you live up to the limit of what public opinion or the law condones at any particular time, you may later find the rug pulled out from under you. At times these changes come gradually, but at other times the change is abrupt and catches many off guard. Criminal penalties were not assessed for insider trading during the first thirty-five years the legislation against it existed. It was only when the legal theory of misappropriation of property was applied to insider trading that the penalties became severe. That was a sudden shift in approach.

Bad practices appear to occur in cycles, taking different forms each time. Years ago public accounting was one of the most respected professions in both the United States and the United Kingdom. Businesspersons would rail at their accountants for being obstructionist, pleading with them to "Tell me what I can do, not what I can't do!" Be careful what you ask for. Gradually, over many years, public accountants began to give "creative" advice on what clients could do. They felt they were falling behind, as a profession, in compensation, so they began to move to "value added" billing rather than billing by hours served. They saw their fees increase dramatically from consulting business based upon the sharing of the value created. Traditional accountants were left behind by management consultants. To add to their misery, pressure was placed upon the accountants to produce more consulting business from their clients, in addition to the normal accounting fees.

Perhaps because of the increasing focus on consulting business, Arthur Anderson grew sloppy on the margin, and a previously unthinkable number of their clients were forced to restate earnings and pay fines to certain government agencies. The bad practices were becoming endemic, and no one seemed inclined to blow the whistle. The same practices were occurring at the other major public accounting firms, yet Arthur Anderson became the firm caught out and made an example of.

From the federal government's perspective, the last straw came when Enron collapsed, with clear cooperation from Arthur Anderson, and Arthur Anderson appeared, at least on the surface, to be covering up its role in the process and obstructing justice. Once again a series of small bad practices by fundamentally good people over a long period of time—practices that no one in leadership appeared to have the common sense and courage to stop—brought about the demise of a major and previously highly esteemed enterprise.

These bad practices also engendered equal and opposite bad practices from the federal government, which, during a time when the firm was attempting to reform from within and make restitution, announced an indictment of the firm—thereby destroying its core competence and client base—long before the facts were in. In this case eighty-five thousand employees were affected, and the stock market lost close to 20 percent in value, in part resulting from the uncertainty created about the viability of any major business firm that might become subject to such pressure.

A better approach might have been for the government to go in with a scalpel rather than a broom. Paul Volcker, the highly esteemed ex-head of the Federal Reserve Bank, had offered to lead a restructuring team at Arthur Anderson, which under his leadership might have been developed as a model for the rest of the profession.[1]

AVOIDING THE INCREMENTALISM
OF BAD PRACTICES

It takes dedication to a core set of values to avoid "getting along by going along" and becoming ensnared in an environment of subtly increasing bad practices. My friend Lynn Sharp Paine, professor of ethics at Harvard Business School, suggests we consider four factors apart from risk and reward when analyzing a business decision. Professor Paine has been dedicated to making ethics important at Harvard, and when things become important at Harvard, it tends to influence the business school curriculum elsewhere as well. I am honored to have shared a speakers' platform with Lynn and to have been able to sit in on a couple of her classes. I respect her work immensely.

In her recent book, *Value Shift*, Professor Paine suggests that if a company is to meet the performance standards desired by society today, it must develop a moral center that is oriented toward both social and economic responsibilities. Such a moral center reflects a set of answers to the fundamental questions every individual or institution must come to terms with. For businesses the questions can be framed around four main themes.

1. *Purpose.* What is the company's purpose? Besides creating wealth and using resources efficiently, what is the company's contribution to society? How do its products and services add value to people's lives?

2. *Principles.* What are the company's guiding principles? What precepts guide the conduct of its people in carrying out its purpose? What are its nonnegotiable standards? Its ideals and aspirations?

3. *People.* What is the company's concept of the person? Who counts as a member of its moral community? Whose interests are considered in its decision making?

4. *Power.* What is the scope of the company's power and authority? To whom and for what is the company accountable? How is decision-making authority to be allocated within the organization?[2]

To summarize Professor Paine, every ethical challenge at work can be resolved quickly and easily by being good and honest. To be good, one must know what the good is. When the crisis comes, it is too late to try to make that determination. One must be empowered by the organization to do what one considers to be the good. One must also be open to hearing views of others as to what is appropriate under the circumstances. By being good yourself and being open to hearing others, you may avert the crisis. If, for example, a colleague asks you to approve a phony document, you should, of course, refuse. You should demur not because you are trying to improve your colleague's ethics but because you are concerned about yours.

As always, it is important to examine one's motives. Becoming an ob-structionist to a person who is overbearing and unpleasant is not a good example of positive ethical behavior. When analyzing or confronting an ethical issue, it is best to clinically strip away the personalities involved, as they may unconsciously skew your analysis.

THE LEADER'S ROLE

A true leader becomes a benchmark, a fixed point. When we are all moving together, there is no sense of motion. When one person stops, he or she becomes a fixed point for the others, from which they can regain their bearing. Sometimes stopping becomes too abrupt, and the leader is left behind or, if not thoroughly grounded, loses footing and begins to be swept out to sea. In that case the leader becomes like a swimmer fighting a rip current. Some areas are more prone to rip currents (landmarks and even printed signs can point those out), just as we know some businesses are more prone to dilemmas—those we can prepare for. But rip currents and dilemmas can also appear suddenly, with no predictability. In either case, instead of striking directly for the shore, against the current, exhausting himself and perishing, the leader must parallel the shore, in line with his beliefs, to keep from having the current take him. A true leader has integrated a sense of ethics so that the intuitive response, under pressure, is the correct one.

A LIFE OF INTENTION

Just as my Harvard Business School professor suggested we always read with a purpose in mind, one might also lead one's life intentionally. Great works of art, such as Dante's *Divine Comedy* or T. S. Eliot's *Four Quartets* are said to read us, as we read them. They force us to confront ourselves and examine who it is we really are. If we begin to lead our lives with purpose, we can begin to answer the basic questions: What do you want your legacy to be? How do you want to be remembered?

For better or for worse, many of us are remembered for the single worst thing we have ever done, the action that attracts notoriety. What is your end game? When can you stop being good? When do you attain closure on defining your character? The only appropriate answer is: never.

Michael Milken revolutionized Wall Street. He helped transform the telecommunications industry, and he had a significant role in the wealth creation of the 1990s. For all the energy, creativity, innovation, philanthropy, mentoring, and sponsorship that he accomplished, Michael Milken will always be remembered as a Wall Street fat cat who went to jail. There is nothing he can do to erase that. He will continue to have his friends and his defenders, but the stigma is permanently attached to him.

Al Taubman is one of the most successful shopping center developers ever. Trained as an architect, he designed a different type of space in which merchants could sell their goods. As a result of his unique design, sales productivity in Taubman centers far exceeds the average. Taubman was one of the most respected innovators in the real estate business. After his career, enjoying great wealth, he fulfilled a lifelong passion for art by purchasing a controlling interest in Sotheby's, the art auction house. He needed no further wealth. Sotheby's was a deeply respected leader in its field. Yet somehow Taubman became enmeshed in a scheme to set prices in the art auction business, was convicted by the courts, and, at age seventy-two, served a year in prison. He protests his innocence. The acts for which he was convicted appear completely irrational on the surface. Still, his wonderful legacy has been severely damaged by what appears to many to be an abuse of power and a sense of being above the law.

There is obviously much more to life than material success. We need a deeper sense of values to sustain us through short-term and long-term setbacks and disappointments. We need something to fall back on in the event of the unexpected crisis. We need a depth of consciousness to allow us to live in the tensions of life and to reconcile the irreconcilable.

BALANCE AND STABILITY AMID CHANGE

Personal ethics is formed and reforming and thus changing over time. Good business ethics is not constant over time or across cultures. How then can one maintain a stable moral compass over the normative swings of society? One way is to attempt to live out a balanced life. Balance involves physical, mental, and spiritual well-being as well as emotional self-control and maturity. To be balanced one needs to be in harmony with oneself, one's family, and one's various communities of interest and to have a passion for some aspects of life outside of oneself. Achieving balance means living in the paradoxes and oppositions of life. One becomes comfortable with both being in solitude and being in community, with being nurturing and being aggressive, with earning wealth and giving it away, with living a deeply secular life and a deeply spiritual life.

One of my heroes from Morgan Stanley, John Barr, is an accomplished investment banker with a distinguished combat record in Vietnam. He has also published six collections of poetry; served as president of the Poetry Society of America and chairman of the board of trustees of Bennington College; taught at Sarah Lawrence College; served on the board of Yaddo (a retreat for artists located in Saratoga Springs, New York); and been named president of the Poetry Foundation.

When asked how he could become both a successful businessman and a poet, Barr responded, "A businessperson [cares] about making something happen, making something better in a world of external activities and affairs. . . . A businessperson is trying to make sense of things in the external world, that's where things get settled. The business of the poet is to make sense of things in the internal world. For a poet, nothing has happened unless they've made sense of that in the context of a poem. They're different arenas, but they both have the same end. I view a businessperson and a poet as a response of the self to the chaotic universe. It's a way to establish order in a disorderly universe. That's where I think the two converge."[3] How has he made it work? Barr explained that he wrote poetry "on airplanes, in hotel rooms, in the back of a taxicab. . . . sometimes I'd wake up at three or four in the morning. . . . I write lines on the edges of train schedules and whatever I can."[4] For me, John Barr is a classic example of an integrated life.

We need to find a balance between professional interests and personal interests, between work time and family time. Family life can be deeply rewarding; it can help sustain us when things go awry; and we can even learn much about setting priorities, time management, and managing and leading people from the family experience.

It takes a great deal of self-discipline to see that we spend weekend and vacation time together. I purposely avoided golf, tennis, and competitive sailing in order to spend more recreational time with my family. Major family events were entered on my day-timer in ink and planned ahead for. When I lived in Manhattan, I purposely traded Friday evening time for Saturday morning time in the office. When I moved to Connecticut, I worked late Friday night if I had to and kept the weekend free. I would work through my briefcase on the commuter train. On weekends, I would purposely put work off until after the children had gone to bed Sunday evening, when I would then cram for the week ahead.

In those days, without cell phones and instant messages, I was able to separate myself entirely from the office upon occasion. Today one can call home—and the office—from a cell phone while on the summit slope of Mt. Everest. Despite the pressure to stay in touch, I would strongly recommend that hardworking businesspeople intentionally schedule some time during the year when they leave their cell phones at home.

One of the major lessons I gleaned from my eleven-week submersion in the Himalayan wilderness was how little news of substance I actually missed. Upon returning home, I dutifully caught up on the various financial publications and periodicals. I missed hardly any data that could have had a fundamental impact on my decision making. For me, this was one more proof of Warren Buffet's adage that we should focus on the big things and not the daily noise and chatter.

We need to develop positive communities of interest outside of work in order to sustain our well-being and dissipate our excess energy. If work becomes our sole source of fulfillment we will lose our sense of perspective and fail to recognize the deeper patterns that are possible in an examined life. Not only is outside activity necessary for our physical and emotional health but we can also gain and hone useful skills, either in solitary study and thought or in other communities, that can make us more effective in the job environment. Through a broadened outlook on life we become more interesting to our professional clients. Once again, the more concerned we become about others and their points of view, the better chance there is we will do the right thing because it is good for them, not just good for us.

CONSTANCY AND FLEXIBILITY

Leadership has more to do with basic values and integrity than with specific management techniques. A leader must have developed a strong sense of self, the detachment to remain constant through the twists and turns of a career, the commitment to remain a rock of integrity on whom others can depend, and the courage to go against the grain when required. A leader has a vision of life that is multidimensional and nonlinear. It is of course important that the organization be successful and provide opportunities. It is much easier to be strong and respected in an organization that is successful than in one that is struggling for survival.

It takes courage to live out of the depths of one's being and portray a richness of life beyond the surface aspects of success, wealth, and power. Ethical leaders have a level of moral and emotional maturity that sustains them in times of ambiguity and failure. Leaders take risks and make decisions in situations when many significant factors are unknown. Mature leaders know that they cannot avoid mistakes or, on occasion, harm to others. In this sense, a leader loses moral innocence and still has the fortitude to go on trying to do the right thing. A leader lives as much by intuition and experience as by rules. The rules provide a structure for creative living that sometimes soars beyond the rules, much as an improvised jazz solo follows basic harmonic progressions—the freedom to express oneself around a tight theme.

I am reminded of Max DePree's *Leadership Jazz*, in which he states, "[O]ne way to think about leadership is to consider a jazz band. Jazz-band leaders must choose the music, find the right musicians, and perform—in public. But the effect of the performance depends on so many things—the environment, the volunteers in the band, the need for everybody to perform as individuals and as a group, the absolute dependence of the leader on the members of the band, the need of the leader for the followers to play well."[5]

Leaders help develop the culture of an organization and manage its culture and values. Leaders set the limits of what is to be tolerated in terms of risk and practices, and take responsibility for the actions of their people when things go awry. Whatever the organization—whether for-profit, not-for-profit, educational, religious, or volunteer—leaders must have a firm understanding of the basic nature of the enterprise, how long it takes to do things, the key decision points, and metrics for measuring performance. And remember that leadership is not limited to the senior persons in an organization. Leaders are those who command the respect of their peers, subordinates, superiors, and clients for integrity, good judgment, and success. They are the "go to" people, and they are the jewels of any firm.

Global Mores for Global Business

THERE ARE MANY WAYS OF GETTING RICH in the world of business. You may be fortunate enough to invent a widget that revolutionizes the very way we exchange information or fund the work of a scientist who discovers the antidote for the aging process. You might hit the market perfectly and make all the money you feel you need for the rest of your life. For most of us, though, the process will be longer and require more of our time and energy and less reliance on luck. Bob Baldwin, our great leader at Morgan Stanley, had an embroidered pillow in his office on which was stitched the phrase, "The harder I work; the luckier I get." His pillow updates Ben Franklin's adage, "Diligence is the mother of good luck" and the still older Persian proverb, "Luck is infatuated with the efficient."

Perhaps those of us who work at it will be the lucky ones in the end. In building a successful business career, it is possible to create wealth for ourselves instead of riches—wealth that can sustain us to the end of our days. In the end, many of the components that lead to career success—such as setting goals, establishing character, learning, being sensitive to ethics and good practices, dealing with failure, having a vision and a legacy, and leading a balanced life—have led to success in life as well.

CREATING TRUE WEALTH

My definition of wealth in a business career includes physical, mental, and spiritual well-being; continuing opportunities for growth and learning; deep trust relationships, affection, and love within a supportive network of individuals; financial security; and an ability to move beyond self-interest to give and relate to others. It is my opinion that each of these elements requires focus, commitment, dedication, and intention. Each may also require personal sacrifice in terms of what one is willing to trade off in time, developing relationships, working long hours, performing unpleasant work, even performing self-sacrificial and courageous acts to get there.

The experiences and opportunities of life are a platform from which to explore these riches.

The way will not always be easy. One for whom such was the case is recently deceased Admiral James Stockdale. Jim was imprisoned in the "Hanoi Hilton" for seven years, three of them in solitary confinement. Jim's back and one of his legs were broken when he first parachuted in, and never reset. He was partially deaf from repeated beatings. He pounded his face with a stool and against a wall so he was unfit to be photographed or filmed. Nonetheless, he became the leader of the prison, sacrificing himself to give hope to others. He emerged physically broken but strengthened in spirit. For his service in prison he was promoted to admiral and awarded the Congressional Medal of Honor.

Jim and I discussed his experiences, and it's clear that Jim knew who he was. He had meaning in his life: a solid inner core of values. His values were based more on the moral philosophy of the Stoics than on a particular religion. His values sustained him through the darkest days when hope was not enough, and all that was left was faith in a grounded knowledge of how he wished to live and to die.

In an essay, "The Principles of Leadership," Jim wrote:

> The only way I know to handle failure is to gain historical perspective, to think about those who have lived successfully with failure in our religious and classical past. A verse from the Book of Ecclesiastes says it well: "I returned and saw that the race is not always to the swift nor the battle to the strong, neither yet bread to the wise nor riches to men of understanding, nor favors to men of skill, but time and chance happeneth to them all." The test of our future leaders' merit may well not lie in hanging in there when the light at the end of the tunnel is expected but rather in their persistence and continued performance of duty when there is no possibility that the light will ever show up.[1]

Jim's ideals and practices seem far away from today's media reports on both business and the military. Yet millions of professionals in American business do experience and practice business in a positive, ethical, and forward-thinking manner. Unfortunately, through scandals, shoddy performance, and greed on the part of some, corporate America has come in for much negative publicity in recent years. To restore the desired image, men and women of character who understand the difference between true wealth and merely getting rich must listen always to the inner voice that discerns that difference and consistently act upon it.

APPROACHING LIFE, AND BUSINESS, WITH INTEGRITY

It is difficult to speak briefly and in a meaningful fashion to young men and women about leading a life of value. One needs only to sit through a handful of graduation speeches to validate this. One of the best approaches I have seen was written by Howard Gardner, MacArthur Fellow and renowned professor at the Harvard Graduate School of Education, who concludes his recent book, *Good Work*, with a prospective letter to a young relative on how to approach a life of work.

> You—like the rest of us—will find it very difficult to stay on course unless you feel loyal to an enduring tradition. Sometimes your loyalty or trust may be based on religious faith and at other times on the assumptions that traditions devoid of wisdom would not survive the passage of time. If you are lucky, you learned such sustaining beliefs in your family, and you may not even be aware that you have absorbed them. To complement these beliefs, you will need to gain a parallel anchoring in the traditions of your domain, as embodied by teachers, mentors, or paragons whom you admire and from whom you have learned. Without strong foundations in traditions that give meaning to the future, it is hard to keep up professional values under the pressure of countervailing forces. . . .
>
> Next, seek the support of others who share the same purpose. Very few people have the fortitude to act consistently against the grain of the organizations to which they belong—or to resist the field that has wandered from its core values. We are social animals, after all, and we need to feel that our behavior makes sense to others. So find allies, inside or outside the job, or—in the style of a social entrepreneur—consider starting an organization of like-minded peers. . . .
>
> But having strong principles and support may not be enough. You will also need a third vital ingredient—the resolve to stick by your principles.

Knowing what should be done and having the means to do it are useless without personal commitment. In the last analysis, no one else is responsible for upholding the values of your work. Either you live up to the implicit covenant that justified professional status, or you do not (and in that case, you would continue a life of furtive deception). What Harry Truman said in the Oval Office applies to all of us in our less august surroundings—"The buck stops here." Sounds difficult? Not really. For the joy we derive from doing our best work, according to high standards, is rewarding enough, even if we must sometimes struggle in lonely confusion.[2]

These powerful words are yet another way of saying that we need strong values which can sustain us, a web of strong personal relationships among people who can support us, and the courage to trust our good friends and live out our values. Trust is key on personal and professional levels. Indeed, Francis Fukuyama, professor of international political economy at Johns Hopkins, argues in his 1995 book *Trust: The Social Virtues & the Creation of Prosperity* that the central requirement for development of capitalistic enterprises like the modern corporation was a high level of societal trust in others. In societies featuring high levels of trust, individuals were willing to engage in the impersonal transactions necessary for the accumulation of capital, and entrepreneurs were willing to entrust their firms to professional managers. Fukuyama's definition of trust is especially relevant: "Trust is the expectation . . . of regular, honest and cooperative behavior, based on commonly shared norms."[3]

ETHICS IN THE WORLD

When teaching ethics I often talk of expanding the topic both horizontally (that is, globally) and vertically (that is, religiously). As free-market capitalism expands throughout the world, its underlying value system often clashes with the value systems of other cultures. One means of understanding and resolving such conflicts is to search for a commonality of values among differing cultures. A place to start such a search might be in the religious underpinnings of the various value systems. As the enduring variations on the Golden Rule, presented in the opener to Part One, underscore, the purpose of all religions, either explicit or implicit, is to take one out of preoccupation with oneself and into relationship with others and with the transcendent "ultimate reality."

Groups as varied as UNESCO, the Parliament of the World's Religions, and the Minnesota Center for Ethical Business Cultures have come up with lists of the shared values of humanity. UNESCO emphasizes such values as a multicultural consensus of traditions, respect for human rights, meeting basic human needs, and collective security arrangements.[4] The Minnesota Center for Ethical Business Cultures focuses on global corporate responsibility, understanding, common respect, and responsible action by individuals.[5] Such values (which include compassion, fairness, responsibility, honesty, respect, and citizenship), provide a basis for achieving global community. Lynn Sharp Paine, head of the ethics curriculum at Harvard Business School, has developed a list of ten values which distinguish cultures that foster economic growth. They are

- An orientation on the future as against the present or past
- A positive attitude toward work as against work as a burden
- A propensity to save and invest as against income equality
- Mass availability of education as against education for the elite
- Fairness in advancement as against cronyism and connections
- Trust in a broad range of extended communities as against trust primarily in the family
- A strong ethical code and a relative absence of corruption, without resorting to sanctions
- Justice and fair play as against who you know and how much you pay off
- Dispersed authority and broad empowerment as against hierarchy and command and control systems
- Religion as essentially a private matter allowing for plurality and dissent as against orthodoxy and conformity[6]

Paine goes on to contrast institutionalized capitalism—based on an impersonal rule of law, competition, efficiency, opportunity, and achievement—with that of third-world countries, based on personal values such as rule of man, connections, personal ties, obligations, relationships, and loyalties. She suggests that we in the West see an increasing tendency to value achievement over affiliations. Robert Putnam, professor of Public Policy at Harvard, developed this premise in his book *Bowling Alone*. He asserts that society has changed in ways that support Paine's thesis. One example is that people are bowling to perfect their game and score (personal achievement), rather than for the social aspect that had, for so long, been the impetus behind bowling (and other activities) and that fueled the leagues. There are many examples of parents valuing individual performance over team play as they "teach" and encourage their children in little league sports activities. The reasons Putnam cites for civil decline are numerous, including busyness and time pressure, economic hard times, the stresses of two-career families, suburbanization and sprawl, television viewing, disruption of marriage, growth of the welfare state, and changing social attitudes.[7]

We no longer operate on the cycle of nature that I found so appealing in the villages of the Himalayas. Indeed, as Stephen Ambrose has pointed out, we did not adopt "artificial" time zones until 1878 when we had to cope with unified schedules for the newly completed transcontinental railroad.[8]

As institutional loyalties become more powerful, duties to family and tribe are rearranged and become duties to amorphous shareholders. In the early evolution of society, loyalties to family and tribe trumped all others. Indeed, one who was lured to a neighboring village was viewed with dismay. The human gene pool was restricted to where one could reasonably walk. A great breakthrough occurred with the invention of the bicycle. Today, the jet aircraft has completely revolutionized the human gene pool. In the sophisticated West, loyalties to amorphous institutions are expected to be as powerful as personal loyalties. One of the biggest issues we discuss when I teach M.B.A. students is when and under what circumstances one is expected to give up personal friendships in order to protect the employer. When does one turn in a friend for violating company policy? For these and other issues the global marketplace becomes an area of conflicting worldviews where capitalism is seen as inhumane.

How do we reintegrate friendship, reciprocity, and community into such a system? How can one have impartial justice for all without destroying personal relationships? Capitalism appears to amplify the impersonal voice, yet it cannot drown out the personal voice of kinship. The question then becomes how to humanize capitalism and resolve competing rights in the utilitarian model.[9]

Capitalism need not be viewed as inhuman or intangible. Among other things, capitalism creates real wealth, raises standards of living, provides opportunities for personal growth, and, under proper conditions, can even enhance the landscape. I was fortunate in my investment banking career that so much of what I helped produce in financing commercial real estate was tangible, in the form of high-rise downtown office buildings, regional malls, and hotels. Premier developers have a vision of creating exciting gathering places for people and not just physical space. To this day I can travel to almost any major city in the United States and see projects that we helped to finance. When in Los Angeles I delight in the glass structure of the Bonaventure Hotel in the sunlight; in Dallas it is the Anatole Hotel—it is any one of several of Gerry Hines's office towers or of regional malls developed by Ernie Hahn, for example. It gives me great satisfaction to know that, in our way, we helped shape the urban environment of so many cities, provided jobs, and helped form the created community and landscape.

All of us in the business world contribute to the well-being of society in some way, if we live constructive lives. We help create jobs, opportunities, good products, and better procedures. When I have the opportunity to walk the deserted streets of ancient cities such as Corinth or Ephesus, I wonder what they looked like in their heyday, filled with trading, banking, and dealmaking. We business people can choose to see ourselves as part of a five-thousand-year continuum of enterprises dedicated to building cities, creating jobs, creating exchange, and creating wealth. Over the eons people of free will have created systems of trust and respect. Rather than seeing ourselves as marionettes following the motions of some giant puppeteer, we can always see ourselves as part of a broad community extending over time and space, doing our bit to make life just a little bit better, adding to the store of values and stories from which future generations of people can draw.

THE FUTURE

I think back to those classrooms at Harvard Business School more than forty-five years ago, where we were all male, mostly all Anglo-American, many of us former military, and all of us dressed up in our business suits, and compare it to the class I taught this week at USC, where there were males and females, of multiple nationalities, with disparate backgrounds, garbed in t-shirts and cutoffs, and entering seriously into discussion with me. At least superficially, there has been immense change in my business lifetime—change in dress or expressions of sexuality; access of women and minorities to business opportunity; a shift to smoke-free environments; Web-based class syllabuses; and the ever-present e-mails, cell phones, and Internet. Much of what I think about and read indicates that the rate of change will be even greater for the next generations.

Yet the need for core values, emotional maturity, courage to do the right thing, strong mentors, good leaders, and good followers remains unchanged. Indeed, the greater the pace of change, the greater the need for rocks of stability to anchor those caught up in anxiety and confusion. Ethics, for each of us, is our individualized search for what will give meaning to our lives. The fundamental question of ethics, then, is "How shall we live?" Ultimately the real test of an ethical theory is whether we have found fulfillment as a result of living in a way that our chosen ethic commands or we have experienced a lack of fulfillment as a result of living in a way that is significantly different from that ethical theory.

We need to learn to live beyond the boundaries of everyday life and recognize that there is an interconnectedness among all aspects of life. One can also describe this connection as polyphony, which as a musical term is shorthand for the combining of a number of individual but harmonizing melodies, as in a fugue or canon, resonating with Dante's four levels. A complete life, a life of integrity, involves both interconnectedness and polyphony, a balance among family, profession, public life, philanthropy, physical well-being, and the inner spiritual life. The extent to which one is ignored forces the others out of balance. A "life of leisure" can be described as a state of mind that occurs when all such efforts are perceived of as being voluntary, when your work is in synch with your inner being, when there is a blending between work and play.

Business should be seen as building relationships, not doing deals. A businessperson of integrity focuses on vision, values, and valor. There is an immense difference between a business life bound by the limits of the deal and a business life bound by the limits of one's faith and spirituality. We will be far more effective if our values are congruent with our professional lives. These values include service to others, respect, and justice. Faith and spirituality can help sustain moral courage. They provide the staying power through adversity.

A tested inner core of values helps us to set our priorities and to live with the consequences of our actions. My business life has caused me to respect and trust counterparts who may be native Japanese practicing some mixture of Shinto and Confucianism, native Kuwaitis practicing Islam, or a larger group of both cultural and religious Jews. I believe personally that God is intermediated through Jesus Christ, who took human form, but I believe in a generous God who created this world for everyone and who would not deny anyone who is open in whatever way to receiving God's love. Some would say this causes me to no longer be an authentic Christian. I would respond, let it be so. I know of no other way to think of these matters in a world that has become truly global and in which our very survival may depend on seeing all humans as our brothers and sisters.

I have always been intrigued with the existential view of life—that we have the ability to make conscious choices and live with the results of our decisions. We need to take responsibility for our own lives while still acknowledging the role of fate and both good and bad luck in it all. Some say that Kierkegaard was a Christian existentialist; others insist the phrase "Christian existentialist" is an oxymoron, that an existentialist places too great a role on the individual and not enough on God to also be called a Christian. There is obviously a balance to be achieved. My faith can be summarized in the apocryphal Russian folk tale of Jesus in the boat with his disciples amidst a storm on the Sea of Galilee. "What shall we do? What shall we do, oh Lord?" the apostles cry out. "I'll tell you what we are going to do," Jesus responds. "We are going to say a short prayer, and then we are going to row like hell!"

And the rowing is hard. Throughout it all, we must develop the courage to balance our intuition with our rational natures. We must learn to sanctify everyday experience. I trust that you will have the inner resources to create a (life) journey of your own and see the potential in business for adventure, success, and a noble calling.

I am sad that my friend John Gardner was not here to read a draft of this book. His comments would have made it much better. Let's let John have the final word: "Meaning is not something that you stumble across, like the answer to a riddle or the prize in a treasure hunt. Meaning is something you build into your life. You build it out of your own past, out of your affections and loyalties, out of your experience of humankind as it is passed on to you, out of your own talent and understanding, out of the things you believe in, out of the things and people you love, out of the values for which you are willing to sacrifice something. The ingredients are there. You are the only one who can put them together into that unique pattern that will be your life. Let it be a life that has dignity and meaning for you. If it does, then the particular balance of success or failure is of less account."[10]

Notes

PART ONE

1. "The Price of Life: Why an American's Life Is Worth Twice as Much as a Swede's." *The Economist*, December 4, 1993, 74.

2. Ray Smith, "Casualties—USA vs. NVA/VC," Ray Smith, www.rjsmith.com/kia_tbl. html#press (accessed August 17, 2006).

3. Wikipedia, "Gulf War," Wikipedia, http://en.wikipedia.org/wiki/Operation_Desert_ Storm (accessed January 25, 2006).

4. Will and Ariel Durant, *The Story of Civilization* (New York: Simon & Schuster, 1972).

5. Stephen L. Carter, *The Culture of Disbelief: How American Law and Politics Trivialize Religious Devotion* (New York: Anchor Books, 1994).

6. Amitai Etzioni, *The Moral Dimension: Toward a New Economics* (New York: Free Press, 1990).

7. Paul Tillich, *My Search for Absolutes* (New York: Simon & Schuster, 1967).

8. C. G. Jung, *Memories, Dreams, Reflections* (New York: Random House, 1965), 330.

9. Frances Hesselbein, Marshall Goldsmith, and Richard Beckhard (eds.), *The Leader of the Future* (San Francisco: Jossey-Bass, 1997).

10. As described in *A Global Ethic: The Declaration of the Parliament of the World's Religions*, trans. John Bowden (New York: The Continuum Publishing Company, 1994), 71–72.

CHAPTER ONE

1. Eberhard Bethge, *Dietrich Bonhoeffer: A Biography*, rev. ed. (Minneapolis: Fortress Press, 2000), 655.

2. Dietrich Bonhoeffer, *Life Together: A Discussion of Christian Fellowship* (San Francisco: Harper & Row, 1954), 78.

3. Frances Hesselbein (ed.), *Leading Beyond the Walls* (San Francisco: Jossey-Bass, 2001), 174.

4. *The Times of India*, Sunday, Nov. 16, 2003. http://timesofindia.indiatimes.com/ articleshow/msid-284799,prtpage-1.cms (accessed December 23, 2003).

5. Ian I. Mitroff and Elizabeth A. Denton, *A Spiritual Audit of Corporate America: A Hard Look at Spirituality, Religion, and Values in the Workplace* (San Francisco: Jossey-Bass, 1999), 212.

6. Johnson & Johnson Credo, www.ethicon.com/html/ethicon/about.xml?article_ name=credo.jspf (accessed August 10, 2004).

7. Much of the Johnson & Johnson material is derived from the Harvard Business School case "James Burke: A Career in American Business," 1989, President and Fellows of Harvard College.
8. Richard S. Tedlow, "James Burke: A Career in American Business," Teaching Note, 1989, President and Fellows of Harvard College, p. 16.
9. This was one of several times in my real estate career in which I found myself caught in the tension between preservation of open spaces and development. As a hiker and nature lover, this might have presented a conflict for me. Yet over time I became disappointed by the strident and confrontational nature of certain environmental groups. Through association with groups such as the Urban Land Institute and the Property and Environment Research Center, I have supported a more balanced vision of managed growth, aligning good environmental practice with free market forces wherever possible.

CHAPTER TWO

1. Terry Pearce, *Leading Out Loud* (San Francisco: Jossey Bass, 2003), 18.
2. Bartleby.com. www.bartleby.com/59/3/everybodywil.html. Reference to *The New Dictionary of Cultural Literacy, Third Edition*, (eds. E. D. Hirsch Jr., Joseph F. Kett, and James Trefil (New York: Houghton Mifflin, 2002).
3. James M. Kouzes and Barry Z. Posner, *The Leadership Challenge*, 3rd ed. (San Francisco: Jossey-Bass, 2002), 318–321.

CHAPTER THREE

1. Audio transcript of 2003 video on Trammell Crow, provided by Martha Martin, Crow family historian. Personal correspondence to the author, January 17, 2005.
2. Robert Sobel, *Trammell Crow, Master Builder: The Story of America's Largest Real Estate Empire* (New York: John Wiley & Sons, 1989), 2.
3. Thornton Wilder, *Theophilus North* (New York: Avon Books, 1973), 292.
4. Alec Wilkinson, *My Mentor: A Young Man's Friendship with William Maxwell* (New York: Houghton Mifflin, 2002), 175 and 178.
5. *Augustine's Confessions*, Book 11, Verse 13.
6. T. S. Eliot, *Four Quartets* (New York: Harcourt Brace Jovanovich, 1971), 44.
7. Charles Murray, *Human Accomplishment* (New York: HarperCollins, 2003), 457.
8. Murray, *Human Accomplishment*, 458.

CHAPTER FOUR

1. James M. Kouzes and Barry Z. Posner, *The Leadership Challenge*, 3rd ed. (San Francisco: Jossey-Bass, 2002), 25.
2. Mark O'Keefe, "Meet Michael Josephson, Pillar of Character Education," *Newhouse News Service*, 2001, www.newhouse.com/archive/story1a041801.html.
3. Sissela Bok, *Lying: Moral Choice in Public and Private Life* (New York: Vintage Books, 1979).
4. Jonathan Weil, "PricewaterhouseCoopers Partners Criticized Travel Billing," *The Wall Street Journal*, September 30, 2003.
5. Michael Josephson, "Character Is an Essential Competence," *Character Counts!* sec. 403.2, March 25–31, 2005, www.charactercounts.org/knxwk403.htm.

6. Tracy Kidder, *The Soul of a New Machine* (New York: Modern Library, 1997).
7. Thomas J. Peters and Robert H. Waterman Jr., *In Search of Excellence: Lessons from America's Best-Run Companies* (New York: Warner Books, 1983).
8. Meister Eckhart, *Selected Writings* (New York: Penguin, 1995).

CHAPTER FIVE

1. Leo Apostel, *World Views: From Fragmentation to Implementation* (Brussels: VUB Press, 1994).
2. T. S. Eliot, *Four Quartets* (New York: Harcourt Brace Jovanovich, 1971), 58.
3. *Rule of the Order of Saint Benedict*, trans. Luke Dysinger (Trabuco Canyon, CA: Source Books, 1996).

PART THREE

1. Charlie-Pye Smith, *Travels in Nepal: The Sequestered Kingdom* (New York: Penguin, 1990), 60–61.

CHAPTER SEVEN

1. Joseph L. Badaracco Jr. *Defining Moments: When Managers Must Choose Between Right and Right* (Boston: Harvard Business School Press, 1997), 3.
2. Jean-Paul Sartre, "Dirty Hands," in *No Exit and Three Other Plays* (New York: Vintage International, 1989), 218.
3. Badaracco, *Defining Moments*, p. 4.
4. Rushworth M. Kidder, *How Good People Make Tough Choices: Resolving the Dilemmas of Ethical Living* (New York: Fireside/Simon & Schuster, 1996), 118–139.
5. Plato, *Great Dialogues of Plato*, eds. Eric H. Warmington and Philip G. Rouse, trans. W.H.D. Rouse (New York: New American Library, 1970).
6. Kidder, *How Good People Make Tough Choices*, 180.
7. James M. Kouzes and Barry Z. Posner, *The Leadership Challenge*, 3rd ed. (San Francisco: Jossey-Bass, 2002), 45.
8. Paul Tillich, *The Shaking of the Foundations* (Magnolia, MA: Peter Smith Publisher, 1988), Chapter Seven, "The Depth of Existence."

CHAPTER EIGHT

1. *Living the Credo: Making Good Decisions at Johnson & Johnson*, prepared for Johnson & Johnson by Michael Josephson, Josephson Institute of Ethics, 2003, p. 3.
2. *Living the Credo*, p. 46.
3. Vaclav Havel, *The Art of the Impossible: Politics as Morality in Practice* (Berlin: Fromm Int, 1998).

CHAPTER NINE

1. Marak Lewis, "Paul Volcker Rolls Up His Sleeves," Forbes.com, Feb. 4, 2002, http://64.233.161.104/search?q=cache:B_aMZVQBM1AJ:www.forbes.com/2002/02/04/020.
2. Lynn Sharp Paine, *Value Shift: Why Companies Must Merge Social and Financial Imperatives to Achieve Superior Performance* (New York: McGraw-Hill, 2003) 194.

3. Jill Singer, "So What Do You Do, John Barr?" March 23, 2004, www.mediabistro. com/articles/cache/a1356.asp (accessed June 8, 2004).

4. Singer, "So What Do You Do, John Barr?"

5. Max DePree, *Leadership Jazz* (New York: Dell, 1992), 5.

EPILOGUE

1. James B. Stockdale, *A Vietnam Experience: Ten Years of Reflection* (Palo Alto, CA: Hoover Institution and Stanford University, 1984), 122.

2. Howard Gardner, Mihaly Csikszentmihalyi, and William Damon, *Good Work: When Excellence and Ethics Meet* (New York: Basic Books, 2001), 248–249.

3. Francis Fukuyama, *Trust: The Social Virtues & the Creation of Prosperity* (New York: Free Press, 1995), 26. See also Charles M. North and Beck A. Taylor, "The Biblical Underpinning of Tit-for-Tat: Scriptural Insights into Axelrod's *The Evolution of Cooperation*," *Faith & Economics*, Fall 2004, 44, 1–25.

4. United Nations Educational, Scientific, and Cultural Organization, "About UNESCO," UNESCO, http://portal.unesco.org/en/ev.php-URL_ID=3328&URL_DO=DO_TOPIC&URL_SECTION=201.html (accessed January 26, 2006).

5. Center for Ethical Business Cultures, "Overview," www.cebcglobal.org/Overview/Overview.htm (accessed January 26, 2006).

6. Author's notes from Lynn Sharp Paine's speech at a conference titled "Business, Faith, and Ethics" at the Counselors of Real Estate Conference, February 9–11, 2001, Tucson, Arizona.

7. Robert D. Putnam, *Bowling Alone* (New York: Simon & Schuster, 2000), 187.

8. Stephen E. Ambrose, *Nothing Like It in the World: The Men Who Built the Transcontinental Railroad 1863–1869* (New York: Touchstone/Simon & Schuster, 2000), 349.

9. Author's notes from Paine's speech at the Counselors of Real Estate Conference.

10. John W. Gardner, "Commentary: Personal Renewal," *Western Journal of Medicine*, October 1992, 459.

Index